T0165162

Under the Lone Star Flagstick

A Collection of Writings on Texas Golf and Golfers

EDITED BY MELANIE HAUSER

SIMON & SCHUSTER

Simon & Schuster
Rockefeller Center
1230 Avenue of the Americas
New York, NY 10020

Designed by Jeanette Olender
Manufactured in the United States of America

10 9 8 7 6 5 4 3 2 1

Library of Congress Cataloging-in-Publication Data
Under the Lone Star flagstick: a collection of writings on Texas golf and golfers / edited by Melanie Hauser.
p. cm.
1. Golf—Texas. 2. Golfers—Texas—Biography. I. Hauser, Melanie.
GV982.T4U53 1997
796.352'09764—dc21 97-28381
CIP
ISBN 978-1-4516-3663-5

Grateful acknowledgment is made to the following writers and publications for permission to reprint the articles contained in this book:

"Shady Oaks" by Tom Callahan and Dave Kindred, *Around the World in 18 Holes,* Doubleday, 1994. Reprinted with permission of Dave Kindred.

Excerpt from "If You Don't Like What You See You're Too Old to Be Looking" by Gary Cartwright, *Texas Monthly,* May 1978. Copyright © Gary Cartwright. Courtesy of Gary Cartwright.

"Golf Puts Its Heart in the Right Place" by Bob Verdi, *Chicago Tribune,* 1992. Reprinted courtesy of *Chicago Tribune.*

"A Firm Hand on a Carefree Cat" by Myron Cope, *Sports Illustrated,* 1968. Copyright © Myron Cope. Courtesy of Myron Cope.

(Permissions continued on page 319)

Acknowledgments

One thing about books like these: You can't do them on your own. Sure, my fingerprints are all over this, but an anthology is just as much a reflection of the people whose work you see—and some whose work you don't.

I was blessed from the start—and I'm talking about my parents. They've been gone for a while now, but they were around long enough to see their love for the game—they played eighteen whenever they had the chance—finally rub off on their oldest daughter. When I griped, they were patient, knowing one day I'd find out what I was missing. When I did . . . well, I'm just thankful we had time to share it.

I have been truly blessed, too, with a lot of good friends and colleagues. They helped me find some wonderful pieces, generously shared some of their own, and were always there when things had to be sorted out.

You can't do a book on Texas golf without the help of Frances Trimble of the Texas Golf Hall of Fame. There must be something she doesn't know about the history of the people who played here and the game itself, but I haven't found it. That said, you can't do it either without writers like Blackie Sherrod and Dan Jenkins. Their work is just a small part of their contribution. Just knowing I could pick their brains when I needed to . . . well, no two people know more about great sportswriting. Or more Texas tales.

You can't do it, either, without research. Some writers contributed their favorite stories, but a project like this still means endless spools of microfilm and index files. I can't say enough for Sherry Adams at the *Houston Chronicle* and Judy Sall at the *Dallas Morning News.* They're two of the best research librarians in the business—and two of the nicest. They went out of their way to help.

To Terry Galvin at *Golf World,* Jerry Tarde at *Golf Digest,* and Jim Frank and George Peper at *Golf Magazine,* thanks for giving me the run of your libraries. I never knew where something great would pop up, but it often came from one of your files.

Special thanks, too, to reporter/researcher Matt Rudy, whose name you'll see in the future.

To Tim Rosaforte, what can I say? You helped me negotiate the mine field. To Helen Ross, Jo-Ann Barnas Taylor, Chris Smith, Dick Mudry, and Jayne Custred, you're the best. To the writers—too numerous to mention—this book is for you.

To my agent, Scott Waxman, for getting things started, and to Jeff Neuman, the best editor anyone could have. His guidance, knowledge, and love for the game are amazing. He has guts, too, for taking a chance on a rookie.

To Tom Kite and Dave Marr, two true Texans, for the forewords.

To Bob Jewell, a dogged victim of this game, a friend since junior high, a great attorney, and one of the best guys I know. Not necessarily in that order.

And finally, to those people—some of whom don't know a birdie from a bogey—who kept me focused and sane. To my sister Susie, my brother-in-law Roland, my niece Sarah, my nephews Travis and Sam, friends Gretchen, Julie, Celeste, and Jan, you picked me up when I needed it, straightened me out when I was struggling, helped me make the tough calls, and made me laugh. You truly are God's angels. It wouldn't have happened without you.

For my parents, who loved the game; and for the Texans I've been blessed to walk alongside and write about.

Contents

Part III ★ *Ben, Harvey, and Tom*

Part IV ★ *Second to None*

Part V ★ Babe and the Girls

Part VI ★ Characters, Legends, and Lore

Part VII ★ From Champions to Goat Hills

Foreword by Dave Marr

Being born when and where I was is the greatest thing that ever happened to me. Why? Because golf has been my life, and the game is a big part of Texas lore.

Golf is a way of life, as is being a Texan. And being a Texan, to me, is a state of mind. There's a lot of pride in being from Texas—maybe some people think too much. But when you're from Texas, that's special. There's a frontier spirit, a gunslinger attitude in a way, which is why, to me, golf is the perfect game for a Texan. Whenever I saw Ben Hogan walk onto a golf course, it was like there was a new sheriff in town—and he's come to play.

I saw a lot of Hogan when I was an assistant to Claude Harmon at Seminole. He was like a sphinx; even if he liked you, he could intimidate you. But you could set your watch by him. At 9:58 and 30 seconds you would hear his shoes coming down the steps. He practiced from 10–12, had lunch, then played at 1:15. He never had much use for idle conversation; he asked me only one question in three years.

But one morning, he gave me a lesson—just not with a golf club.

When he walked by me that day, I said, "Good morning, Mr. Hogan." Hogan kept walking and said, "Good morning, Dave." Then he stopped. He came back, put his hand on my shoulder, and said,

"Dave, don't ever call anyone 'Mr.' that one day you might have to play." I've never forgotten it. It just shows you the competitiveness of the man and how he got ready to play with every ounce of his being.

I learned a lot growing up at Memorial Park, too, where Robie Williams took care of me. He gave me a job opening up, sweeping the shop, starting the people on the first tee. Even though it was during World War II, tee times could be tough to come by; every now and then I'd assign a time to W. Churchill or J. Stalin or F. Roosevelt. Those times belonged to me and my buddies. I got $5 or $10 a day and I got to play golf. And if I needed anything, I had it.

I met so many great players there, including Tommy Bolt, whom I caddied for, took money from, and eventually played against. Back when I was playing junior golf, certain tournaments allowed the winners to pick their prize, and when I won one tournament in Crockett, Texas, I chose a shotgun. Why? Because someone had told me he'd pay me $125 for it. I thought that one-twenty-five was probably enough that I could retire to the south of France. Bobby Moncrief won another flight at the same event and chose a power mower, which, at the time, was about like winning a computer with one of those MMX Pentium chips.

The dollar signs danced in our heads. After all, you could get a trout sandwich for 75¢ at Bill Williams's Drive-In, which meant for $1.50 we could take a date and live high.

The day after I won, Tommy Bolt came up to us at Memorial—I had put the shotgun in the pro shop; the power mower was in the trunk of Bobby's car—and threw down a challenge. "Oh, young Dave. I see you won a tournament yesterday," Bolt groused. "You think you can beat ol' Tom today, you two boys?"

Two on one? We nodded and said, "Let's go."

Eighteen holes later, Bolt had gone out and shot a smooth little 63 and wiped us out, winning the shotgun and the mower. He was sitting on the wall waiting for the mower when I walked out with the shotgun. Tom turned dead white. He thought I was going to shoot him.

To this day, every time we cross paths, I ask him how that shotgun's handling.

When I look back, I think about the people like Billy Maxwell, Don January, L. M. Crandall—all those and many more who played for Fred Cobb at North Texas State and really got college golf on track. Now we accept all the Tiger Woodses and Justin Leonards and Tom Kites and Ben Crenshaws that have come out of these colleges, but it wouldn't have happened as soon without Cobb coaching at North Texas State in the late '40s. Dave Williams's record at the University of Houston stands on its own.

But Texas golf isn't just golfers. It was also Marvin Leonard, who started Colonial, and a lot of folks like Sid Van Ulm, the wonderful writer and cartoonist with the old *Houston Press,* and Dan Jenkins, who has made a living off of writing stories about Texas.

My life has been so full because of golf. And, if I had just stayed in Texas and never played the tour, that life would still be a rich one because of Texans and their place in what I think is the most wonderful game.

Read on.

Foreword by Tom Kite

Anytime you have the opportunity to read a book about Texans that's written by a Texan, you have to approach it with a little caution because, as everyone knows, Texans are extremely proud of their state and all the accomplishments of those who live there. But when it comes to golf, the pride is justified.

You see, Texans are by nature an untamed and independent kind. The early Texans learned how to handle the ups and downs of just existing; they endured Indian attacks, floods, droughts, and just downright hostile land. They made something of themselves and paved the way for those who followed. More recently, the state has continued to suffer through plenty of misery: when oil and gas prices were high, the state boomed, but as the prices declined and the savings and loans collapsed, Texas fortunes declined right along with them. Many people actually enjoyed seeing Texas down, saying we brought it on ourselves. But even if you are not a big fan of Texas and Texans, you must admire a state that can pull itself up by the bootstraps and bounce back like nothing ever happened. Texans have been doing just that since the early years.

This is precisely the attitude one must have to play golf at a high level, so it should be no surprise that many of golf's champions have been influenced by the state. Whether native Texan or import, if you can compete and succeed in Texas, the rest of the world just seems easy. I know this slaps the hearts of those from the other forty-nine states. Non-Texans either envy what we have or they resent our wealth. But the fact remains that, at almost any given time, nearly one third of the golfers on the PGA Tour have Texas ties.

When you read about the early struggles of Byron Nelson or Ben Hogan, you have to be impressed by the fortitude these men showed just to exist on the fledgling PGA Tour. They grew up during the Depression, and there were just no jobs around. They played golf because they loved it so much, but they also had to be tough; there simply weren't enough jobs to go around for everyone. The axiom that only the strong survive proved true again. One other "tough" guy who came around about that time was Lloyd Mangrum; he was extremely quiet and somewhat antisocial, but on the course he was as tough and unrelenting a competitor as you would want to find. The love of golf enabled the Hogans and Nelsons and Mangrums to bounce back time after time.

Today's players didn't have to endure the Depression or survive when only a few made money at tournaments. Ben Crenshaw and I have been able to take advantage of a growing and prosperous PGA Tour, but the competition is as fierce as ever, with more and more "flatbellies" with textbook swings wanting to try their luck against the best. And even with golf's popularity growing dramatically worldwide, I'm confident Texans will continue to find their way up the leaderboards.

Golf comes easier to some than to others, but it is a struggle for all at some point in time. Texas has been blessed with some of the finest teachers the game has known. Jack Burke Sr. (and later Jackie Burke Jr.), Hardy Loudermilk, Henry Ransom, Ross Collins, and Harvey Penick all dedicated their lives to helping us learn to play better. Now, with Chuck Cook, Hank Haney, and a couple of the Harmon brothers, Dick and Butch, residing in the state, there will always be great players from here.

One needs only to read some of these magnificent stories to realize

Texas golfers are special. And even though most of them are written by Texas writers, you should not assume they are just another bunch of Texas tall tales. They are fact. Most golf writers have an empathy for golfers and a deep respect and love for the game, because they play—or at least attempt to. They understand how difficult this game is—or how easy it can be—but these stories aren't filled with braggadocio just to make the golfers seem more heroic. Blackie Sherrod, Dan Jenkins, Turk Pipkin, Curt Sampson, and Melanie Hauser are among the elite journalists who have chosen to cover golf as their main passion. Not only did they play golf, but they brought golf writing to a state hungry for knowledge about the best players in the world. As a kid growing up, I devoured every column written about golf; through the pictures these writers helped create, I formed my opinions of the golf tour and the men who became my heroes. Oh, how I wanted to become part of their world. Without those storytellers, many of the accomplishments and, certainly, the personalities of the stars would have been unknown to me. And after getting out on tour, I assure you I wasn't disappointed.

It's only natural that some of the finest stories have been written by Texas writers. After all, they have the advantage of being Texan, writing about Texans and being involved with the greatest game of all. It is long past due for them to be compiled into one collection. This anthology will give some insight into what we Texans live and breathe every day.

Introduction

I was sitting in the Colonial pressroom one afternoon, lost in that single-minded world writers crawl into when they flip open their laptops and rest their fingers on the keyboard. Actually, I wasn't working on a laptop—they didn't have them back then. Instead, I was poised in front of a Silent 700 by Texas Instruments—a glorified portable typewriter filled with a roll of thermal paper and some editing keys no one ever could figure out how to use.

The exact year, day, and subject escape me, but the hairstyles, the pseudocomputer, and the polyester shirts I recall were a dead giveaway that it was sometime in the late 1970s. I'd bet my Austin paycheck at the time that if I wasn't grinding on a tome about Ben Crenshaw or Tom Kite—the hometown boys—I was fixin' to take a futile stab at making a Steve Melnyk or John Schroeder or Grier Jones sound exciting. Maybe I was talking about that dastardly fifth hole that borders the Trinity. The one where, if I were playing it, I'd likely putt it off the tee. Or maybe I was writing about Tom Watson, who kept winning Byron Nelsons back then, but couldn't win Colonial.

That doesn't matter. What did were the words. They shot past me, short-circuiting that focus I was desperately trying to find. The conversation was straight out of *Semi-Tough* or *Dead Solid Perfect.*

I turned around and saw Dan Jenkins and Jerre Todd, the commish of the Colonial pressroom, laughing harder than they did growing up. I listened to them tell another tale about Paschal High or maybe it was something about the *Fort Worth Press.* Or maybe it was something about Crenshaw. I just remember feeling as though I'd stepped into a Jenkins novel.

Then it hit me.

Forget the inverted pyramid. Good writing is storytelling. And sportswriters are about the best storytellers you'll ever find. As long as they have something worth embellishing.

Like Texas golf.

You can have your FOR SALE signs at Pebble Beach, your made-for-TV extravaganzas in the desert, your distinguished rosters at Shinnecock and the golfing compounds that keep springing up in Florida. I'll take Texans and the game they didn't invent, but just about perfected.

There isn't a richer history to tap—this side of the Atlantic, anyway—or more tales to unfold. There's Byron Nelson's win streak, Ben Hogan's comeback, Dave Williams's sixteen NCAA titles, and Harvey Penick's uncanny ability to teach life and golf in one quick lesson. Crenshaw's Little Red Masters for Harvey and Kite's windblown Open. Trevino. Lefty Stackhouse. Dave Marr.

And that's just a start.

Golf hasn't been the same since Hogan invented practice. Retirement age got pushed back a little farther when Jimmy Demaret's Austin lawn party for the legends of the game spawned the Senior PGA Tour. As for conveniences, we owe the golf cart to a Houston Country Club member who patented in 1948.

And if you're into numbers, you may yet be convinced that Texas perfected this game. Give or take a passer-through—and Texas hasn't yet met a player the whole state can't claim or adopt—Texans can lay claim to thirteen Masters titles, eleven U.S. Opens, five British Opens, fourteen PGAs, a dozen or so U.S. Women's Opens, nineteen Vardon Trophies (including nine of the first twelve), eight Ryder Cup captains, and two all-time, all-golf records that may never be broken—Nelson's streak of eleven straight and Kathy Whitworth's eighty-eight tour wins (Sam Snead only won eighty-one).

Texas is the kind of place where a poor kid named Trevino could grow up hustling with a Dr. Pepper bottle and wind up winning two U.S. Opens, two British Opens and one PGA. And where Houston's Champions—a rare golf-only club—can boast a membership roster that includes four PGA champions, plus three men (and one golf club) who have been to the moon. It's also a place where, for every great course, there's a nine-hole layout—some right out of *Tin Cup*—to delight your adventurous tastes. The only problem is knowing where to look.

Which brings me back to Colonial. And those stories. And what sets them apart.

Golf writers are as rare a breed as you'll find. They really do walk courses and they don't just interview their subjects, they unravel them. They listen to stories and stories about stories. They put a little Harvey into their work—they take dead aim and don't stop until they know just about everything there is to know. And, more often than not, the relationships they have with the players they write about run deep. They're decades old and filled with trust and respect, not just great one-liners.

What follows is a collection of stories that take dead aim on Texas golf. The idea isn't to enlighten you on every player and place, but rather convey a feeling about the game and the state—a state of the heart. I wish there were room for something on everyone and everything that makes Texas special—Don January, Justin Leonard, Mark Brooks, and Sandra Haynie are among the absent, as are stories from writers Frank Luksa and Sam Blair—but that would require a bound set of volumes.

The intention here is to give you some of the best words ever reprinted on subjects that transcend the confines of Texas' broad state lines. Some are fact, others fiction. Most are written by Texans, the rest by writers who captured the independence, spirit, and legacy of the state and its stars.

You'll recognize most of the writers and many of the stories, although nips, tucks, and excerpts have been taken along the way so everything will fit into one neat package. Some stories are on their third or fourth tweak, but they just keep getting better. Others, written before your time, allow a glimpse into the game—and newspapers—past. There are even some observations from Harvey Penick.

The chapter on Hogan is assembled to take you through his life and put his career in perspective; the chapter on Ben, Harvey, and Tom to give you insight into three Hall of Famers from Austin whose lives and careers are inextricably entwined. There's Jimmy Demaret's Technicolor world, where a piano, a tune, and a room full of friends late at night was as important as golf and Byron Nelson's streak. Babe will make you laugh; Betty Jameson's sad story may make you cry.

And about Fred Couples, Lanny Wadkins, Steve Elkington, Tommy Bolt, and Charlie Sifford: Yes, they're transplants, but ones whose places in the game you can't overlook. The Sifford piece, by Jim Murray, takes you back to the days of poll taxes and segregation—even at water fountains; it takes more than one piece to explain Trevino.

The selections on Colonial and Preston Trail reveal their twenty-something age, yet stand up against time. Not much has changed. At Colonial, the pressroom site has been moved (three times, I think) and is now on the indoor tennis courts; the drink du jour is a holster filled with a thirty-two-ounce margarita; and the lookin' and ratin' is now done by the women, too. Preston Trail doesn't host the Nelson anymore, but it's still—like Houston's Lochinvar—a place where women aren't allowed.

Lefty Stackhouse and his temper, and hustler Dick Martin are as legendary as they come. So is Tenison Park, where the pros got sent home C.O.D. As for Goat Hills? It stands alone in Texas lore.

The collection is meant to entertain the way Jenkins did in the Colonial pressroom—to give readers a feel and not worry where those lines between fact and fiction blur. But you might learn a little too—about the first major held in Texas and the day the Texas Open folks hijacked Gene Sarazen from a train.

Enjoy.

Part One

Bragging Rights

Blackie's Texas

Blackie Sherrod

Golf Digest, *February 1987*

As you may have heard over the grapevine of tom-tom, this is Sesquicentennial Year in Texas. That historical significance has had a heavy influence on us buckaroos from Baja Oklahoma. The chief effect is that it sent a lot of us to pronunciation school. Some of the old nesters, after spraining their veteran tongues in an effort to pronounce the danged thing, said to hell with it. They would just wait another fifty years and call it Centennial Deuce. It was of such fierce independence that the West was won.

However, because of this special year, researchers have dived headlong into brittle old records and chronicles and diaries, many etched on buffalo hide with a Parker quill, to renew the colorful past.

Besides, it gave them something to do, while the government was messing around with oil prices. We don't have a recession in Texas, understand, but our boom is worse than it's been in a long while.

Texans have been known to, uh, stretch the truth a tad, and there's probably a heritage for it. It got pretty lonesome around the campfires at night, after all the traveling-salesman jokes got told for the forty-eleventh time, so imaginations frequently ran wild. So perhaps certain aspects of the state's history, pertaining to golf for example, are better presented as cold, substantiated facts.

To start with, it has been fairly well documented that golf was not invented in Texas, regardless of what you may have picked up down at the pool hall.

Golf began, of course, to the east of here, across the pond, some say. But early on, some wealthy Texans bought the American rights from King James IV of Scotland, shipping them over from Edinburgh and carting the unwieldy things south by covered wagon. It was quite a task, let me tell you.

Texas, after all, offered local natural facilities for golf. There were abundant prairie-dog holes, and gutta-percha abounded in every stream. The weather was conducive to year-round participation with only an occasional day off to let a tornado play through. It rained every year or so, just enough to keep grass hopeful of eventual salvation.

Besides, the hardy defenders of the Alamo discovered that a mashie niblick came in rather handy for close infighting and drawing lines in the dirt. Brassies were frequently used for stirring chili and fending off the pesky Comanche. (Later on, of course, Texas pioneers moved west and settled Colorado and built the Grand Canyon with the original sand wedge.)

After the state gained its independence and subsequently annexed Uncle Sam as a business partner, roughly one billion golf courses sprang up around the territory. Then in the late '30s, when the professional golf tour showed signs of survival, Texas began rolling hotshot players into the business like pints out of a bootlegger's buggy.

Some of the early names were Lighthorse Harry Cooper, first golfer to win the Vardon Trophy while playing in buckskin. Ralph Guldahl nailed two U.S. Opens together and became the first chap ever to manage a subpar Open. For this he was awarded two ears and a tail, although historians fail to tell us of what.

Byron Nelson and Ben Hogan, riding bareback pintos and living off jerky, left caddie ranks at Glen Garden Club in Fort Worth to conquer the world.

Nelson once won one hundred consecutive tournaments, or maybe it was eleven, with an average round of 68.33 strokes, leading Hitler's generals to sue for peace in our time.

Hogan invented the steely stare, later adopted by bankers everywhere, and pronation, and cornered the market on international golf acclaim.

Lloyd Mangrum, acting his look as a riverboat gambler, would give any pilgrim three a side and relieve him of his poke.

Jimmy Demaret could sing all night and shoot 64 by dawn's early light.

Mind you, these Texans rattled around the country in battered jitneys with a long rubber hose with which to siphon fuel from unsuspecting tanks, addicted to three-hundred-dollar purses and peanut-butter sandwiches. They took everything that wasn't chained to the back porch and they all sprang from the same roots.

Scientists rushed to examine these creatures, much as they flock to a dig when Piltdown bones are unearthed. Was there something in the Texas water, in the air? Were these characters lacing their barbecue sauce with dope?

Theories were a dime a package. Texas golfers played 360 days a year, whereas weather in most other areas limited activity. Texans learned to play on Bermuda greens, it was said, and anyone who could putt on Bermuda greens could knock them in blindfolded on truer surfaces around other sectors of the nation.

Texans learned to hit the ball off hard dirt, hit it squarely and exactly for there is less margin for error than on fluffy fairways. They learned to play in the wild winds that swept off the plains, learned to keep the ball low if needed, sail it high if air travel was desired, play the bump-and-run, to use the putter in strange situations.

The "Texas wedge" was a putter used from the frog hair and out of bunkers and, occasionally, to whop a rattlesnake.

(Mike Souchak once told of his first visit to the Odessa Pro-Am, a legendary West Texas hustle haven, figuring he could fleece a bunch of redneck rubes out of their brogans. He got a rude awakening the first day when he walked down a fairway and met a native foursome on an adjoining hole. They had on hard hats, slick shoes, they were ten under par, cussing, and throwing clubs, said enlightened Mike.)

There was a second echelon of Texans—Jack Burke, Ray Gafford, Ernie Vossler, Doug Higgins. Then a coach at North Texas State, Fred Cobb offered the first collegiate golf scholarships and turned out polished competitors like Don January, Joe Conrad, Billy Maxwell, and a host of others.

Then Dave Williams at the University of Houston enlarged the idea, producing Rex Baxter, Jacky Cupit, Kermit Zarley, Marty Fleckman, John Mahaffey, Phil Rodgers, Homero Blancas, Babe Hiskey, Tom Jenkins, Fred Marti, Rocky Thompson, Bill Rogers, Bruce Lietzke, Fred Couples, and a regiment of others. Dave Marr, Charles Coody, Dave Eichelberger, Bert Weaver, Terry Dill, DeWitt Weaver, Butch Baird—all those guys were developed in Texas college ranks.

Lee Trevino became a rather prominent fast-draw Texan, but he came from dirt floors instead of grassy campi. Trevino captured more of golf's imagination than any Texan except Hogan. Said he wanted to win enough money to buy the Alamo and give it back to Mexico. Instead he won enough money to buy Mexico.

Then, even the Lone Star loyalists had to admit, the Texas crop became skimpier. Instead of our cup runneth over, our cup runneth out.

California and Florida began flooding the circuit with a bunch of flat-bellied surfers, all hitting the ball beyond the clouds and putting with the confidence of a pickpocket at a detectives' convention.

Ben Crenshaw was heralded as the next dominating Texan, but he spent so much time in the woods Deane Beman made him an honorary bear. His Texas teammate Tom Kite has proven much more consistent, but to this date, anyway, no one has mentioned him in the same sentence as Hogan and Nelson and Trevino.

So the Sesquicentennial State—there's that goldurn word again—no longer dominates the golf tour.

Perhaps this young waddy, Scott Verplank, can mount the flag back on the ramparts. He'll get a bigger buildup even than Crenshaw because, as a tender collegian, he played against the pros and beat 'em. Some of his home statesmen claim the Dallas kid is the best amateur who ever took up the stick, but then you know how Texans love to brag. I mean, this Verplank kid will soon be driving a Cadillac so big, one of its accessories is a Ford.

Magic Deal

Dan Jenkins

Program, U.S. Women's Open, 1991

The golfer hit the ball, the ball went up in the air, the ball came down on the green—and backed up. Yeah. Spun backwards. Magic deal.

That's the first thing I remember about Colonial.

I was eleven years old. I was at the U.S. Open of 1941, the little pasteboard ticket on my belt, the little striped polo shirt on my concave chest, the little moccasins on my feet, my dad having a cocktail in the old original white-frame clubhouse.

"This is the National Open," my dad said, tying the ticket firmly on my belt. "These are the greatest golfers in the world. Go watch them. I'll be in the clubhouse."

That clubhouse was sure bigger than the ones at Katy Lake or Worth Hills. Probably had more than one cold-drink box in there.

Anyway, I slid down the hill to watch golfers at the ninth green. That's where the balls kept backing up.

"Geeagh, look at the ball back up!" I would say to anybody near me in the gallery. "How can they do that?"

"Backspin," somebody explained.

"Backspin? Boy, nobody better do that at Katy Lake or Worth Hills—they'll get in a fistfight."

Of course, it was impossible to get backspin at Katy Lake or Worth Hills, the only two golf courses I had ever seen until that first day at Colonial.

Katy Lake, a nine-hole course that would later become the Seminary South Shopping Center, the place where I had played my first round of golf ever at the age of eight, had sand greens. The only thing that ever backed up at Katy Lake was the rake.

And nobody ever backed up a shot on the rock-hard Bermuda greens at Worth Hills, which later became—tragically, if I may say so—part of the TCU campus. Worth Hills was where I had reamed to improve my score by discovering mulligans and refusing to count strokes I didn't like.

But there I was at Colonial, at the National Open, which was what everybody called it then, gazing at grass that laid down flat. Bent greens. Very mysterious.

It was every bit as mysterious as the sight of golfers wearing pants without a belt.

"How do they keep their pants up with no belt?" I asked people in the gallery.

Nobody knew. This was Fort Worth, after all.

That night, I entertained my grandparents with tales of grass that laid down flat and men wearing pants with no belts.

"Don't be silly," my grandmother said. "Grass doesn't lay down flat and pants won't stay up without a belt."

"Golfers wear pants with no belt," I insisted.

"Well," my grandmother said, "golfers might but people don't."

Those bent greens at the National Open at Colonial were responsible for the only period in my life when I was interested in agronomy.

I soon built my own nine-hole course that played from my grandmother's front yard to her backyard to the vacant lot next door to my aunt's yard across the street. I planted bean cans for cups, and with a lawn mower, a garden hose, and a pair of scissors, if I say so myself, I groomed the finest greens south of Berry Street and west of Hemphill.

The grass never would lay down completely flat, and I never had a pitch shot back up, unless it struck the side of the house.

I would hit shot after shot to the dreaded No. 4, located between a bed of iris and a fish pond, but the ball never backed up. Then my life took a funny turn.

It was a decade later that I found myself playing Colonial in college golf matches, leading the TCU Horned Frogs to something less than first place in the Southwest Conference.

There I was, three-putting on grass that laid flat down. This, I might add, was a considerably tougher Colonial than the one you see today. The greens were the size of place mats, and huge old trees hung over them. Uncultivated ditches bordered several fairways.

Take the famous No. 5, for example. It's still a great hole, but in those days, it was impossible for anyone but Ben Hogan to play. The fairway was narrower because of a watery ditch that ran along the left side. No bail-out. The green was smaller, it sat closer to the Trinity River, and the overhanging limbs protected it from any second shot in flight.

Take No. 13, please. This seemed to demand a prodigious shot across a combination of waste and water where anything short, right, or long was lost.

Take No. 15, once the second hardest par-four on the course. Why? Because there were trees that are no longer there which required you to hit a hook-fade off the tee in order to find the fairway, and then you faced a second shot to a tiny green with water on the left, out-of-bounds on the right, and your pocket if you were long.

But I could make the ball back up by then, especially when I didn't need it to do that.

Which is my other vivid memory of Colonial. My voice ringing out through the pecan trees, as I yelled more than once: "That's right! Now back up, you lousy, rotten . . ."

Once Upon a Green

Turk Pipkin

Texas Monthly, *April 1994*

I was eight years old when my dad took me to the sun-drenched links of West Texas and taught me how to caddie. Though his golf bag weighed down my shoulder and practically dragged the ground, somehow I slogged around eighteen holes without falling too far behind. That night, completely exhausted, I fell into a heavy sleep, dreaming of my day in the company of men as we walked on playing fields of green.

Caddying became a glorious summer job: toting bags, fixing divots, and tending pins, not even knowing how much money I had earned for the round until the golfers had settled all bets and I had cleaned the clubs and replaced them in the spacious trunk of a big Lincoln or Cadillac. I'd wait with eager anticipation as either a five or a ten was peeled off a money clip and handed over. Ten bucks meant I'd done a good job, that I'd been part of a team. After I finished caddying, I usually played a few holes myself, experimenting with what I had seen. Somewhere along the way, I learned about the sweet mysteries of golf, gambling, profanity, and bad jokes. My skin was tan to the bone ("Like a wild Indian," my friends used to say), a badge of honor that proved I was training for a way of life that I would come to love and to miss. Never again would the sky seem so blue.

Life, as we all know, is no longer so simple, and neither is golf. Vast hordes of players now ride electric or gasoline-powered carts, frequently on curbed cement paths, parking and rushing to the far reaches of the hole like nervous lemmings. Not knowing the yardage to the green, they carry a jumbled selection of clubs, none unfortunately ever the right one, resulting in a hike back to the cart. The price of participating in this ridiculous spectacle is a tiring five-hour round, instead of the invigorating three hours that it would take the golfer to walk with a caddie—if one were available.

The once-proud golf tradition of young caddies who earn while they learn has long since fallen victim to courses that depend on cart revenue, to increasingly lazy golfers, and to a generation of kids who would rather watch TV than work for modest wages. The few professional caddies working in Texas are mostly lifers who eke out a living on the most private and most expensive courses in the state.

Not that long ago, carrying a bag was perhaps the best introduction to the game. All my current golf buddies started as caddies. Wearing shorts and high-top sneakers with laces untied, my friends and I carried for a grand assortment of golfers: kindly men who bought us hot dogs, show-offs who tipped for every piece of good advice, beer hounds with a six-pack and a bag of ice stuffed into their monstrous bags, and cheats who slipped us an extra five and said, "Make sure I get good lies." They were doctors, oilmen, ranchers, and a few hotshot golfers who supported themselves by winning modest tournament prize money and gambling on the side. There was even a crazed club-tosser who claimed that Lord Balfour once said, "It is better to smash one's club than to lose one's temper." I have never met a former caddie who does not look back with great fondness upon his days as a beast of burden.

Legendary Texas golf instructor Harvey Penick started his eighty-year career in golf as a caddie at the Austin Country Club in 1912. "I was eight," says Penick—taking a break from signing numerous copies of his new *Little Green Book*—"and the bigger boys would've chased me off if it hadn't been for my brother Tom, who was caddie number one. Any boy who caused trouble for me would've had to whip Tom, which they couldn't do. We made twenty cents for nine holes, fifty cents for eighteen if you did a good job. With only six to eight clubs, the bag wasn't too heavy, and we didn't have to read the greens because they were all level and made of sand. The main thing, because the rough was so bad, was to watch that ball."

Penick and his fellow caddies were allowed on the course only with someone else's bag on their shoulders. He recalls, "One day my buddy

Charlie and I decided we had fifty cents, and we went out and played. We were on number eight when the pro raised up out of the bunker and wanted to know what we were doing. He told us to leave the course right then and go get our money back. After that, we played in a pasture and teed the ball up on cow dung." To this day Penick refers to himself as a grown caddie still studying golf.

Former Professional Golf Association, Masters, and U.S. Open champion Byron Nelson, now eighty-two years old, started caddying when he was twelve in Fort Worth. "I was going to school, of course, and I asked some of the kids where they got their dimes and quarters, and they said they caddied over at Glen Garden Country Club," he says.

"The caddie master at Glen Garden was Harold Akey, and he taught me what I needed to know. Then he told the first guy I caddied for that I was new. The guy said that if I didn't lose a single ball, I'd get an extra quarter. I was very excited about that, but then he sliced his very first tee shot into the rough, and I never did get that quarter." Byron Nelson's fellow caddie at Glen Garden was a tough young kid named Benny Hogan. Between the two of them, they would go on to win 115 PGA events, remarkable proof that they learned how to do much more than just find golf balls while they worked out of Mr. Akey's caddie shack.

Among the ranks of celebrated former caddies are Bill Clinton, Jesse Jackson, and even Bill Murray, who drew upon his own caddie-shack memories to steal the heart of the best movie ever made about the game. Jerry Jeff Walker refers wistfully to his golden days as a caddie at New York's Oneonta Country Club, a wooded and hilly tract. Caddies were allowed to play after six, and with his fellow loopers, Jerry Jeff often played until it was too dark to see the ball, racing daylight to use every last second of the sun.

There seems to be a move afoot to revive some of that young passion before it is lost forever. Both the United States Golf Association and *Golf Digest* have been touting caddie crusades intended to restore the game to its finest form. Caddie shacks are now referred to by the

USGA as caddie houses and are supposed to be wholesomely free of drugs, alcohol, tobacco, and profanity. Participants in caddie training programs are taught a basic understanding of the game and such life lessons as punctuality and "professional demeanor."

I can only hope this puritan approach won't also take all the fun out of caddying. In my caddie days, "professional demeanor" meant helping one's employer win his match—period. No one cared if we pitched pennies or turned green smoking Swisher Sweet cigars behind the pump house; no one cared, that is, as long as we knew the yardages and repaired the ball marks on the green. Jerry Jeff—hardly a model of professional demeanor in his adult years—doesn't think he picked up any bad habits at the caddie shack. He has, however, identified one hint of his future compulsive behavior: He once drank so many Pepsis at the golf course—thirteen in one day—that the caddie master cut him off cold turkey.

In many parts of the country, the ultimate caddie payday is selection for one of the two hundred annual Chick Evans Caddie Scholarships, which provide full tuition and housing to former caddies at fourteen universities. No Texas courses participate, but River Oaks Country Club in Houston is now recruiting caddies sixteen years and older at local churches and schools.

One theory why Texas lags behind in the caddie revival is that our scorching summer weather discourages golfers from walking during the three months that young people are available to caddie. Maybe that's why a good hat and gallons of iced tea were among my first lessons when my dad taught me to caddie. I was just tall enough to reach the flag when he showed me how to keep it from flapping in the wind as I tended the pin, being careful all the while to keep my shadow off the line of the putt. My father felt the caddie's most important job was to keep his eye on the ball, mark its location, and be able to walk straight to it. He also taught me how to read the greens in case my opinion was asked and to keep my mouth shut at all other times.

Again it was my dad—a good judge of character and a man who seemed to know everyone—who taught me how to find this gainful employment, just as he had taught me to address all players as "sir" and, most importantly, to walk tall when I had that bag on my shoulder, no matter how much it weighed. Of course, what he was teaching me was not simply how to be a caddie but how to get along in life.

While I have been writing this story, my father has been lying very ill in the hospital. He had been having trouble walking and had gone in for knee surgery. Complications followed, and as I stood by his bed, all I could think was that he had just wanted to play a little more golf. And I, of course, just wanted to caddie for him one more time.

I still remember how he used to switch all of his clubs from his heavy tournament bag to a plaid canvas bag that had once belonged to his father. He paid me five dollars a round, often depositing it directly in my bank account. I don't remember how I spent the money; the important thing was that I had earned it.

So passed the summers of my youth until one June, when I discovered that I had grown from caddie into golfer. Thirty years later, I can honestly say that, despite thousands of rounds and countless hours of practice, reading, and instruction, most of what I know about golf I learned with someone else's bag on my shoulder.

Part Two

Hogan

Hogan

Dan Jenkins

Fairways and Greens, *June 1994*

Ever since I was a kid and heard it "live" on the radio, and read about it in the newspaper, and saw it happen in a newsreel at the Hollywood Theater in Fort Worth, I've vigorously contended that Ben Hogan, my idol from the same hometown, won his first National Open in June of 1942, even though it came at a time when I couldn't find a Hershey bar anywhere because America and chocolate had gone to war.

This feat of Ben's, of course, has turned out to be terribly inconvenient for certain historians, inasmuch as it gives Hogan five Opens instead of four, or one more than Bobby Jones and Jack Nicklaus, not to forget Willie Anderson, who used to bring the monsters to their knees with rounds of 81.

Okay, that championship in '42 wasn't formally called the U.S. Open—it was the Hale America National Open Golf Tournament.

Okay, it wasn't played at Interlachen in Minneapolis, where the '42 Open was originally scheduled—it was played at the Ridgemoor Country Club in Chicago. Interlachen backed out as the host club a few months after Pearl Harbor, basically, I assume, because many of its potential gallery marshals and rough-growers had gone off to fight Germans and Japanese.

Okay, the championship wasn't run exclusively by the blue coats and armbands—it was only cosponsored by the U.S. Golf Association, along with the PGA of America and the Chicago District Golf Association.

Okay, the proceeds at the Ridgemoor didn't go to the USGA to invest in turf experiments—they went to benefit the United Service Organizations and the Navy Relief Fund.

And, okay, Ridgemoor was not as properly manicured as the normal Open course, which is to say that with the war on, the late Joe Dey didn't have the work force to grow the rough up to everybody's knees, shave the greens down to marble, and reduce Ridgemoor's par from 72 to 70.

But to all of those things I have always said: So what?

It behooves me to remind everyone that they played a "wartime" Masters in April that year, which Byron Nelson won, and historians count it. They played a "wartime" PGA in May that year, which Sam Snead won at Seaview in Atlantic City, and historians count it.

So what's wrong with counting the only National Open that was played in '42, particularly since it was won by Ben Hogan and not by Joe Zilch?

I've never had a problem putting Ben's victory at Ridgemoor in 1942 in the same lofty category with his great triumphs at Riviera in '48, Merion in '50, Oakland Hills in '51, and Oakmont in '53.

I might add—for whatever sentimental value it might have—that Ben didn't use to have a problem with this either.

There was this day, I recall, when Ben returned to Colonial Country Club in Fort Worth after winning at Merion in '50. Somebody said, "Congratulations on your second Open, Ben."

"Third," Ben responded quietly as he walked away.

There was this day at Colonial when Ben returned from winning at Oakland Hills in '51. Somebody said, "Congratulations on your third Open, Ben."

"Fourth," he said, smiling, going about his business.

Not to imply that Hogan ever went around campaigning for a fifth Open. Ben does consider that he won a major at Ridgemoor.

Well, look. Hogan has these five gold medals, see? They still highlight the Ben Hogan Trophy Room at Colonial, and all five medals look exactly the same, like the kind of medal they give you when you win a U.S. Open championship.

I say a man who owns five gold medals for winning U.S. Opens has won five U.S. Opens.

One day I delved into the newspaper microfilms to refresh my memory and strengthen my argument about that championship in 1942.

It seems that a record 1,540 golfers entered local qualifying at sixty-nine sites around the country. It also seems that sectional qualifying was held in Toronto; Boston; Chicago; Kansas City; Denver; Bloomfield, New Jersey; Atlanta; Detroit; Minneapolis; Buffalo; Cincinnati; Tulsa; Dallas; and Los Angeles.

I ask you: What were they doing holding nationwide qualifying tournaments if there wasn't going to be something similar to a U.S. Open at Ridgemoor Country Club in mid-June of '42?

Here's a paragraph from the Associated Press report of the opening rounds:

"There was a furor of excitement in the locker rooms when officials of the United States Golf Association ruled that the irons of Sam Byrd of Ardmore, Pa., were too deeply scored and that he could not use them."

I ask you this: What was the USGA doing inspecting grooves—or ruling on anything else—if this was not a U.S. Open?

This championship unfolded the way most U.S. Opens do. Otey Crisman, a "little-known pro from Alabama," tied Mike Turnesa for the first-round lead. Turnesa held the thirty-six-hole lead by three strokes over Hogan, who shot a 62 in the second round. Hogan moved into a fifty-four-hole tie with Turnesa at 203, as Jimmy Demaret became a strong contender, only two shots back.

With only four holes to play in the final round, Demaret led by two strokes, but Hogan played the last four holes in two under for a closing 68 and a seventy-two-hole total of 271, while Demaret played the last four holes in three over and wound up tied with Turnesa for second.

HALE AMERICA IS FIRST MAJOR TITLE FOR TEXAS BEN.

That was the headline in the *Fort Worth Star-Telegram.*

The lead on the AP report of June 22, 1942, reads:

> CHICAGO, June 21—Tiny Ben Hogan, never before a winner in a major golf tournament, crashed to a dramatic victory in the Hale America National Open Sunday with a 72-hole total of 271, 17 under par for the distance.
>
> The 29-year-old Texan stood off a late challenge by colorful Jimmy Demaret. Demaret led Hogan by two strokes through 68 holes, but Hogan, refusing to blow up under pressure, picked up five strokes on the last four holes to triumph.

I have only one last thing to ask: If that wasn't a U.S. Open in '42, how come Hogan won it?

The Accident

Bo Links

from Follow the Wind

It was past six o'clock, and Hogan would be back any moment. The card catalog told me they had the other reference I needed. This one was located on the first tier, not far from where I was standing. It was right under one of the black windows, in a spot where there was plenty of light, for the sun's bright spears penetrated this part of the room unaffected by the color of stained glass.

I was turning the pages frantically, for I did not know the exact date to look for. It was the year after my brother was born but a different month. Probably in February. But was it the first or the twenty-eighth? The advertisements told of men's suits selling for under $35 and two-bedroom houses going for about $12,500 in a nice area.

There he was, on the cover of *Time.* Big and bright, Bantam Ben Hogan smiled like a champion. It was January 10, 1949, and he had just completed a staggering run of championship golf, becoming the first player in history to capture the U.S. Open, the PGA Championship, and the Western Open in the same year. The glory of his game now transcended the confines of a golf course and, like one of his drives, carried far and true. If this magazine cover was any indication, Ben Hogan's name was hurtling down the middle of that wide fairway known as mainstream America.

Sifting through the books and papers, I found a hard-news story that told about the Phoenix Open. He shot 270. Lost a playoff to Demaret, but they were all saying he was starting out just like he had left off. It was odds-on he would be the leading money winner once again. The loss at Phoenix was his first defeat of the 1949 campaign; he had already won twice, at Long Beach and at the Crosby. It was a scintillating opening month, and the rest of the year held great promise.

But now, in the afterglow of his quick start, Hogan was going home to Fort Worth to rest until the Masters, which wouldn't be played until April. He was going to be ready. The Hawk had never won that one, and he wanted it badly.

Then I saw the article I had been looking for. It was all there, just as I'd heard. The place was somewhere east of Van Horn, Texas; the date, February 2; the time, about 8:30 A.M.; the weather, hazy sunshine—at least it was hazy until a dense fog covered the twisting highway, Route 80. He had just checked his tires because he suspected a flat; instead all he found was ice on the pavement, so he cut his speed down to almost nothing. He started up again and was inching along, barely going thirty, when four headlights came bearing down on him. Two of them belonged to a huge Greyhound bus, driven by an impatient Alvin

H. Logan, who was trying to pass an Alamo Freight Lines semi. The bus was barreling right at Hogan as it tried to pass the truck. There was nowhere for the Hawk to turn: a culvert was to the right, and that plodding six-wheeler was dead ahead on the left. It was his shiny, spanking new Cadillac against a runaway bus. Fractured pelvis. Broken collarbone. Three busted ribs. Broken ankle. Bladder injury. Massive contusions to the left leg. Hogan's entire body was reshuffled like a deck of cards.

The article said he saved his wife's life by covering her body with his own. Hogan's own account of what happened was, well, classic Hogan: "I just put my head down," he later said, "and dived across Valerie's lap, like I was diving into a pool of water."

As for Valerie, it was nothing but a feeling of hopelessness. "It was the end," she recalled to a reporter. "A situation in which we had no chance." In a touch of irony, only moments before, the Hogans had been discussing the highway hazards that confront professional golfers, men who travel so much but are seldom involved in collisions.

In the early seconds after impact, the Iceman was lying so still that Valerie thought he was dead. When she felt him twitch, she knew he hadn't left her; she also knew she had to do something fast, but she was pinned underneath him. She wriggled free, after which she stopped a man and woman who were driving by.

Hogan himself would later recount the postaccident trauma in the forget-me-not parlance of a man who had just brushed off death. "I remember my leg was hurting," he said, "and I asked somebody to hold it. Then I started getting very cold and asked them to cover it. I passed out again—I guess I passed out a dozen times before the ambulance finally got there. I don't remember them putting me in it."

It wasn't like the sirens pulled up right away. The postaccident scene was horrific, the tangled wreckage blocking the highway, people milling about. Valerie said she aged a hundred years in an hour and a half. Her husband kept getting grayer and grayer. "Mrs. Hogan said it was ninety minutes after the crash before an ambulance arrived to pick up her husband," one article reported. "Confusion in the crowd that gathered was blamed for the delay, several believing that others had already summoned an ambulance."

If the Hawk had his way, they would have taken him on to Pecos, a town eighty-nine miles ahead on the route they'd been traveling. At least that's what he said to the ambulance driver after regaining consciousness. Was it delirium? Or a commonsense suggestion? The professionals were acting out of instinct. The Hawk couldn't move; all he could do was think, so that's what he did. And when he thought, he was guided by sound principles. He wanted to keep going east. Why? It was closer to home in Fort Worth. Did Hogan know they were taking him all the way back to El Paso? Not likely. "If he'd have known that," Valerie said later, "we would've had real trouble with him."

The ambulance stopped briefly in Van Horn so that X rays could be taken, then continued on to El Paso, a full 119 miles distant. They checked him into a Catholic hospital called Hotel-Dieu. The doctors who attended him were named Villareal, Cameron, Fenner, and Green.

What could Bantam Ben have been thinking about during that long ride to El Paso? About the Open and PGA Championship he'd won the previous year? About the money and the glory? The short thumb? About the fools who were standing around gawking at the wreckage, assuming someone else had made the call to the ambulance people? Or about just hanging on to the thread of life long enough for doctors to have a shot at saving his mangled body?

The newspaper said it all so matter-of-factly: "The physicians expressed confidence that Hogan would be able to play golf again." They weren't so sure, though: ". . . but would not venture to guess as to when."

Some of them were even more glib, if that was possible. It was "dollars to doughnuts he would be back on the tournament trail sooner than expected." Easy for them to say.

Reading on, I learned that two weeks after the original surgery, a nasty blood clot moved from Hogan's legs up to his chest, through the right half of his heart, and into his lungs. When the Iceman complained of chest pains, the physicians investigated and knew right away that they had another emergency on their hands, arguably more life-threatening than the accident itself. Not only was there a blood clot in the danger zone, but they detected another one, lower down. Would it move? No one knew, but they couldn't take any chances.

Knowing they needed an expert, the local team of doctors picked up the telephone and called the Mayo Clinic. They were told to find Alton S. Ochsner, a renowned professor of surgery affiliated with Tulane University in New Orleans. But there was a problem. Even if they could reach him, there was no direct flight from the Crescent City to El Paso. Hogan was fading fast. His blood count was dropping, and everyone knew the obvious: They were going to run out of time unless something extraordinary happened.

It was a desperate hour, but fortunately for Hogan, his brother Royal had an idea. He called Brigadier General David E. Hutchison, the commander at Biggs Air Force Base, located near the hospital. When he finally caught up with Hutchison, he put forth a simple question: Could the general help the Hawk, a man who had served two years in the Air Force during wartime?

The answer came with action, not words. The general put together a B-29 crew in the middle of the night—3:30 A.M. to be exact—and sent them screaming through the air to New Orleans. They returned to El Paso by 11:30 that morning, having touched down in Louisiana barely long enough to get Dr. Ochsner on board.

No one knew if they had acted in time. The doctors in El Paso had thinned Hogan's blood to prevent further clotting. His hematocrit was down to 17, which meant the percentage of red cells to overall blood volume was drastically low. It was approximately one-third of normal. If the number dropped much further, Hogan's heart probably would fail. One of the wire services prepared an obituary.

The first thing Dr. Ochsner did on arrival was to order several transfusions. He restored Hogan's blood count as best he could, and although it was well below what was normally considered a safe level for surgery, he knew he could not wait any longer. For two hours, the greatest golfer in the world was under the scalpel, clinging to life. The surgical team cut a wide incision in Hogan's abdomen and tied off his vena cava, the vein that feeds blood to the heart from below. If it hadn't been done, there was a danger that a third clot might form and float up from one of Bantam Ben's legs and cause a fatal lung clot. The words "pulmonary embolism" hung over the surgical team like a storm cloud.

While Hogan was in surgery, Valerie and Royal were in the hospital chapel praying for a miracle. She had no way of knowing what was going on in the operating room, and all she could do was look within herself and hope for the best. Finally, late in the afternoon of February 19, the danger passed. Hogan was gaunt and weak. He was twenty-six pounds underweight, but he was alive.

He required around-the-clock nursing care. Valerie actually moved into the hospital with him, and when Hogan's night nurse took ill, she filled in, dutifully staying beside him until dawn for weeks on end.

When June rolled around, Cary Middlecoff and the others were in Chicago, attacking Medinah, while Hogan was hobbling on ankles so swollen they could not be encased in ordinary footwear. A pair of unlaced GI boots had to make do. Hogan pushed on, walking when he could, as far as he could. The surgery had disrupted the circulation in his legs to such an extent that swelling and pain in the lower portions of his body had become a daily experience, particularly when he moved around. How would he ever walk a golf course again?

I wonder if Hogan ever read any of those articles. How could those reporters know of his pain, of the torture he put his body through after diving desperately to save the woman he loved? He was Bantam Ben, the Hawk, the Iceman, the King of the Links—and yet when the bugle sounded the call of distress, he answered the summons without hesitation, risking everything. Some would say after the fact that the leap across Valerie's body actually saved not one life, but two, for the steering wheel was pushed clean through to the backseat from the impact of the collision. Had Hogan not moved quickly, he would have been back there with it.

It was not a lonely time when he—and he alone—could only wonder if the touch, the feel, would still be there when the doctors cleared him to swing again. *If* they cleared him to swing again. What if he couldn't do it anymore? What then? A club job giving lessons on Tuesday morning? No, thank you. That was not for him.

Well-Wishers Greet Hogan at End of Fifty-nine-Day Journey

Jack Murphy

Fort Worth Star-Telegram, *April 2, 1949*

Ben Hogan stretched his gaunt frame beneath a warming sateen comforter in the "hospital" room of his new home at 24 Valley Ridge Road late Friday afternoon, thus ending a pilgrimage that began fifty-nine days ago.

A few moments earlier, a broad smile had creased his features as a small gathering gave him a spontaneous volley of applause at the T&P depot.

He was lowered cautiously and deliberately from the Texas Eagle's rear car, a halting and clumsy process that somehow seemed out of step for the champion of America's links.

But Hogan by now has regulated himself to inactivity and confinement. His smile seldom departed as he was wheeled the length of the tracks and carried down precipitous steps leading to the waiting room.

Exploding flashbulbs marked his route as friends rushed to his side to shake the left hand he proffered from beneath a reddish brown blanket. His mother, striving to hold back tears, hovered anxiously at his head, bending over him occasionally for hurried words of welcome.

An emotional moment rivaling, perhaps surpassing, his triumphs in the PGA and National Open tournaments came at the end of a torturously slow ambulance ride to the home that he left two days after Christmas.

"See, the rosebuds in the yard," said Mrs. Hogan, as he was carried from the driveway to the front door of his home in Westover Hills. "See them?"

"I see them, they're wonderful."

Wheeled inside, he was aided by his brother Royal and an attendant to the made-over bedroom off the dining room.

Beside his bed he found gayly colored flowers, a walker to be used during convalescence, and countless greetings from friends.

"The newspapermen would like to see who the cards are from," suggested Mr. Ralph Walters, Hogan's brother-in-law.

"Sure, sure, open them," answered Ben.

One card bore the name of Rags Matthews, TCU's all-American end of another era.

"I remember when I used to slip under the fence to watch Rags play," Ben said, smiling again.

"Is this your bedroom?" a reporter asked.

"No, we didn't have any furniture in here. I guess it's a good thing. We're turning it into a hospital room."

While his immediate family and a nurse hovered in the doorway, Hogan good-naturedly submitted to reporters' questions.

"Ben, can you give us any idea when you'll be back playing again?"

"I don't think anybody can tell."

"Were there many letters and wires while you were at El Paso?"

"A tremendous amount of letters, flowers, calls, and wires. People have been great. People you don't even know have taken an interest. They've just been great."

Hogan was reminded that his home—in which he had lived only

eight days before his accident—was burglarized in the second week of his stay at El Paso.

"I don't know what's missing, but they took a Christmas present Bing Crosby sent me. I saw Bing in California and told him that the present had arrived after I left. He wouldn't tell me what it was.

"It was still in the package when they broke in here. They unwrapped it and took whatever it was.

"They also took a watch that was given to me for being captain of the Ryder Cup team last year. And a watch I got for winning the Motor City Open at Detroit."

Further such burglaries were avoided, Mrs. Hogan said, when the services of a night watchman were obtained.

Though the trip home was smooth and uneventful, Hogan had passed a restless night, sleeping no more than thirty minutes at a stretch. Friday morning, he was haggard and worn and complained of aches in his back and legs.

"Ben said I wasn't much of a nurse," grinned his pretty wife. "I slept all night." It was her first night in bed in three weeks. She had been in a chair beside his hospital bed until dawn each morning after a night nurse became ill.

All discomfort faded, however, in the happiness of being home. Mrs. Hogan tried, almost unsuccessfully, to keep back her tears. And Ben just grinned and grinned.

"It's great to be back," said the man who had won a miraculous battle with death.

Flattery

Gene Gregston

Fort Worth Star-Telegram, *July 23, 1953*

NEW YORK—For the most part, New York's writers have been captured by Ben Hogan, just as have all the major golf titles in the world. It took our Texan the better portion of twenty-eight years—a long haul in the athletic domain—to make both conquests because these metropolitan scribes, like those championships, are not easy to come by.

One, in particular, is famous, or infamous as the case may be, for his barbed-wire typewriter, but even Jimmy Cannon of the *Post,* though getting in his minimum requirement of "digs," had to succumb to the politeness, charm, and humble attitude of Hogan.

It appeared that Cannon may have done so unwillingly, resisting to the last, but Cannon, like Carnoustie and Oakmont and the Masters, finally bowed.

The battle progressed as follows, quoting Cannon:

> New York, many a visitor claims, is a hostile city where all people remain strangers forever. Those who know Ben Hogan tell me he is a calculating man, withdrawn and chilly.
>
> "Even when Ben says hello," a golfing journalist explained, "he looks at you like a landlord saying pay the rent or get out." [Note: See, there's a cleverly turned bit of spadework into Hogan.]
>
> They enjoyed each other's company, the city and the man who have reputations for being cold. Of course, this affair wasn't spontaneous. But Hogan excited the people who stood in the heat and watched him go up Broadway in an open car to City Hall. He seemed touched by their adulation.
>
> [At Toots Shor's] there came the sound of cheering. The drinkers moved away from the bar and started toward the foyer as Hogan

came through the turning, glass-paneled door. They applauded and this wasn't rehearsed. He turned around, looking at them, slightly embarrassed by this demonstration. It wasn't planned and neither was what Thelma Knight, the hatcheck girl, said:

"Let them climb Mount Everest," she said. "We play golf."

It was good to hear, the way she said it.

They were waiting for him and again they applauded when he entered the room. There were Jim Farley and Ford Frick . . . Stan Musial . . . Red Schoendienst . . . lonesome George Weiss . . . Gene Sarazen . . . Tommy Armour . . . District Attorney Frank Hogan . . . Bernard Gimbel . . . Gene Tunney . . . Don Ameche . . . Grover Whalen . . . Jimmy Demaret . . . Horton Smith . . . Herman Hickman . . . and Shor, who picked up the tab.

"Is there anything else in golf you would like to do?" I asked him, and it sounded like a silly question because he has done it all.

"Yes," he said. "I just want to keep playing. I just hope I don't wear out too soon. Look, I'd rather win than lose. I like to win. I don't like to lose. But I hope I can continue to play a long time. Golf is my life. Competition is my life."

The famous people were standing behind their chairs on the dais. Ben Hogan, the cold man, who was being feted by the cold city, took a sip of his drink.

"I'm up on the clouds so high," he said, "I don't think I'll ever come down."

Thus, Cannon wound up giving Ben a fair shake, although the next day he lived up to his reputation by printing a little incident which was not complimentary in its connotations. It said Ben took a $5,000 check from a representative of A. S. Barnes, the publisher, for advance royalties and didn't say thanks.

Who knows, maybe the Barnes man should have said "thanks" to Ben for his golf and his appeal that provided the book's contents, its selling power, and more than the $5,000.

Another writer explained, "Cannon has to get in so many of those barbs a day, that's his style."

And, despite this and similar isolated cases that have cropped up this week, Ben's had the percentages heavily in his favor.

Figuratively speaking, Ben will have this city in his hip pocket when he returns to Fort Worth Friday.

He admitted that New York's welcome was the hardest course he's ever played. But the fact is, they just don't come too tough for Hogan.

Another Day, Another Man

Dan Jenkins

Fort Worth Press, *May 5, 1959*

In the most strenuous of courses and under the most disturbing kind of conditions, perfection was born again in the man who invented the word. Ben Hogan was suddenly back on top. And all seemed right in the world of golf, if not timeless and changeless.

It happened in six holes yesterday in that playoff for the Colonial National Invitation tournament. Fred Hawkins moved in on Hogan like a young, ambitious prizefighter, landed a couple of stinging blows, and then got knocked out with counterpunches.

Hogan's game was as right as it had ever been as he sculpted a beautiful one-under-par 69 to batter down Hawkins's 73 on a day when Fred's round might have been good enough against any other man in the sport.

It had been six long years since Hogan won a tournament on American shores. And since he is nearing forty-seven years, it had been said that he would probably never win another. The fleeting years and the lack of competition, plus the pressures of running a club-manufacturing business, had seemed to have taken a toll on his mind and body.

But there was Hogan yesterday, bent into the galelike winds, which promoted gusts up to forty-five miles per hour, hitting shots unknown and unlearned by others in the trade, planting himself firmly for deadly putts on swaying carpets, thinking out his shots with the deliberation of a Greek philosopher, and then performing them with the alarming consistency of a machine.

The calendar was being ridiculed before your very eyes.

All of the action was packed into the second, third, fourth, fifth, sixth, and seventh holes, a path that includes the most decisive stretch on Colonial Country Club's 7,021 yards of deception.

On the second and third holes the two men played one super shot after another until Hawkins took an advantage with a twelve-foot birdie on the difficult third hole.

Back on the second hole, Fred had flipped a beautiful approach out of the rough to within ten feet of the hole and Hogan had followed it with a low, skipping wedge shot that ran onto the green and came to rest a couple of feet away. Both birdied.

Then Hogan had played a remarkable two-iron around a bend of trees and onto the third green, only to see Hawkins smash a four-iron inside of him—and make the putt. Fours are against the law on No. 3, and Fred had made three.

But now they're at the fourth hole, a dangerous par-three requiring a long iron shot with the lashing wind directly behind them, angrily capable of blowing a shot clear out of control. Hawkins pulled his shot to the left of the green. And, again, Hogan cheated the wind with a stunning two-iron that hit forty yards short of the green and bounded up the slope and onto the putting surface, ten feet from the cup.

After Fred chipped up to the flag, leaving himself a five-footer for par, the playoff's most melodramatic moments began. Ben addressed his birdie putt. He backed off. A cement mixer had come churning down the road, snarled in the traffic of those unemployed who didn't purchase tickets and were peering over the fence at this curious Monday-afternoon overtime. While the gallery purred, Ben waited. It seemed like an hour. And finally he stroked the putt to assume command. Hawkins missed his par.

At the doglegging fifth hole, hardest on the course, Ben played down the middle off the tee and safely onto the green for par and let the wind undo Hawkins. Fred's tee shot soared high toward the turn of the Trinity River, but he hadn't allowed enough for the wind. His shot sailed over the trees and into the drink. He staggered out of it with a double-bogey six—and Hogan went three shots up.

Ben faltered briefly on the sixth hole, missing a three-footer for bogey, giving Fred a breath of life. But the two-shot advantage was quickly increased to four strokes on the seventh hole.

Here, Hogan played another of those trick shots, a low, run-up approach that skidded along the fairway, under the wind, and bounded up on the green within nine feet of the hole. Hawkins went over the green, chipped back, and missed his putt while Ben sank his for a bird.

So on the fourth, fifth and seventh holes, Hogan picked up six strokes by playing two-under-par golf. From the seventh to the clubhouse, Hogan managed his lead with safe blows—and it was hardly any contest at all.

"It was the finest golf I ever shot under those conditions," Ben said.

Whatever year this must be, that was Hogan at his best yesterday.

Hogan Even Took an Eleven on One Hole

Dick Peebles

Houston Chronicle, May 14, 1971

"If you're a golfer, you've had your problems," is the philosophical way Ben Hogan took the six-over-par nine he had on the 228-yard par-three hole Thursday in the opening round of the Houston Champions International at Champions Golf Club.

Hogan, who was forced to withdraw from the tournament on the twelfth hole when his left knee went out on him, said he had hit a number-three iron a little fat off the tee and it landed in the ravine fronting the green.

The fifty-eight-year-old all-time great went into the ravine to see if he could play his ball, but finally decided it was unplayable. It was while he was scrambling down the embankment that Hogan was seen to grab at his left knee.

"I may have hurt it there," he admitted.

Instead of hitting a ball from the drop area, Hogan trudged back to the tee with the same number-three iron and drove off again. Again, he went into the ravine.

Out of golf balls, Hogan borrowed one from one of the players in the following threesome. He wasn't sure if it was George Archer or Raymond Floyd.

He swung again and again hit into the ravine.

He borrowed another ball and this one he hit onto the green, then two-putted for a nine.

Asked why he did not hit a ball from the drop area, Hogan said, "I thought it was an easier shot from the tee."

Visibly disappointed over the turn of events after playing so well in practice rounds, Hogan said he will return to his home in Fort Worth today and undergo therapy on the knee in hope that it will be healed enough for him to play next week in the National Invitation Tournament at Fort Worth's Colonial Country Club.

"Don't ever grow old," he said to a friend as he climbed into a cart that carried him back to the clubhouse.

Showing that he still has a sense of humor, Hogan told about the time in the 1940s that he took an eleven on a three-par hole during the Jacksonville (Fla.) Open.

"It was in the third round," he recalled, "and I had started the day one stroke out of the lead. It was raining, and when I parred the first six holes, that are real good holes, I felt that I probably was either leading or tied for the lead.

"During practice rounds and the first two rounds of the tournament, the pin had been on the left side of the green that had a ridge going up the middle of it. It was a simple little seven-iron shot. This time the pin was on the left.

"I hit a seven iron and saw the ball land on the green," he continued. "Then my caddie says to me, 'Mistuh Hogan, I think we is in the water.' I said, 'What?' He said, 'Yes, suh, I think we is in the water.'

"I didn't know there was even any water over there," said Hogan, "but when we got down there, sure enough there it was in the edge of the water in the white sand. I figured this would be an easy shot. Nothing to it. I rolled up my pants leg and hit the ball. It came out, struck the bank, and, as I looked up, I saw it trickle back in. So I swung again. The ball came out, but again it rolled back in. By this time, I had muddied up the water so badly, I couldn't find the ball.

"So I went back across the water and dropped my ball in a pile of sand. I swung and hit that one in the water. Then I hit another to the left side of the green where I didn't want to go in the first place because I didn't want a downhill putt, and I two-putted for an eleven. I finished with an eighty-one or eighty-two. I forget which.

"When I got back to the hotel, my wife Valerie asked me what I shot. I told her eighty-one or eighty-two. She said, 'You're kidding.' I assured her I wasn't, that I had taken an eleven on a par-three hole. Then she got mad. About that time, from our corner room we could hear a newsboy down on the street yelling, 'Extra! Ben Hogan takes eleven on a par-three hole!'

"She believed me then," grinned Hogan. "Let me tell you, that night at dinner I had a lot of friends. The next day I shot a sixty-seven and finished up in the money."

With that The Hawk stubbed out a cigarette in an ashtray and finished cleaning out his locker. He was headed home to Fort Worth. The

1971 Houston Champions International had lost one of its biggest attractions.

(Editor's note: More than Champions lost that day. Hogan's last shot here turned out to be his last ever in competition.)

Where Ben Hogan Is the Man in the Window

Tom Callahan and Dave Kindred

from Around the World in 18 Holes

As Ben Hogan polished the silverware, I watched his hands. Tom and I waited at a nearby table. Hogan did each piece carefully, first the fork, then the knife and spoon. He rubbed each with his napkin and returned it to its proper place. He sat alone at a table for eight in a corner. Now and then the four other men in the room stole glances at Hogan's back. It was eleven o'clock in the morning.

Someone once asked Hogan how he would like to be remembered and he said, "As a gentleman." At eleven in the morning, he wore a gray sports coat, blue slacks, white shirt, and blue tie. He smoked a cigarette, his lighter placed just so by the package. He sipped from a glass of white wine. His hands moved slowly and surely.

Ted Williams met Hogan late in Ben's prime. The man whose hands made him one of baseball's best hitters said, "I just shook a hand that felt like five bands of steel." Hogan's hands then were as brown as rawhide. Now they were an old man's blue. Only two weeks earlier, with no fanfare, he had turned eighty-one.

Every morning, Hogan came to his corner table in the grill room at Shady Oaks Country Club. He always sat in the same place. He faced the window through which he could see the eighteenth green and up the wide fairway. For years he had lunch and then carried a five-iron a half mile to a spot hidden inside the course. There he hit balls. He might carry seven or eight balls and walk after them for the exercise. On the way, he said hello to everyone he passed.

At his practice spot, he liked silence. Mickey Wright was the best woman player ever and a fellow Texan. She often went to Fort Worth to watch Hogan hit balls. When she asked if he minded, Hogan said, "Not as long as you don't say anything."

Hogan last played competitively in 1971. His contemporary Sam Snead stayed out there by using unorthodox putting strokes, first croquet-style and later sidesaddle, dignity be damned. Not Hogan. If he couldn't be Hogan, he would become a ghost. He appeared only on his terms. He said no to Jack Nicklaus, whose Memorial Tournament honored the titans: Bobby Jones, Walter Hagen, Arnold Palmer.

When years passed and Hogan was not chosen, Callahan asked Nicklaus about it. "I'm not going to lie to you," Nicklaus said. "We invited Hogan our second year and he refused. He said, 'I don't want to be eulogized while I'm alive.'"

At Shady Oaks, in private, Hogan kept hitting balls because that's who he was, a man who hit balls. "Hogan invented practice," Jimmy Demaret said. A hard man who once heard a famous player ask for the secret to his swing, Hogan told him, "The secret's in the dirt. Dig it out, like I did."

Even at age seventy-seven he produced awe. "Fifty years older than me and hitting four-irons a hundred and ninety-five yards," said the Shady Oaks pro, Mike Wright, one of those kids Tommy Bolt called flat-bellied limberbacks. "One day a member playing with Mr. Hogan said, 'What'd you hit, Ben?' Mr. Hogan put his seven-iron back in the bag. He takes a six and hits it within three feet of the first one. He puts the six back and hits an eight-iron to six feet. He's got it surrounded. It doesn't take a genius to figure out the moral of that story."

Hogan quit hitting balls in 1991. He no longer could make a full swing that satisfied him. His friend Bolt had said of the young Hogan,

"Ben applied himself to each and every shot completely. He never in his life took no ol' funky-butt swing." In his old age, Hogan said, "I could chip, but what fun is that?"

Still, if you went into the Shady Oaks bag room in the summer of 1993 and there went to space number 51, you found a Hogan bag, a deep burgundy, its label the Ravielli line drawing of Hogan at impact. There you found the bag filled with Hogan clubs, the forged beauties his company made at his command. He hadn't hit a ball in two years, but he left the clubs there. He paid for the space, the same as everyone else. He never asked any favors.

I watched Ben Hogan's hands because I had seen them in 1967 when they were sure and strong and looked like the hands of a man who had worked at life. I watched Ben Hogan light a cigarette and I thought of my father's Lucky Strikes. These men were born a month apart in the fall of 1912, Hogan and Dad.

An upset stomach sent Dad to a doctor. He came home and died in two weeks. With so far to go, we ran out of time. Seeing Hogan's hands again, I wanted to tell Dad about his grandson and great-grandsons, Jared and Jacob who were four when Santa Claus brought them baseball gloves. Dad would have wanted to play catch.

A kid sportswriter at his first Masters in 1967 saw Red Smith roll three or four pieces of white paper into his upright Smith Corona typewriter. "You know he's not a real newspaperman if he puts only one sheet of paper in the typewriter," Red liked to say. He sat three rows from the back of the Augusta press barn, the right side of the right-hand aisle. He used both hands to insert the paper into the typewriter. His hands trembled. Red was sixty-one years old.

The kid saw Hogan on the practice range, the third man from the right end. Every shot with every club flew two yards left of the target and then fell two yards right, a fade two decades in the making, the ball dropping in the caddie's shadow.

Hogan was fifty-four, soon to be fifty-five, and he had a bad knee, left over from the car wreck that nearly killed him in 1949. At every step there was an old man's hitch. Hogan. Ben Hogan. The Hawk. All those Aprils ago, he shot 66 the third day of the Masters. His 30 on the back nine tied the record. It left him two shots out of the lead. He last had won a major tournament in 1953, the year he dominated golf, winner at Augusta and in the U.S. Open as well as in the only British Open he ever played, bringing the Carnoustie beast to heel.

That third day in 1967, early in the afternoon, the kid sat in the press barn wondering what a real sportswriter would be doing—when Hogan began his run: four straight birdies around Amen Corner.

A seven-iron to seven feet at the tenth. A six-iron to one foot at the eleventh. A six-iron to the twelfth, leaving a fifteen-foot putt that caused him to say, "I am still embarrassed to get before people and putt. Hell, I'm even embarrassed to putt when I'm alone, but the only way to beat this thing is to play. I hear children and ladies saying, 'For God's sake, why doesn't he hit it faster?' So I say to myself, 'You idiot. You heard them. Why don't you hit it faster?'"

He made the putt at the twelfth. He reached both par-fives, the thirteenth and fifteenth, with four-wood second shots for two-putt birdies. A kid's first Masters and Ben Hogan was on fire, his scoreboard numbers changing from black to the subpar signal of red, a red 2. The kid heard someone say, "We better get out there."

The kid first saw Hogan coming up the ascending cathedral aisle that is Augusta National's eighteenth fairway. Hogan walked through applause, thousands of hands clapping, a waterfall's roar. He started the day as an heirloom on display; he became a contender. He became the Hogan who had survived the car wreck and won the U. S. Open the next summer. At every green the galleries recognized the Hawk in full flight. Even Hogan, who didn't hear Carnoustie's train, heard Augusta's worshipers.

"I'd had standing ovations before," he said, "but not nine holes in a row."

At the eighteenth, Hogan put a five-iron second shot twenty feet above the hole. The kid sportswriter sat in press bleachers rising next to the green. He saw the little man in the white cap standing over the putt that day. He sees him still.

Embraced by cathedral silence, Hogan stood over the downhill putt. He stood over it and waited. And then he touched the ball gently, just started it rolling. Down the hill. Murmurs now. The ball near the hole. And then it dropped from our sight. Hogan had made the thing.

He made it for his 30, for the 66. Hurrahs raised the cathedral's roof then, and Ben Hogan took the warmth of the people and thanked them by lifting high his flat white cap. It was late in the day and his shadow fell long on the green. The kid saw this, and he was glad, and he hoped the old man, a hard man, liked it.

Hogan loved it. In the clubhouse later, he told a dozen reporters, "There's a lot of fellas who have got to fall dead for me to win. But I don't mind telling you, I'll play just as hard as I've ever played in my life."

The young hero Arnold Palmer sat off in a corner. He changed his shoes and listened. Hogan sat under a sunlit window framed by lacy white curtains. He was balding, his hair gray and white at the fringes. His face was hard and dry as a Texas summer. He would shoot an aching 77 the next day and never again play in the Masters. Not that it mattered. All that mattered was this moment, Hogan again Hogan, a man telling us again who he was.

The twilight sun came through the white lace curtains. It fell soft and golden on Ben Hogan's face one more time.

Tom and I had come to Shady Oaks at the invitation of the club's pro, Mike Wright, who now reached behind his office door to an old box of golf clubs leaning in the corner. "These are Mr. Hogan's second-to-last set of clubs," he said. "He's got the last set at home. He says he's working on them. But here. I want you to look at this."

At the end of a pilgrimage, many a believer has picked up a holy relic as proof, certain that his faith is well placed. I picked up Ben Hogan's five-iron.

"How's it look?" Wright said.

The five-iron's face looked all wrong. It looked as if someone had twisted the face to increase the loft while pulling the toe back from square. Someone, in fact, had done just that. The pro said, "Mr. Hogan did it. And feel the grip, too."

The grip was very thick and a ridge ran along its bottom side. The ridge forced my hands into a weak position on top of the shaft. Hogan had been very busy with these clubs.

"People forget how important equipment was to Mr. Hogan," Wright told us. "He thought of each club as a piece of jewelry. He designed the club face and grip over the years to help discourage the hook he'd had as a young player. I took this club to the range one day and I couldn't hit it. I hit every ball over the right-field fence."

I should pause here. Over the years, I tried many times to arrange interviews with Hogan. The best I did was a letter or call of "thanks, but no thanks." All that stuff was a long time ago, he said, and when you get to be an old man, you'll understand that memory fails. His secretary said, "You wouldn't want to embarrass Mr. Hogan," and I always said, "No, of course not, I'll write the piece without him."

In Calcutta when we decided to go to Fort Worth, Tom and I had no idea if we could meet Hogan. But we had to go. It would be good to shake his hand, maybe say a word or two, but if that couldn't be done, even if we couldn't even see him across the room, at the least we would walk the Texas ground he had walked. So from Pebble Beach we called Mac O'Grady.

When Mac explained to Mike Wright the journey we had made, the pro first hesitated—"I'm reluctant"—and then said to come ahead, he would introduce us to Hogan. Wright avoided writers because he respected Hogan's desire for privacy. Wright also said he wanted no publicity for himself. In the end, he agreed to help us for one reason alone: "I want people to know the Mr. Hogan I know."

Too young to have known Hogan as a player, the pro knew Hogan as a warm and kindly gentleman who once upon a time made history. Wright's cubbyhole office was a Hogan museum, its bookshelves heavy with Hogan theories and observations. On the wall, a 1955 *Life* magazine cover advertised Hogan revealing "The Secret" of his swing.

The pro showed us a small "golfer's watch" made in the 1950s to be attached to the belt. It carried Hogan's name on the face.

Wright took us into the pro shop's workroom, where he set up a television monitor. He wanted us to see his favorite videotape. It showed Hogan, maybe sixty-five years old, in his signature flat white cap and gray sweater, hitting balls at his Shady Oaks practice spot. Mike said, "I've talked a lot about the swing with Mr. Hogan. But he told me, 'Don't tell anybody. It's a secret.' And I never have."

We asked to go to Hogan's practice spot. On the way, the young pro parked the golf cart. If we wanted to know Mr. Hogan, we should hear this story.

"I was twenty-three years old, the assistant pro, when the Shady Oaks golf committee asked me to come to a meeting settling the head pro's estate. As far as I knew, it wasn't an interview for the head pro's job. But Mr. Hogan asked me if I had written a letter to the golf committee saying I was interested in the job. I said I had and he offered to proofread it for me.

"He said, 'Now, you know the committee is going to interview you for the job, don't you?' I said they just talked about a 'meeting,' but I assumed the job interview would be part of it. So Mr. Hogan asked me, 'What are you going to wear?'

"'What I've got on,' I said. A nice golf shirt and slacks. I didn't want to go in there wearing a suit and have the committee think I was being presumptuous. I'd just go in the way I went to work every day. Mr. Hogan told me, 'No, go buy yourself some clothes and let me pay for it.' I said I wasn't comfortable doing that. So he took off his sport coat and handed it to me. 'Wear this,' he said.

"His coat was too small, though, and, with all due respect to Mr. Hogan, it smelled of smoke. So I went to Sears and bought a coat, shirt, and tie, all for under sixty-five dollars. They even ironed it. Still, I took Mr. Hogan's coat with me to the 'meeting.' It was, in fact, an interview. When I got done, I went back to the shop. Mr. Hogan was still at the club, past the usual time when he left, and I gave him back his coat.

"I got the job the next day. I don't know if Mr. Hogan recommended me. I do know he supported me. And I also know he could have put an X on anybody he didn't want."

Grantland Rice called Hogan "soft as a fire hydrant." Henry Longhurst described him as "a small man, normal weight, no more than 140 pounds, height about five feet nine inches, with smooth black hair, wide head, wide eyes, and a wide mouth which tends, when the pressure is on, to contract in a thin, straight pencil-line. You could see him sitting at a poker table saying, expressionless, 'Your thousand—and another five.' He might have four aces, or a pair of twos."

Sam Snead remembered Hogan's eyes. "Ben'd put those steely blues of his on you. Boy. That came from his days dealing cards. He dealt in Vegas or somewhere, to make ends meet. That's how he learned that stone face. He got so he wouldn't even let Jimmy Demaret play gin rummy 'cause Jimmy's eyes'd get real big if he got good cards. Not Ben's. No, sir-eee."

This was the Hogan who in eight years, 1946 to 1953, won four United States Open championships, two Masters, two PGAs, and one British Open. This was the Hogan who came back from that terrible auto accident, came back the next summer, limping in pain, to win the U.S. Open. In 1950 Gene Sarazen called Hogan "the most merciless player of all the modern players" and said, "His temperament may derive from the rough, anguishing years of his childhood or the hostility he encountered as a young and overdetermined circuit chaser. Whatever the reason, he is the type of golfer you would describe as perpetually hungry."

Hogan was nine when his blacksmith father had health and money troubles. One night in the family's Fort Worth living room, Chester Hogan rummaged through a valise. Another son, Royal, thirteen, watched his father search the case. The boy said, "Daddy, what are you going to do?" In answer, the blacksmith shot himself above the heart. He died the next day, Valentine's Day, 1922.

To help support his family—his mother, brother Royal, and sister Princess, eleven—the little boy named just plain Ben peddled newspapers at a railroad station. Soon he heard of money to be made caddying at nearby Glen Garden Country Club. Some Saturday nights little Ben Hogan could be found asleep in a bunker at Glen Garden. The first caddies in line might carry twice on Sundays and earn an extra sixty-five cents.

As a teenager, Hogan three times was embittered by Glen Garden. At fifteen he seemed to have won a caddies' tournament in a sudden-death playoff, only to be told the playoff was a full nine holes. He then lost to the club prodigy, a skinny kid a foot taller by the name of Byron Nelson. The next year the club captain chose Nelson for a junior membership, saying, "Byron Nelson is the only caddie who doesn't drink, smoke, or curse." Without the membership, Hogan could enter no club tournaments. He could not even practice at the course where he had come to love the game. The club captain refused Hogan permission to hit balls in the caddie area. At sixteen Ben was too old for that, the man said.

By her account, Clara Hogan tried to warn her young son off golf, telling him he had no future in the game. "When I finished speaking my piece," the mother said, "Ben stood there and his eyes just blazed. He said, 'Momma, someday I'm gonna be the greatest golfer in the world.'"

He quit high school before graduation and turned pro at nineteen. In his first tournament, he tied for thirty-eighth and won $8.50. The year was 1932 and the Depression was on. While trying the golf tour, he also worked in oil fields, garages, a bank, a hotel, and as a gambling house's dealer and croupier. Years of small successes and large failures led to a moment early in 1938 when golf didn't seem worth the effort anymore.

Living on oranges and staying in cheap motels, Hogan came to the Oakland Open with eight dollars in his pocket. Sam Snead saw Hogan the morning of the tournament's final round and told the story in his autobiography:

"I remember Ben standing outside the Claremont Country Club beating his fists against a brick wall.

"'What happened, boy?' we other young pros asked.

"'I can't go another inch,' groaned Ben. He was as close to tears as that tough little guy can get. 'I'm finished. Some son of a bitch stole the tires off my car.'"

His Texas contemporaries had surpassed Hogan. Byron Nelson, out of the same caddie yard, won the New Jersey and Metropolitan Opens. Jimmy Demaret won the Texas PGA. Ralph Guldahl won the Western Open and the 1937 U.S. Open. Ben had told his wife, Valerie, that 1937 was the decision year. "Now or never," he said.

By January '38, with no money to get out of his Oakland motel, his Buick jacked up by thieves, a man whose father killed himself in the family living room would have found sympathy if he said he'd felt enough pain, it was time to quit, his doubting mother had been right after all.

Instead, Oakland shaped Hogan's career. A Texas sportswriter wrote that Hogan played the Oakland final round "with a set jaw, lips locked into a tight smile that was not a smile, and eyes of steely intensity," a portrait of the Hogan the golf world would come to know.

He shot a 69 that day to finish second to Harry Cooper and earn $380. It was enough to put tires back on the car. It was enough to convince Hogan he could go on. He won his first tournament in March 1940. In 1959 he last won a tournament. In between, *whatever the reason,* Hogan became Hogan.

Tommy Bolt, Hogan's buddy, could play some himself. He won the 1958 U.S. Open. "Ben was the greatest golfer you ever dreamed of seeing," Bolt said. "Arnold Palmer and Jack Nicklaus are great. But listen, pal. They couldn't carry Ben's jockstrap. Only way you beat Ben was if God wanted you to."

We came to the place where Hogan hit balls. It was out of the way, but hidden only in the sense that people who saw Hogan there gave him those moments alone. He dropped balls and hit them from the crest of land rising gracefully from a narrow creek two hundred yards away. There on the Hogan hill at Shady Oaks, Mike Wright felt as if he were not alone.

"Mr. Hogan is here somewhere, peering around a corner, watching," he said.

The young pro said someday it would be nice to put up a little statue on Hogan's hill.

Even with Mike's assurance of an introduction to Hogan, Tom and I didn't count on it. Things happen.

As we stopped for lunch after nine holes, we first went to the locker room. There we turned a corner toward the washbasins. And very nearly ran into the ghost.

In his coat and tie, Ben Hogan moved one hand across his thinning hair. He dropped a towel into a bin. He moved to his right a bit and passed these strangers coming in, all sweaty. Here's what Hogan said, and I know because I wrote it down. He said, "Hello."

Here's what Tom said after Hogan passed us, and I wrote it down because Tom, a hard case, is not easily impressed. (He once insulted Sonny Liston so spectacularly that he and the fearsome heavyweight champion of the world fell to wrestling around a hotel room, their nose-to-nose dance rearranging the furniture it didn't destroy.) Here is what Tom said in the Shady Oaks washroom: "Hogan. It's Hogan. It's like seeing Babe Ruth."

During lunch with Mike Wright, we watched Hogan polishing the silverware, smoking, asking for a second glass of wine. Then Mike took us to Hogan's table, where the great man rose to greet us with a smile and a twinkle in eyes once thought of as steely. He looked trim, fit, and lively. He couldn't have been more gracious to two reporters appearing at his table.

"Please, sit down, Mr. Hogan," I said. But he continued to stand by the table, the better, I supposed, to keep these things brief. Hogan always came to his work with a reason for everything he did, even for matters as simple as a cap. It was said he wore the white flat linen cap because it worried him less in the Texas wind than the wide-brimmed hats of the '40s. Sounds right.

"Welcome, welcome," he said. "It's so nice to have you here."

I told him there were traces of Hogan all over the world. "So we had to come see you."

"It's good to see you," he said.

At a mention of the 1967 Masters, he nodded and smiled but said nothing. The walk up the eighteenth fairway would have been forgotten, too. We had walked the ground of Carnoustie's sixth hole, made famous by Hogan's work there, the work so well known that historians speak of Hogan's Alley. Tom began to tell about his eagle putt. "Mr. Hogan, your hole at Carnoustie, I almost . . ."

Only to be interrupted by Hogan. "I can't remember every hole. It was so long ago, you know."

"That's all right, Mr. Hogan," Tom said. "They all remember you."

Tom's favorite memory was Hogan's surprise appearance in the press barn during Masters week of 1977. "I asked you if you ever played the perfect round, and you said you 'almost dreamed' it once: Seventeen straight holes in one, and then you lipped it out at the eighteenth." Tom looked at the smiling old man. "You said you were mad as hell."

Hogan laughed. "I think that's right."

As Red Smith used to say when he had the raw material for a column, we were rich by now. Hogan had been with us on this journey: his image on the Iceland pro shop's door . . . the Wee Icemon oblivious to the Carnoustie train . . . a French mademoiselle with a Hogan bag . . . a "Big Ben Hogan" driver for sale in Johannesburg . . . a turbaned Indian conjuring his name . . . my own bag of Hogan Radials, the clubs too good for their sorry owner . . . and now we had touched the ghost, made him real.

We would go play the back nine. Tom said, "You know, Mr. Hogan, playing the eighteenth hole here with you watching through this window, that's a lot of pressure."

"Aw," Ben Hogan said, "it's a baby golf course."

Weren't they all babies to Hogan? We said our thanks and goodbyes, and on the way out we shook hands. Hogan's hand was wide and strong. I wrote down his last words to us that afternoon. He said, "Enjoy your game. Come back."

We saw him one more time. We played the eighteenth. He was the man in the window. Smoke curled from a cigarette. We fairly well butchered the hole.

Part Three

Ben, Harvey, and Tom

Golf's Teacher of the Century

Mickey Herskowitz

Golf Digest, *May 1977*

Harvey Penick discovered golf in an era of knickers and niblicks, a more romantic time before Social Security, the electric cart, and television, when a pro entered a country club through the kitchen door, if he entered at all.

He was among the first of the homebred pros to take over from the Scotsmen and Englishmen who were, in this country, the game's first teachers. Herbert Warren Wind said so in his book, *The Story of American Golf.*

"If you want to look it up," says Penick, striking a note both modest and scholarly, "it's in the revised edition."

By any reckoning, this is one of the great golf teachers of our time. Or his time. Which means, naturally, of any time. He is eighty years old, an age, as Casey Stengel once put it, "when you look around and a lot of your friends are no longer breathing."

But Harvey Penick is still going strong. His students have carried his name and his message across the land. He is indelibly a part of the history of the sport, revised or otherwise. A caddie at eight, promoted to the golf shop at twelve, a club professional at eighteen, he never had time to turn amateur.

When he entered college it was as a coach, not a student, at the University of Texas. He held the job for thirty-two years, most of them without pay. For forty-eight years he was the pro at Austin Country Club, until he retired in 1971, to be succeeded by his son, Tinsley. Harvey is still their starter, still gives lessons, still comes to the club every day as pro emeritus. He was honored recently as "Teacher of the Century" by the Southern Texas PGA.

A golf course is to Harvey Penick what a park bench must have been to Bernard Baruch: an office, a front porch, a place to teach and take the sun and lay a little philosophy on those who happen his way.

He has never had a high profile, a hot name in the news, a name known to the average fan. But the player whom the average fan "hero-worships," that player knows about Harvey Penick. Wherever they gather and play, he is quoted and talked about with a respect and reverence rare in sport. "I went to Texas in 1952 because of Harvey," says Davis Love, Jr., a former tour player and teacher in the Golf Digest Schools. "I grew up in El Dorado, Arkansas. If you went to an amateur tournament in the South and Southwest, you heard about him. Everybody knew of him."

Ben Crenshaw remembers the best advice Harvey ever gave him. The year was 1975, and Ben was mired in a dreadful slump after his brilliant rookie campaign. He seemed to have misplaced his swing. After six months on the road he returned to Austin and sought the soothing counsel of his mentor.

Recalls Crenshaw: "Harvey said, 'Before we do anything else, let me see your swing.' I hit four or five balls and he stopped me. He put his hand on my shoulder and said, in about as harsh a tone as he ever uses, 'Ben, don't ever wait this long again to come back and see me.'"

When Davis Love [Jr.] left the pro tour to become the assistant pro to Wesley Ellis at Mountain Ridge Country Club in New Jersey, he was struck by a sudden and disturbing thought: He knew nothing about teaching someone else to play golf. He did the obvious thing. He put in a call to Harvey Penick in Austin.

"I said, 'Mr. Penick, I'm up here now in New York, and I've got about a month before the snow is off the ground and I have to start teaching folks. What do I do? I've never taught before.' He asked me, 'Have you ever played a musical instrument?'

"I said, no, I hadn't. He said, 'Go out and buy one, take two or three lessons, and call me back.'

"I went out and rented a clarinet. That was why I left the tour; I wasn't making any money and I couldn't afford to buy one. I found a woman who gave lessons out of her home, and the day of my first lesson I drove up to her house, nervous and worried about doing the right thing, about embarrassing myself in front of her. I didn't know the terminology, wasn't sure what she was talking about. I went through all the things people feel when they're faced with taking a lesson from a golf pro. And then it hit me. This was what Harvey had in mind. He knew I'd played golf since I was three, and everything I did came naturally. So I had to learn what it was like to be on the other side, to be a student.

"That was nineteen fifty-nine or sixty. I've been calling him for tips on how to be a better teacher ever since."

Tom Kite recalls one of Penick's favorite tricks, a little show-and-tell. "He likes to teach by example," says Kite, "rather than with words. One of the big problems with a swing is the so-called 'coming over the top.'

"Mr. Penick would never use that phrase. He avoids the language that might mean one thing to you, and something else to another player.

"He put a grass-cutter, a sickle, on the end of a golf shaft. Had a blade about an inch wide with a sharp edge on both sides. It laid flat against the grass. If you swung over the top, that thing got stuck in the ground. It got you used to just clipping the top of the grass. After you swung a few times, Harvey put the golf club back in your hand and said, 'Now swing the same way.' It was so simple, and it worked."

Crenshaw has a similar story to tell. "One day he was giving me a putting lesson, and he asked if I was pushing or pulling the ball. I said, 'I think I'm pulling.' He left me on the green and went into the golf shop and brought out some talcum powder. He picked up my putter and sprinkled powder on it. Then he said, 'Just stroke this putt.' I tapped it and he said, 'Now look at the face of your putter.' And, sure enough, it left a powder mark on the heel, not the center.

"It was about as simple a trick as I've seen. His genius lies in that clear-cut, nonmechanical way of teaching," Crenshaw says.

A year ago, a psychologist from North Carolina came to Austin to spend two days with Penick. He was curious about Harvey's successes with Crenshaw and Kite. "How can you work with two such different types?" the man wanted to know.

"It's easy," said Harvey. "When I'm giving lessons to one, I don't let the other hang around."

Recently, a visiting West Coast professional asked if he still gave lessons to old people. The question startled Penick for just a moment. "Well, sure," he said, and he proceeded to tell him about a club member named Jim Swearingen, "Eighty years old, same as me, I guess that's old. I still give him a lesson once a week. Been seeing him for fifty years. The only trouble is, if he pops the ball a little he can't see it. He's like me. He can't see the ball unless he tops one about fifty yards."

When Harvey isn't around, Mr. Swearingen works with Tinsley Penick, who told the fellow from California: "Yeah, he has the same problem as my dad. They both knock the ball out of sight."

Harvey is a modest and unselfish character, for whom the satisfaction of teaching others is as strong as the joy of playing. And although you will never get Harvey to admit it, his level of play was once quite high. He began his professional career, in 1924, by beating Lighthorse Harry Cooper in an exhibition match at the Austin Country Club. He held the course record there for years, with a 63, until it was broken by Jimmy Demaret. He qualified for the U.S. Open and the PGA, and once teamed with Ben Hogan on the Texas Cup team.

But Harvey capsules his playing career in one sentence: "The year I qualified for the National Open, I went up and saw Sam Snead drill one like a bullet, and on the train going home I decided I better specialize in teaching."

When an English pro named Jim Smith left Austin for the opening of a new course at Cherry Hills in 1923, the directors offered the job to Harvey Penick on the condition that he finish high school. He received a guarantee of $50 a month, a percentage of what he sold in the shop, and whatever he earned from giving lessons.

"I don't believe the game has actually changed a bit," he says. "You just have thirty good players now to every one you had back then. But the fundamentals are the same now as they were for Harry Vardon or Walter Hagen. Of course, they used to have a lot more golf shots. Had to, with the lies you got over in St. Andrews. Now with all these lush fairways and carpet greens, it's mainly a driver, putter, and wedge.

"When I was a coach you could take those boys and mold them. I used to think if I got a boy early enough, I could make him a player. You can't do that anymore. Today the competition is so great, they have to prove themselves by the time they leave the juniors."

He has coached, or instructed, hundreds of young players who have gone onto the tour or into teaching jobs. He won't name them for fear of slighting someone. But you can start with Don January, Don Massengale, Mickey Wright, Betty Jameson, Betsy Rawls, Kathy Whitworth, Wesley Ellis, Terry Dill, George Knudson, Davis Love, Jr. and the current sunshine boys, Kite and Crenshaw, and you haven't scratched the surface.

What Harvey does best, as they say in Texas, is put the hay down where the mules can get at it. "He has a way of pointing out foibles," says Crenshaw, "that makes things so clear you wonder why you didn't think of it yourself. When he suggests an adjustment and a player succeeds on the next few shots, one of his favorite lines is, 'Just because the medicine tastes good, don't take the whole bottle.'"

After speaking at a PGA seminar in Georgia, Harvey was stopped by a club pro looking for an argument.

"Those guys who played for you at Texas were good players before they ever got to college, isn't that right?" the pro asked Penick.

"Yes, sir, that's true," he said.

"This Crenshaw kid, he had a name for himself before ever going to college, right?"

"Yes, sir."

Now a crowd started to form.

"You didn't have to do a lot of teaching with Crenshaw. He was already a complete player in college, right?"

"Yes, sir," said Harvey, starting to walk away.

"Tell me," said the pro, pressing his luck, "when was the first time you worked with Crenshaw?"

"I believe he was five years old when his father brought him around."

If the pro had quit one question earlier, Penick would have been perfectly willing to let him think that he had upstaged a legend. The man has an ego the size of a pinpoint.

Penick concedes that he may have one advantage over most teachers: "I've probably seen more golf shots than any man alive, and too many of them were my own."

He doesn't put form ahead of substance: "You don't have to be a stylist to play golf; a person who has to look too good doesn't always make the best competitor"—and he's not overly impressed with someone who hits the ball a mile ("the woods are filled with long hitters"). He has been called the golf pro's pro. He doesn't teach golf. He teaches people. . . ."

. . . It was Penick's custom not to watch his players compete in a conference tourney. "When they went out on the course," he says, "I'd already taught them all I knew. After that they were on their own." But there was always a telegram waiting for them at the first tee, containing just three words: TAKE DEAD AIM.

Davis Love Jr. paid Penick the ultimate compliment a year ago. He took his seventeen-year-old son, Mark, to Austin so Harvey could coach him during the Christmas holidays.

"It was the first time I've ever taken a lesson," Mark says, "that I didn't think, Oh, no, here's something else I have to remember."

There is a fairness and gentleness in Harvey Penick's teaching that is almost Talmudic. You have no reason to disbelieve him when he says, "I care just as much about the player who is trying to break ninety, or just get the ball airborne, as the one who is out on the tour."

As a further test of his patience, he once gave lessons to his wife of fifty-six years. Helen Penick is a lovely lady whose game is so erratic she claims that when people ask her how she is playing she replies, "Under an assumed name."

The lessons did not last long. "He was not very enthusiastic about it," she says. "He told me I could play well enough to enjoy it, so go ahead."

Davis Love Jr. seems to say it for everyone when he observes that, "Harvey is such a remarkable individual, if you're around for very long you're going to belong to him. He has the type of personality that inspires you to do your best, to please him. He never raises his voice. I don't think he knows any cusswords."

If he knew any, he surely would have used them during a plague of back problems dating back six or seven years ago. He was operated on for removal of a disk, suffered a broken back and underwent a bone fusion, and wound up with arthritis. His doctor told him, "I don't know anything about golf, but you're just about worn out."

Well, not quite. In a span of two weeks in mid-1985, he was inducted into the Texas Sports Hall of Fame, was the honorary starter for The Legends tournament in Austin, and gave a clinic for the Diabetes Association. "I can still hit some trick shots," he says, "but I have to hit 'em real easy.

"It's funny. I told the doctor, when I'm teaching I don't seem to feel any pain. He said it was because pain has to travel through your mind. When I'm concentrating, my mind blocks it out. That's okay, I figure, because I teach with my heart."

Gentle Ben: At Peace with Himself

Melanie Hauser

On Tour, *July 1993*

The first streams of morning light have begun to filter through the plantation shutters, just enough light to outline the wall of books behind the desk, kick up a bit of dust, and give this nook the warm feeling of an old library filled with treasures.

As your eyes adjust, they dance from object to object—a pair of old British lithographs, antique golf clubs, a lighted cabinet filled with leaded crystal and the trophy of Augusta National Golf Club given to the Masters champion, scads of photographs and trophies, and a collection of golf books that would make Bobby Jones, who has his own place of honor in one corner, proud. The large desk is cluttered with stacks of paperwork, messages, and business files. A low table is filled with Ryder Cup scrapbooks and coffee-table books on golf architecture and Texas art.

A painting of a Longhorn hangs over the sofa, a University of Texas letterman's blanket is draped on the cushions. Pictures of Harvey Penick and Charlie Crenshaw, a double-take look-alike of the late Alabama football coaching legend Paul "Bear" Bryant, face each other from across the room. A construction-paper stegosaurus, colored crayon-green, teeters on the edge of a cushion.

It is here that Ben Crenshaw, the golf historian, pores over his collection of rare books; here that Ben Crenshaw, the architect, spends endless hours sketching holes and course layouts; here where Ben Crenshaw, the father, whiles away an afternoon teaching five-year-old Katherine to identify native Texas birds.

All those sides you rarely see of Ben Crenshaw flow together gently in this cozy room. The golfer's trophies and money clips, the scholar's nineteenth-century books, the young phenom's burnt-orange blanket, the businessman's briefcase, the dad's treasured dinosaur, the dreamer's visions.

He pulls a book off the shelf and launches passionately into another story, and you see there is no way to separate this man from the game. Like Jones, Crenshaw promotes golf, not himself. Like Jones, he is the consummate gentle man.

As he winds his way through the story, you think back to the first time Crenshaw's engaging grin, floppy blond hair, and ageless swing captivated you. To that Sunday afternoon on Augusta's tenth green when, after a decade of turmoil, he raised his arms to celebrate a sixty-foot putt and put a lock on the 1984 Masters. To his first days on the PGA Tour when, after dominating the game as an amateur, such incredible expectations were heaped upon his slender shoulders and a putter named Little Ben.

In some ways, Ben Crenshaw hasn't changed much over those past two decades. The blond hair is shorter and tiny crow's feet now dance around his eyes, but the warm smile still crinkles his nose and makes you realize this forty-one-year-old is still golf's golden boy. Even after all these years.

If anything, his desperate love for the game and its history have only grown richer with age, his knowledge greater, his gentility more graceful. His thoughtful words come deeper from his heart.

"He's like a nice warm blanket," said longtime friend Dave Marr. "He's grown and matured, but he hasn't really changed."

Yet he has. Crenshaw's game is still as erratic and emotional as ever, his putting stroke as velvety-smooth and extraordinary as it was at seventeen. But while he's still upset by his inconsistency, Crenshaw no longer lives and dies with his fluctuating performances and emotions on the golf course.

Despite winning seventeen tournaments and more than $5 million in his career, he admits he played his best golf in high school and college and that he doesn't have the drive he did at twenty or thirty. He doesn't worry about expectations unless they are his own.

He understands this capricious game still holds many challenges for him, most of them not in tournament golf.

"It doesn't bother me anymore that I didn't turn out to be whatever," he said. "It's just very safe to say that, rightly or wrongly, my priorities have changed, but I'm comfortable with it. I'll never be a one-dimensional player again, but a lot of people still want me to be. They want me playing thirty to thirty-five tournaments a year across the world. I'm past that stage in my life. I just can't do it."

After years of playing and studying the world's great courses, Crenshaw is ready to build a great one. Or two. Or . . . well, you get the picture.

Next to wife Julie and daughters Katherine and Claire, the greatest love in Crenshaw's life right now is his burning desire to design courses with his close friend and partner, Bill Coore, whom he joined in 1985.

Ben Crenshaw finds it harder to keep his concentration focused these days as he begins the transition from PGA Tour player to golf-course architect.

Their latest project is scattered across Crenshaw's dining-room table. A proverbial field of dreams, a Scottish heaven called Sand Hills just above the unlikely city of North Platte, Nebraska.

"This may be the best property any architect could hope for in a long time," Crenshaw said. "It's truly nature-made. We saw it and we went berserk.

"If you saw it, you'd swear you were in Scotland. It's mind-boggling."

Crenshaw envisions a prototypical Scottish golf club. No real estate. No nothing. Just golf. Traditional less-is-more golf.

He shows off the current routing, complete with deep natural bunkers and flowing fairways. After ten minutes, he's still going. The more he learns from books by Jones, Alister Mackenzie, Donald Ross, and the other great talents who turned rolling acres into land art, the happier Crenshaw is.

"Talk about passion," Julie Crenshaw said. "His eyes just light up when he talks about building golf courses. I think you have to have a gift to look at a piece of raw land and know there's going to be eighteen holes there."

That Crenshaw's eyes have turned toward design should come as no surprise. Crenshaw has never just played great courses. He felt his way around them, absorbing the beauty and history within. He has studied the golfers who played them, the tournaments played on them.

He can name the U.S. Open champs in order. Give him a course, he'll give you a tale. Maybe a dozen. Want to know an obscure bit of trivia? Crenshaw's the man.

CBS-TV announcer Ben Wright, himself a trivia buff, is always trying to outfox Crenshaw. One day Wright thought he had him when he asked, "What were Francis Ouimet's practice scores on the Saturday and Sunday before he won the 1913 U.S. Open?"

Crenshaw shook his head, declared it a darn tough question, and asked for a clue. Wright told him they were identical scores.

"Yes," Crenshaw said a few seconds later. "I've got it. They were eighty-eight, eighty-eight."

He was, of course, right.

What's most amazing about Crenshaw's vast knowledge of the game is that he didn't become serious about studying its history until he turned pro. Until then, the game was just, well, a game. One he dominated almost from the time he picked up a club.

"I can't remember it being easy, but it was fun," said Crenshaw, who also played football, basketball, and baseball growing up. "I must have had a knack for it."

Knack? By the age of eleven, he was shooting 74 and by seventeen he was beating players twice his age. His senior year at Austin High, he won eighteen of nineteen tournaments. He left the University of Texas at the end of his junior year in 1973 after winning three NCAA individual titles, one of which he shared with Austinite and UT teammate Tom Kite.

Talk about legends. He was Superman, Jack Nicklaus, and Arnold Palmer rolled into one. At least it seemed that way. Especially the day Brent Buckman, Crenshaw's former college roommate and the head pro at Austin's Barton Creek Club, met Crenshaw at Austin's Morris Williams Golf Course.

"I was a freshman [at UT] and was out there practicing," Buckman said. "Austin High was playing a match, so I decided to hang around and see this kid.

"Come time for the number-one players to tee off and Ben wasn't there. Suddenly, I heard tires screeching and a big old Buick 455 Grand Sport pulls into the parking lot. The trunk flips up, Ben grabs his bag and runs to the tee. Everyone else has teed off.

"He teed the ball up, didn't even tie his shoes, and damn near drove the first green."

Another legend has Crenshaw opening a city junior tournament with rounds of 62–61 with two holes in one. He swears it's not true, but what the heck. It sounds so good his friends tell it anyway.

But his best real stretch of ball-striking? Crenshaw said it happened at Austin's Fourth of July Firecracker Open at Lions Municipal Golf Course when he was seventeen. In the span of four holes, he either drove or narrowly missed three 350-plus-yard par-fours and started the streak by reaching a long par-five in two with a driver and a five-iron.

"I'd never done that before nor since," Crenshaw said. "I'll never forget those four holes. I shot a sixty-four that day and won the tournament by seven or eight."

Crenshaw had no fear back then. There wasn't a par-five he couldn't reach in two, a course he couldn't handle. "I really do feel in my heart in high school and college I played my best golf," he said. "I don't know why. Maybe I didn't think. I just did."

He shook his head.

Somewhere along the line he got a bit defensive and started questioning himself and his swing. He started listening to guys on the driving range and tinkering with his natural swing.

"I played my best on tour when I was simply comfortable over the ball, I was confident in my aim, and I just let it happen," he said. "I'm still that way to this day."

When Crenshaw won the first professional tournament he entered—

the 1973 Texas Open—and the expectations were heaped on him, little did he know how many ups and downs lay ahead.

A year later, his mother, Pearl, died and Crenshaw fell into the first of a series of slumps. The next period came in 1980 when his fluid swing broke into tiny pieces. Then there was his divorce from first wife Polly Speno in 1985 and, a few years later, his battle with Graves' disease.

"My performances mirror the way I feel about myself very closely," Crenshaw said. "I have a tendency to get down. My emotions get very low and it's very hard for me to figure out little ways to make the down periods better."

Perhaps the toughest stretch began in 1984, just after the Masters victory and decision to divorce. Ironically—or perhaps fortunately—that coincided with the beginning of his blissful relationship with Julie.

The two met just before Crenshaw won the Masters, having been introduced at the Los Angeles Open. Julie, who is thirteen years younger than Ben, didn't know much about the game.

"When he won the Masters, I remember saying, 'Oh, how nice,'" Julie said. "Can you imagine? I had no idea."

But she did know there was something special about this gentle man.

"He takes time for everybody, he's very thoughtful, and he's a very emotional person," she said. "Those are the things that drew me to him. It's great that he does that to people. That's why they love him so much."

Yet, when he lost twenty pounds and was struggling with what would be diagnosed as Graves' disease, some of those same people wondered if Crenshaw was battling a cocaine problem.

"I'd say that hurt worse than anything," Crenshaw said. "It was something I couldn't take, I couldn't fathom. I didn't know how to deal with it."

At the same time, even close friends were questioning his decision to marry Julie so quickly after his divorce. "I don't know if they put the blame on me," she said, "but they didn't think I was helping."

Now they know she was.

Julie believed in him, nursed him through the illness both physically and emotionally, and he bounced back midway through 1986. Crenshaw's eyes dance when he talks about his wife and daughters. They're his staunchest supporters and his greatest delights.

The name Gentle Ben never fit as well as it does late at night when Julie finds her husband, book in hand, asleep beside Katherine. Or when the simplest of things touches him.

"The slightest little thing can bring him to tears," Julie said. "He's so emotional, so passionate about things. He took Katherine to *Beauty and the Beast,* and he cried."

Crenshaw's tender side came from his mother, one of the sweetest, kindest people, he said, anyone ever met. One afternoon, ten-year-old Crenshaw was depressed because he couldn't find anyone to play golf with at Lions Municipal so he went alone. Pearl joined him on the fifth hole and walked the rest of the way with him.

"I see his mother in him every day," Julie said. "She was so sweet; everyone loved her. She never said anything bad about anyone."

Neither has her son, who, like his mom, has trouble being tough. Even with tarantulas.

"One day we found one in the house and he wouldn't kill it," Julie said. "He captured it in a coffee can and said, 'We've got to put it back where it belongs.' So, he tossed it into the creek, can and all."

That vulnerability is what has always drawn people to Crenshaw.

When his game was tearing him apart, he was honest, telling people he felt as though he was in a straitjacket, that he just wanted to be somewhere on the course. When he won the Masters and said it was for his friends, you knew he meant it.

"I'm an open book," he said, "and I don't mind it."

Neither did Bobby Jones, the one man Crenshaw has always put on a pedestal. He has studied Jones so thoroughly, he can tell you how the man thought, how he played, what he wrote, and even what he wore.

"In his writings, no one has opened themselves up like that," Crenshaw said. "He opened up his soul. He told people about his occasional weaknesses, about the mental side of golf and the way you play it. He always said his worst fear was having a big lead and squandering it and looking like a fool.

"Not many people have said things like that. His books have a very human quality about them. They're open and honest. They're his thoughts alone."

Those Jonesian thoughts are a lot like the ones running through Crenshaw's head. Perhaps the biggest disappointment is that the two never met. Crenshaw hoped for the chance at his first Masters, but Jones died just before that.

"I never met Bobby Jones, either," Buckman said. "But if I ever got the chance, I'd probably think he was a lot like Ben."

Maybe more than Buckman thinks. Jones, the consummate amateur, had a rather famous putter named Calamity Jane and retired from the game at twenty-eight. Although he only consulted on two courses, his visions for Augusta National and Atlanta's Peachtree and his writings helped shape others' ideas.

At forty-one, Crenshaw and his equally famous Little Ben are still going strong, although his concentration isn't what it once was. And, while he isn't ready to retire, he has started the transition.

"One thing that bothers me more than anything is inconsistency," Crenshaw said.

"I can be really good at times and just pathetic at times. I have a lot of low periods, then it will come back up. I'll have confidence and I feel as capable as anyone . . . I feel good at times, but I've got to confess, they're less and less."

Crenshaw would love to win again at Augusta. He'd like to play in another Ryder Cup. But he'd also like to build golf courses. And spend time with his family.

Balancing it all is getting tougher with each opportunity like Sand Hills. Buckman has seen his friend wrestle with the changes and knows how difficult it has been.

"He's finally at peace with himself," Buckman said. "Instead of doing things for other people, he's doing things for Ben."

And, he hopes, for posterity.

Golf Puts Its Heart in the Right Place

Bob Verdi

Chicago Tribune, *June 22, 1992*

Never mind throwing any more clubs. Hold the profanity, too. And don't balance the ball the next time you reach that pond in regulation.

Golf means well, after all. Golf should be forgiven. Golf is fair and good and just. It wasn't always that way, but Tom Kite won the ninety-second U.S. Open Sunday, so golf deserves some kind words for a change. Golf gets a mulligan.

If golf were as cruel as it's supposed to be, this forty-two-year-old Texan would have gone through life with that asterisk next to his name, that millstone around his neck, that stigma attached to his every move. Tom Kite, winner of more money than any player in history, but the best player never to win a major. He gave a few away, had a couple taken from him in broad daylight, and, last April, he wasn't even allowed to do either.

When the game's finest gathered at Augusta National for the season's first of four big events, Tom Kite was back home in Austin. His invitation didn't get lost in the mail. Nobody ever licked a stamp to send it. His record hadn't been so terrific lately, though it was not nearly as flawed as the Masters's policy for determining its field. Other golfers knew he belonged and so did the galleries and so did the people who run the tournament. They sent Kite a note, and they'll probably fix the loophole in the system, but that couldn't get him anywhere near the TV set.

"It would have hurt him too much to watch," wife Christy was saying. "To watch the Masters, which he loves so much, would have hurt. So he cut some trees in the backyard and went to practice and was gone most of that Sunday."

When he returned, the Masters was over.

"Well," Tom said, "I know you were looking at it. Who won?"

"Freddie," Christy said.

"Good," said Tom. "Good for Freddie. He deserves it."

The sport will second that notion in Tom Kite's behalf now, because golf has paid off a huge and outstanding IOU. Kite has always been a credit to the game, even when he seemed to be getting shortchanged. Not once did he complain about that Masters injustice, because he didn't feel it would be proper. That's Kite's style, though. Years ago, before he won all those nonmajors and the $7-million-plus that goes with it, Kite was in the hunt at the Hall of Fame Classic. That is, until he invoked a penalty on himself as he settled over a tap-in from about six inches.

"My ball moved before I putted it," Kite said.

"But nobody saw it," he was told.

"I did," Kite said.

You get the idea. He's always had the highest respect for golf, even when golf was giving him a face full of slaps. His parents and teachers urged him to forget golf because he lacked size. At the University of Texas, Kite's slight shadow was dwarfed by Ben Crenshaw's presence. And every week, before most of the other players arrive or after they've departed the practice range, Kite's out there beating balls. Because he wants to, because he has to. The back of Kite's neck bears the fine, leathery look of patience and perseverance.

Victory at Pebble Beach Sunday demanded those qualities, more than the perfect swing or the textbook grip or any of that other stuff you find in golf manuals. Magazines and instructional films aren't much help when you have to bring a six-iron in over the whitecaps of Carmel Bay on No. 7, a par-three of 107 yards. Did we say victory at Pebble Beach? This was victory at sea. The gray dome of clouds that hovered over this course for the first three rounds was shooed inland by Pacific gales. The greens didn't bite, but the wind did.

Before it ended, some of the best golfers were blown from the leader board toward Nevada. Scott Simpson, 88? Payne Stewart, 83? Davis Love III, 83? Raymond Floyd, 81? Dr. Gil Morgan, who once had a seven-shot bulge at twelve under par, wobbled in with an 81? Was this Seventeen Mile Drive or Three Mile Island? For a spell there, it seemed that the winner by attrition might be Colin Montgomerie, who finished at even-par 288 as the final twosome strolled the sixth fairway. Give him the trophy and count the bodies later.

But Kite ignored the small-craft warnings and somehow carved a 72 out of the landscape. Par was better than good enough. Par was terrific, courageous, weatherproof. And the grinder did it. Which is why Christy Kite ran for the phone in the press tent, to talk to the kids back home about what Dad had accomplished on Father's Day.

Tom Kite put an end to an unplayable lie—that he couldn't win a major.

Golf's conscience is clear.

One from the Heart

Melanie Hauser

Golf World, *April 5, 1996*

Ben Crenshaw couldn't stop talking. Or pointing things out. The first tee. The locker room. Magnolia Lane. The eighteenth green. The people. The warm, rich feelings. The beauty.

Crenshaw chose his words carefully. As always, they were passionate; they came straight from the heart. Claire, who will be four in a few weeks, was busy exploring the nooks and crannies. Katherine, at eight, was finally beginning to understand why this place called Augusta National meant so much to her dad.

He talked about treasured friends there like Council Dandridge, the man in charge of the locker room. He showed her pictures of Bobby

Jones and Ike; of the early line drawings of the course; of the members who will always have special places in his heart.

The Crenshaws had stopped by a month of Mondays ago to have lunch and shoot some TV promos for the Masters. When they walked into the Trophy Room, the waiters didn't have to be introduced. Ben and Julie were part of the family. And the girls? They recognized Katherine and Claire from their Christmas cards.

"I want you to know how special your daddy is here," one waiter said, launching into a story.

A few hours later, the family was on a plane to Orlando and Katherine was sitting with her father. He told her how much it meant to him to have her see the place where he won two majors; to begin to understand the place he truly loves.

"He started crying," Julie Crenshaw said. "You could see just how much Augusta means."

Crenshaw's vulnerability is what draws us to him; his passion is what intrigues and touches us. You can't separate the man from the game or the emotions. As he talked to Katherine, you knew there was more to it. Thoughts of Harvey Penick were resting in the back of his mind. It had been eleven months since he laid his longtime teacher to rest; eleven months since he stood sobbing on Augusta's eighteenth green after saying goodbye by winning Harvey's Little Red Masters.

The moment, the week, the emotions, will never be equaled nor totally understood.

Just treasured.

Their conversations always ended the same way. The frail old man would offer his hand—palm up—to Crenshaw to shake, then hold for a few seconds. It was a loving gesture, one born nearly four decades earlier and nurtured by two hearts that now somehow seem entwined.

As Crenshaw's strong hand enveloped Penick's weathered one, the memories and lessons swirled together; the master's simple message was reinforced. Penick would lift his head as best he could and remind his pupil to take dead aim. Yet when the two parted for the final time, Penick didn't offer his hand. He realized he didn't have to.

From his bed that Sunday, he ordered Crenshaw to pluck an old hickory-shafted Gene Sarazen putter out of his bag in the garage, then asked him to putt on the bedroom carpet. Penick checked the grip and the setup.

He watched the pendulum swing. He knew the hands could feel a line and speed better than any others he had seen. He knew all the boy had to do was trust. He told him just that.

"He searched long and hard for his words and how and what to say to people," Crenshaw said of Penick. "He would study the pupil once he held out his hand to shake it. He would study your countenance. Before the lesson began, he knew what kind of person you were."

Or with Crenshaw that day, what he needed.

Thirty minutes later, Penick was satisfied and sent Crenshaw on his way.

"After Harvey gave him his last lesson, Ben came back into the den where Julie and I were playing with the girls," said Helen Penick, Harvey's widow. "He didn't say a word until he left. Then he just said goodbye."

Looking back, she had a feeling a bit of Harvey went with him.

"All the time," she said, "I felt Harvey's hand was on Ben's shoulder."

Seven days later, Penick took his final breath.

Early on that morning of April 2, Tom Kite had stopped by the Penick home on his way to Austin Country Club, where members were dedicating life-sized statues of Penick and Kite. Then Penick had listened and watched as another of his favorites, Davis Love III, won in New Orleans and qualified for the Masters. Late that afternoon, Joan Whitworth, a close family friend who was chairing a cancer tournament at the club the next day, dropped by.

"We talked for a few minutes and he told me he was sorry, but he wasn't going to make the tournament," Whitworth said. "By the time I had driven over to the club—what is it, five minutes at best?—he was gone."

Not long after Whitworth returned to the Penick house, Christy Kite stopped at the club on her way home from a gymnastics meet and heard Penick had died. She found Tom on the golf course and broke the news to him. While Tom went to the Penick house to help out, Christy called Augusta National, where the Crenshaws had gone after Ben missed the cut in New Orleans. The receptionist took the number and promised to look for them. No more than fifteen minutes later, Ben and Julie walked in to have dinner with Masters tournament chairman Jack Stephens and were handed the note. When Julie saw the message, she knew.

"I wasn't going to let Ben hear it on the phone," she said. "I called Christy and got the details, then I went in [the dining room] and pulled him aside.

"We went out on the porch and I told him. We stood there and cried. It was really bad for about fifteen minutes, but then we regained our composure and went back in."

Dinner companions Stephens and Pat Summerall weren't sure what to say. They knew what Penick had meant to Crenshaw; they could see how devastated he was.

"You can imagine how they felt," Julie said. "But Ben was fine. He sat there and celebrated Harvey's life and reminisced."

Penick had never fully recovered from a bout with pneumonia, so both Kite and Crenshaw had prepared themselves for his death. Yet when they talked that night, both were still numb.

"Ben talked about coming back [to Austin], but really, there wasn't anything he could do here," said Kite, who helped the family make calls late into the night, then boarded a plane to Augusta himself. "I had actually already come up with a plan for what we could do. It was for me to get over there, get a practice round in, then for us to fly back to the funeral [on Wednesday]. He agreed."

When they hung up, Crenshaw let the tears flow.

"In retrospect, I couldn't believe what was happening that week,"

Crenshaw said. "I think all of us [who knew Harvey], whenever we left Austin, we knew it could happen, and we hated the thought that we might be away."

Yet perhaps it was for the best. While Kite was caught up in a swirl of phone calls and details and family, Crenshaw was a thousand miles away as he grieved his loss. As Crenshaw cried that night, first on the veranda, then again at his rental house, there was a peace enveloping him.

As he had so many Masters previously, Crenshaw came to Augusta searching. His game seemed a wreck. All he wanted was to make it through four rounds.

He had failed to do that at New Orleans, but in retrospect, perhaps that was simply fate stepping in. Now he had a few extra days to work things out. To trust. To take dead aim. To let Augusta National finish what Penick had begun.

Crenshaw's emotions were in check when he arrived at the course Monday, but his game was still a mess. Shots were flying in all directions.

"I played with him the first two rounds at New Orleans," Love said, "so I know where his game was. He was frustrated and I think some of it had to do with Harvey's health. Plus, his [big] toe was hurting him pretty badly.

"I really don't think he had any expectations. I think he just hoped he would make it through."

When Ben Crenshaw and Carl Jackson found each other some twenty years ago on the grounds of Augusta National, little did they know what lay ahead. Crenshaw was golf's golden boy, Jackson one of Augusta's best caddies. Both were soft-spoken and genuine. Both had a childlike vulnerability. Both approached their work from the heart.

Over the years, they forged an unbreakable bond. They won together in 1984 and came close a half-dozen other times. No team knew the course better than these two. No pair knew each other better, either. Yet when Jackson arrived at the course Monday morning, he didn't know what to expect. Would Crenshaw be able to put Penick's death behind him?

A few swings into that first practice round, Jackson saw the problem. But telling his man about it was a different matter altogether.

"He was reaching at the ball so bad," Jackson said. "I was glad when the round was over and he said he needed to go out to the practice tee. I saw what was bad, but I don't consider myself an expert. I was just waiting for an opening to make a suggestion."

He got it the next morning. As Crenshaw hit balls, Jackson pointed out that he had the ball positioned too far up in his stance and his shoulder turn was a bit looser than usual. Crenshaw liked what he heard and hit four balls using Jackson's suggestions. It was all he needed.

"I saw the spark that morning," Jackson said. "Then Ben paid me a compliment. He told me it was the best session he had had in a long time. I knew he believed he had finally found something to make him play better."

Crenshaw knew Love was struggling too, but with a different problem. Love's late father had been another of Penick's devoted pupils, and Love wasn't sure whether to fly to Austin for the funeral. Both Crenshaw and Kite had told him to stay put and work on his game. Love, whose friendship with Crenshaw has blossomed because their wives are great friends, was touched by Crenshaw's gesture.

"Ben told me, 'Look, you're playing great. You've got as much chance to win as anyone. You need to stay and practice,'" Love said. "He was almost discounting his game. But what he told me . . . I knew that's what my dad would have told me to do, too.

"It was great that Ben went out of his way to ease my mind about my decision."

Five days later, the storyline would take another strange twist. Come Sunday, the two friends would challenge each other in one of the most mystical and emotional finishes in Masters history.

• • •

The bright sun was creeping above the azalea bushes when the Citation II lifted its wheels off the runway at tiny Bush Field Wednesday morning. The trip would take just under two hours, but to the six passengers—Julie and Ben Crenshaw, Tom and Christy Kite, Terry Jastrow, and Chuck Cook—it felt more like an eternity. They were going home to lay Penick to rest; alternately to celebrate and grieve his life; to put—for a few hours at least—their preparations for the biggest tournament of the year out of their minds.

In Austin, the day had dawned gray and dreary, and when the jet landed a light drizzle was falling. All of Travis County, it seemed, was in mourning.

When Charlie Crenshaw and his oldest son Charlie arrived, they scrounged to find seats in the chapel foyer. Scotty Sayers, Ben's combination friend, agent, and business manager, sat closer to the front and kept an eye on Crenshaw. Sayers and old friend Randy Smith, the pro at Dallas's Royal Oaks Country Club, were worried he wouldn't make it through the service.

"He was emotional, but I think he cried all his tears Sunday night," Sayers said. "I remember him telling me Harvey's body looked so peaceful, as though the pain was finally gone."

There was a peace surrounding Crenshaw that day that surprised everyone, even his father and older brother. They realized it before the service when they found their way to the pallbearers' room to check on Ben.

"That was the first time I had seen him since Harvey died," said brother Charlie, who took lessons from Penick, too, but played baseball at the University of Texas. "He looked real calm and collected. I was surprised. He said he had been crying a lot, but at that point he was calm."

After the service Crenshaw paused before getting into the limousine and walked over to his dad and brother. He had a huge smile on his face and gave them both big hugs. The look in his eyes took both of them by surprise.

"He told me, 'I really think I'm onto something,'" brother Charlie said. "Then he told me about Carl helping him with his swing. I looked at Daddy and said, 'I don't think I've ever seen him with such conviction.' It was like he had new life in him."

Or perhaps just with him.

"When you think about someone who meant so much to your life, you think about all the times and all the things he taught us—you try to absorb as much as you can," Ben said. "In a lot of ways, it was a very appropriate time for him to go. It was a week when he would be on everyone's mind."

And have his hand on one shoulder.

Kite and Crenshaw were emotionally and physically exhausted, and slept much of the way back. Yet when the plane touched down about 5:30 P.M., both players went to Augusta National to practice. The range was almost deserted, but Love was one of the few still there. He asked about the funeral.

"I felt sorry for them," said Love. "I'd just hit balls and played the Par-3 [contest] and they'd been back and forth across the country. You know it had to be tough on them.

"Tom seemed in a furious rush when he came to the tee. But Ben seemed to be more relaxed."

Crenshaw hit a few balls, then moved to the putting green where he lined up three putters—Little Ben, his trusty Wilson 8802; the Cleveland Classic 8802 clone he had taken from Sayers's office; and a black 8802 he had bought in San Antonio. He and Sayers discussed the greens and the pros and cons of each putter.

"I figured he would practice with the others, then go back to Little Ben," Sayers said. "He always does."

This time, he didn't.

Fort Worth banker and Augusta member John Griffith was staying with Crenshaw and knew there was a problem. It wasn't unusual for Crenshaw to pick up a putter at night and tinker in the den, but this week was different. Griffith could see something didn't feel right, so he wasn't surprised when Little Ben was banished to the locker and Sayers's putter—dubbed "Little Scotty" at the house—was put in the lineup.

Crenshaw putted by himself until dark. Somehow the serenity of a lone golfer at work on a beautiful night seemed fitting.

"The progression of the day was nice," Sayers said. "It was so peaceful out there. To me, it set the mood for the week."

The rain and gray skies moved over from Austin and settled into Augusta as the tournament began. But nothing, not the weather nor a poor performance from playing partner Ian Baker-Finch, would get Crenshaw down. With the funeral behind him, Crenshaw's focus sharpened. He was trusting himself again. He knew, deep down, he had a chance.

He put Jackson's suggestions—moving the ball back in his stance and taking a tighter shoulder turn—right to work. They were the same things, he said, Penick would have noticed had he been there.

"I started off the tournament and I felt I was working on something positive," Crenshaw said. "I was hitting a lot of shots with authority and making some putts. And nothing helps your confidence more than seeing you do what you're trying to do."

Crenshaw bogeyed the first hole, but got the shot right back. It was solid golf—the kind that gets you in at par or better. He didn't get caught up in Baker-Finch's opening 79, but rather stitched together a comfortable opening 70 and set the tone for the week.

"I was a little worried," Sayers admitted. "Sometimes with Ben, he'll sympathize with a player like that or [the bad play] will rub off on him. It didn't affect him."

That night, the Crenshaws tossed their annual barbecue. In addition to the ten people—three of them named Julie—staying in the five-bedroom house, the crowd included close friends, corporate friends, and Rob Gillette, the head of Crenshaw's fan club, "Ben's Battalion." Gillette stayed through Saturday, then kept a promise to his wife and drove home to Maryland to teach Sunday school. He watched Crenshaw win on TV. Someone else used his badge.

• • •

Pat Oles was busy scurrying from shot to shot. The Advance Man, as Julie Crenshaw called him, was the Team Crenshaw member who scanned each hole for potential trouble and set the scene to those outside the ropes on every shot. He would dart through the crowds and stake a claim to the best viewing spots, then alert the team to any disasters that had befallen players in the groups ahead. Crenshaw, with a chuckle, called him Rommel, as in the field marshal."

"I was just like everyone else who was with Ben," said Oles, an Austin developer and close friend. "We all got involved in the tournament. It was almost like we were out there playing the shots with him."

On Friday, when Crenshaw faced an over-the-hill, around-the-break, to-the-back-of-the-green, no-one-could-read-this forty-foot putt at the fourteenth, it was Oles who found the perfect vantage point—and line—from behind the green. While Crenshaw and Jackson sized it up from the front—a process that seemed like it took several minutes—the team shook their heads from the back. Little did they know it would be one of the biggest shots of the week.

"We thought there was absolutely no way he was going to get it anywhere near the hole," Oles said. "It could easily have been a four-putt. But Ben studied the putt for a long time. Then he knocked it eighteen inches from the cup."

Walking to the next tee, Jackson shook his head. "Julie," he said through the gallery ropes, "that was the meanest putt I've ever seen. If he had asked my opinion, I would have told him to putt up there and take his bogey. But he had other magic in his mind."

Most reported it as simply another putt in Crenshaw's second-round 67. Jackson and those inside the locker room knew better. If a putt like that didn't throw a scare into the field, nothing would.

"Hole by hole, round by round, my golf was marked by a certain continuity," Crenshaw said. "You weren't seeing any highs and lows. The little mistakes I made were retrieved quickly. I had gotten a little more confidence hole by hole, so it was starting to knit together pretty well. Those are the types of things that build confidence."

The possibility of a storybook ending hovered around Crenshaw all day Saturday. But he dismissed any thoughts of it from his mind and politely sidestepped the questions. He had been in these situations before and it hadn't worked out.

He knew better than to look ahead. . . .

Still, about 6:30 P.M., the phone rang at Charlie Crenshaw's house in Austin. It was Julie telling her brother-in-law he better get on the next plane for Augusta.

The toughest thing about being in contention at Augusta is the wait. On the weekends, the leaders don't tee off until two P.M. And no one can sleep until noon. Least of all, Crenshaw.

"It's interminable," he said. "It's the toughest part of the week. The anticipation is so great. You want to go out and get to the battle. You have a lot of time to think about it."

A decade ago, Crenshaw would pass the mornings on the driveway, shooting hoops with Sayers and anyone else from the house who cared to join in. With all the residents now forty-something, with less forgiving muscles, the routine was less strenuous. When Charlie Crenshaw arrived at the house around noon Sunday, his little brother had his wedge in his hand and was chipping pinecones. Everyone there took a turn.

"He was very calm, out there in the yard," Charlie said. "He just looked at me with a smile and said, 'Let's go see what happens.' He just got in that zone."

Not long afterward, Ben stopped a conversation in midsentence and walked down the driveway.

"He just stood there and stared," Charlie said. "It was like he was pondering the day."

Or taking dead aim.

Brian Henninger just shook his head in disbelief. How in the world, he wondered, could a player pull both of his first two drives Sunday and be two strokes ahead of his playing partner who striped it? How could anyone make birdie on No. 2 from just this side of the ditch filled with azaleas left of the fairway? How did his Cinderella story become Crenshaw's amen?

"Ben had a couple of great saves on the first two holes," Henninger said. "I pretty much piped it on those holes, and he's all over the place. He's one under after that, and I'm one over.

"Then everything transpired in a Gentle Ben-ly sort of way."

It was the second hole, too, that caught Jackson's attention. Like everyone else, he was thinking Crenshaw's tee shot was buried in the azaleas, but when he got down there, it was on the edge of the fairway.

"We made birdie from there, and that's when I started to believe it was going to be our week," Jackson said. "Everybody who's going to win the Masters knocks in a few long putts or chips in, and he wasn't getting those. Ben's breaks were just coming in other ways." . . .

At No. 9, Crenshaw gambled with his approach and won, made birdie to turn two under for the day and set the stage for the back nine. By then, even the hardest heart was cracking. You didn't need a psychic friend to tell you what was happening. You could almost see Penick's hand resting on Crenshaw's slight shoulders to guide, to nudge, to assure. Jackson and Crenshaw barely said a word to each other as they made the turn.

"Over the years we've had a saying: 'It's time to reach deep,'" Jackson said. "We knew this was the time. It was happening without us saying it. I could see that fire in his eyes. He was reaching as deep as he could."

No one looks at scoreboards more often than Crenshaw. Yet Sunday, he hadn't peeked at any of them as he neared the fifteenth green. Julie Crenshaw and Sayers were walking up the right side of the fairway when a roar went up from the eighteenth green.

"That's Davis. He's finished," Sayers said. "It's Ben's tournament to win or lose now."

Crenshaw heard it, too, and looked—finally—at a scoreboard. He saw that he and Love were tied.

"That meant, of course, I had to make one more birdie," Crenshaw said.

That meant, of course, this tournament was over.

Inside the scoring tent, Love was thinking the same thing. He told himself one of Harvey's boys was going to win. Only his scenario had him—not Crenshaw—slipping on the jacket.

"Ben had three holes left and I thought I had won the tournament," Love said. "With sixteen, seventeen, and eighteen to go, usually it's the guy who's in the cabin who wins."

This time Penick and Crenshaw had other plans.

When Crenshaw stepped to the sixteenth tee, there were no questions in his mind. He saw the shot perfectly—a crystal-clear six-iron with a hint of a draw. He saw the shot working its way toward the hole.

Back in Austin, Helen Penick was toasting yet another birdie—this one to be. Earlier, when Crenshaw nearly holed his approach at No. 9, she and friends Susan Watkins, Carrell Grigsby, and Joan Whitworth had popped the cork on a bottle of 1983 Dom Perignon. Simon & Schuster, publishers of Penick's series of tomes that began with the *Little Red Book,* had sent the champagne to celebrate Harvey's ninetieth birthday the previous October 23.

The champagne had been flowing as liberally as the foursome's tears. And when he birdied sixteen and seventeen?

"Boy," Helen Penick said, "did we toast those two."

Larry Gatlin opted to strut. The member of country music's Gatlin Brothers singing group had arrived in Augusta early Sunday, watched Curtis Strange and Jay Haas for a while, then dropped back to watch Crenshaw, his oldest tour buddy. Now he was whooping and hollering with the best of them.

With friends in high places—like Ken Venturi in the CBS tower at eighteen—Gatlin can always rely on getting the best seat in the house. Which is why he left at fifteen and headed to the tower.

"Ben looked like a man on a mission, and that can look two different ways," Gatlin said. "You can clench your teeth and set your jaw and stalk the golf course. That's what a guy like Curtis would do. Ben was the other way. He was totally at peace with himself.

"Instead of going out there and making himself win, he let himself win."

Gatlin heard the roar when Crenshaw birdied sixteen, then arrived in the tower just as Crenshaw, who had flipped the prettiest little nine-iron approach thirteen feet from the seventeenth pin, made an improbable left-to-right birdie to take a two-shot lead.

Crenshaw called it "one of the best putts I ever made. It was just like a dream. I saw the ball go and it was just like in slow motion. It slowly turned and went in."

Sitting in the Butler Cabin, Love and Jack Stephens watched the putt roll across the monitor screen. When it was halfway to the hole, Love knew it was in; he knew it was over. Ben Crenshaw wasn't going to double-bogey the seventy-second hole. He turned to Stephens and said, "Ben's going to win. I'm going to the pressroom and get [my interview] over with before he comes in." . . .

On the tee, Crenshaw plucked a four-wood from his bag and let his tee shot rip. His eyes were focused on what he had to do. His heart was exploding.

"All of a sudden it was like, 'I can't believe this,'" he said. "This week, these circumstances, this man who gave me my life in golf. How could a guy be so lucky? I couldn't believe it. And I couldn't believe I was playing the kind of golf you dream of. I didn't count the bogeys until later, but I only had five all week. I'd never played a major tournament with just five bogeys."

The lump in his throat was the size of the Augusta clubhouse. He could see that second green jacket and Harvey. He could hear cheers. He couldn't hold it in. He brushed away the tears.

"The people were all congratulating him too soon," Jackson said. "I can't handle flattery real well and I don't think Ben can either, even though he gets it all the time. He just said, 'Wait a minute. I've got one more shot here.'"

Saying it and pulling it off were two different things. He came out of the eight-iron shot and it came up short.

"I was not in good shape hitting the second shot," Ben said. "I was just mentally starting to break. That was probably good for me because it jolted me back and told me I had some work to do."

Crenshaw flipped his chip ten feet past the pin. Amazingly, it held up.

"The next day when I played the golf course, I threw a couple of balls down there and you'd be amazed at how, if you were tentative with that chip, that ball could hit the slope and run all the way back down," CBS's Jim Nantz said. "I got nervous just thinking about it."

Julie and Charlie Crenshaw were near tears as they stood behind the green. They squeezed hands and prayed.

The best putter in the game had to get down in two to win. He had to. No one wanted to think, What if? They'd seen enough disasters at eighteen and more than a few come-from-behind miracles before.

"Ben played the hole like a lot of us would have," said United Press International's Mike Rabun. "Only he made the last putt."

When the ball finally disappeared from sight, Crenshaw's putter dropped to his side and those slender shoulders began to shake. Tears were streaming down his cheeks as he doubled over and his hands reached up to cradle his face. Jackson walked over and reached down to steady him as he let go. . . .

Julie Crenshaw sobbed as she watched the tears roll down her husband's cheeks. Officials at the scoring tent urged her to walk out and give him a hug. She said no.

"I told them Carl would take care of him, it was their time," she said. "I wasn't going to get near him until after he signed his card. He still had a job to do."

The emotions were churning inside Jackson, too. When he saw Crenshaw collapse, he said to himself, What do I do now?

What he did was just a reaction. "I tried to do what I could for him.

I wanted to tell him anything to make him feel better," Jackson said. "So I told him I loved him. And I had goose bumps everywhere."

When Crenshaw went into the scoring tent, Jackson stepped to the side. He wanted to stay out of the way, yet he didn't know quite what to do. "I looked around and I made eye contact with Julie and Charlie and they're all over there boohooing," Jackson said. "Finally Chris [Mazziotti, Henninger's caddie] told me to get the flag out of the hole and keep it for a souvenir."

Henninger congratulated Crenshaw and embraced him. "That's when I realized it was such a private quest and that he had somehow done it," he said. "He buried the feelings enough so they didn't affect his round, but at the same time, they were still there."

A year later, Crenshaw can chuckle about the moment but only for a few seconds. As he begins to describe it, that lump starts growing in his throat.

"When that last putt dropped, I dropped," he said. "It was such a relief it was over. I was thinking of so many things. I was thinking of the little guy starting out in golf, of Harvey and my family. And I was thinking I was lucky.

"Carl literally had to peel me off the floor. His actions reflect the way he is—he's a very kind man. I was happy for him; very proud for him. He's guided me around there so many times and there he was picking me up off the deck. That was a good hug."

The card signed, Crenshaw walked behind the tent where he and Julie shared a hug and a few tears. Next up was his brother. They buried their faces in each other's shoulders and cried.

"I just told him, 'You're the greatest in the whole world. This is your day. I love you,'" said Charlie, who didn't make it to the Masters for Ben's first victory there in 1984. "I felt like I was about ten years old."

Oles and Sayers got into the festivities, as did another old friend, Mary Beth Ryan. Then Gatlin came along. Finally, the Crenshaws jumped in a cart and headed for the Butler Cabin. . . .

Crenshaw sobbing and Jackson steadying him. The picture was in just about every newspaper in the country the following day, the moment frozen and etched in our minds. The man behind it? CBS executive producer Frank Chirkinian.

"The greatest thing I ever did," Chirkinian said, "was not cutting away to the heroes shot where the crowd goes wild. I stuck with Ben."

Once Crenshaw was standing and the cheering in the Penick house had died down, Helen Penick told Susan Watkins to pick up the phone, call Augusta National, and make sure this message got to Ben: "Harvey and Helen send congratulations and love on this special day."

It was almost dark when Crenshaw jumped onto a cart with Augusta National press chairman Charles Yates and started toward the clubhouse and a round of drinks on Augusta National. Before he cleaned up, Crenshaw called his father. Big Charlie, who had walked every step in 1984, doesn't come anymore because he can no longer walk the hills.

The Gatlins collected their things, then went to the porch to meet Yates so the four could sing their traditional goodbye—"Let the Lower Lights Be Burning"—on the porch. Just then, Jack Stephens walked by and asked if they were going to join Crenshaw at the dinner.

Larry said thanks, but they didn't want to intrude. Plus, his brothers didn't have coats or ties. Stephens told him not to worry, the members wanted them there. Ties materialized out of thin air.

Augusta members consider Crenshaw family—he's the son some never had and the brother the rest of them wanted. So as you might expect, the dinner was filled with toasts and more tears.

"We didn't eat much," Julie said. "We just held hands under the table. We were still in shock. It was just such a special time. It was the first major we won together."

The phone in the clubhouse rang. It was the Loves, who never saw Crenshaw to congratulate him, calling from their home in Sea Island, Georgia.

"I told him, 'I'm thrilled you won. I know Harvey's happy, too,'"

Love recalled. "You know Ben. He starts saying, 'Oh, I just got lucky.' He was excited for me, but he kind of apologized for winning. I just told him everyone was happy for him and to enjoy the night."

Love paused.

"Even if I go on to win five Masters, [last year] will still be one of my favorites. Having a part in a storyline like that was incredible."

In order to be in compliance with the pilot's rules, the Crenshaws' jet had to be off the ground by eleven P.M., so Stephens introduced the Gatlins. When Crenshaw won his first Masters in 1984, they celebrated with him, too, just not at the club and hardly in the same way. In '84, they greeted him by standing on their heads just inside the door of their rental house.

"Usually, we would sing three songs but because of the time, we just sang 'The Eyes of Texas,'" Gatlin said. "Ben and Julie and their group all did 'Hook 'Em Horns.' It was a very wonderful moment."

After they finished, Stephens, an Arkansas native, stood up. "This is the one time I'll allow it," he joked. "But I'll tell you one thing, you boys might not be able to come back."

Long after Crenshaw left, the Gatlins appeased Stephens. "We sang 'The Eyes of Arkansas' for him," Gatlin chuckled.

State troopers were waiting to escort the Crenshaw party to the airport. The jet lifted off before eleven, and once the plane had cleared Augusta, Crenshaw picked up the phone and called Helen Penick.

"He said he'd gotten the message and was on his way home," she said. "He just called to say thank you."

Everyone tried to sleep on the flight, but no one could. When the jet touched down in Austin about one A.M., it was greeted by a minicam, a reporter, and Sayers's wife. The team dispersed to their homes. No one went to bed.

Sayers had his children tape the final round, and he stayed up until four A.M. watching the replay and crying. Oles and his wife launched into a shot-by-shot for their baby-sitters—the kids' grandparents—and didn't fall asleep until nearly five A.M. The Crenshaws tossed and turned until five, but were awake an hour or so later.

Ben got up and made the coffee as he does every day, then drove to the supermarket to get a newspaper. Julie was sitting in the library when he walked in the door with a grocery sack tucked under his arm. It was filled with all the newspapers from around the state.

"You won't believe this," he said. "It's all over the front page. All of them."

"He just burst out bawling," Julie said. "He was so touched."

So was Harvey.

So was golf.

The Rarest Kind of Genius

Tom Callahan

Golf Digest, *February 1997*

Grumpy, frumpy little coot that he is, Tom Kite will probably take this the wrong way. But he has very quietly been reprising the heroics that have distinguished his career and are just right for a forty-seven-year-old captain in a Ryder Cup year.

Ever since fate cast him as the proverbial blind date next to Ben Crenshaw's perennial prom king, Kite has been insulted by practically every compliment in the book. "Tom is the rarest kind of genius," Johnny Miller once noted. "He has the ability to do the same thing every day all day long."

Yeah, and so's your old man.

To Kite, any cloying reference to his work ethic is just media code for myopia from a truly nearsighted society that simply has never been able to picture him dribbling a basketball with one hand. "I didn't grow up playing basketball," Kite said through tight lips several years ago. "I never worked at it. But I can assure you that if I had wanted to be a pretty good basketball player, I would have found a way to be a pretty good basketball player."

Nobody doubts it. That's the point.

For years, Kite was the leading money-winner who had almost won a lot of majors. When he finally triumphed in the 1992 U.S. Open, a cymbal clashed. Kite shot par at Pebble Beach on a day when the top twelve suitors were a combined 100 over par, when Ray Floyd, Mark Brooks, Scott Simpson, Mark Calcavecchia, and Paul Azinger couldn't break 80.

Rather than receding then, as Open champions are apt to do, Kite threw a little thirty-five-under at the Hope and trumped that with another victory in the L.A. Open. But the slump eventually fell upon him, and began to settle in.

Chuck Cook, a Texas teacher, flew back to Augusta with Kite and Crenshaw following Harvey Penick's funeral in 1995. At different times, Cook had tutored both players, though Tom rather more than Ben, Tom being much more inclined toward instruction. Sitting on the plane, Cook thought he could see the Masters played out in the sad eyes before him.

Kite was reverting to steel. Crenshaw was a mess. "I honestly thought Ben would withdraw," Cook says, "and Tom would win." Of course, Ben won. Tom missed the cut.

The famous archrivals were pitted in a Shell match last September that, Kite's rancid putting aside, was beyond poignant. So emphatically was Crenshaw outdriven and generally outshot that it was hard to think of them as contemporaries. Kite looked more like, well, the athlete. But Crenshaw chipped in at the first and second, and with ten fewer putts, won the day.

Trying everything he could, even nonwooden drivers, Kite climbed up from the pit of 104th on the '95 money list to sixty-sixth last year. He felt poised to turn a larger corner at the British Open, but a Thursday 77 sent him back to the range. Cook, who was tending to Corey

Pavin at the time, dropped by for just a second and came away shaking his head. "He's enjoying the process of fighting his way out of the slump," Cook said. "What a player he is."

"What an athlete," someone else muttered, never mind who. With a 66 the next day, Kite reentered both the tournament and the picture.

Near the close of the year, Tom went to Spain to win something called the OKI Pro-Am and, after giving Valderrama a glimpse of his game face, returned to California to partner Jay Haas in another mild victory. Kite was off the schneid. The Ryder Cup lay ahead, and Seve Ballesteros wasn't the only captain hoping to play in it.

If he wasn't a killer, Kite would still be the right commando to send after the Cup. His credentials begin with seven singles matches through the years, of which he has lost none. More than any of golf's matinee idols, he is the picture of the Ryder Cup player.

His voice may have been the loudest one shouting down Olympic golf in Atlanta, which is surprising in a way, because Kite knows the Olympics. He has a teenage daughter, Stephanie, who aspires to them. "She's every bit the competitor I am," he says, "if not more so."

She's a gymnast. When you think of those little-girl gymnasts marching tin-soldierly from apparatus to apparatus—to sugarplum music—and then consider that one of them may have the heart of Tom Kite, all you can say is: Yikes.

The Ryder Cup is its own Olympics, Kite would say, where the captains provide the gymnastics.

Part Four

Second to None

A Golfer Second to None

Melanie Hauser

Houston Post, *May 26, 1989*

Ben Hogan isn't just the best Texas golfer. He may have been the best player—period—ever to pick up a club.

And Ben Crenshaw is just about the best putter from Texas—or anywhere else for that matter—ever to grace a slick-as-a-tabletop green.

But the perfect Texas golfer?

Just about everyone agrees he would roll putts like Crenshaw and hit shots as dead solid perfect as Hogan. After that? It's simply a matter of opinion. And imagination.

To a Texan, perfection is more than knocking a nine-iron stiff for birdie to win Colonial or an emergency press at eighteen. Tall tales, colorful language, and quick tempers are as much a part of playing a solid eighteen in the Lone Star State as pulling off a bump-and-run into the green or lifting a few cool ones in the clubhouse. After all, low scores and major championship victories are great, but if a Texan can't toss clubs with a flair and be entertaining after he's won a U.S. Open . . . well, just imagine what Augusta National would be without Amen Corner.

The Lone Star State has raised, bred, and bestowed green cards on more great players than any other state in the union. Hogan. Crenshaw. Tom Kite. Byron Nelson. Lanny Wadkins. Fred Couples. Morris Williams Jr. Steve Elkington. Jack Burke Jr. Jimmy Demaret. Lee Trevino. Lefty Stackhouse. Tommy Bolt. Lighthorse Harry Cooper. Dave Marr. There are more combinations and permutations of swings and grips and temperaments than acres of land between the Rio Grande and Red rivers.

Dan Jenkins grew up in Fort Worth and knows just about every player from Ralph Guldahl to Stackhouse to Crenshaw. Jenkins his ownself figures his perfect player would start off with Hogan driving the ball in the fairway and hitting the long irons and fairway woods and Nelson hitting the short irons. Semi-Texan Bolt, who lived in Houston for a spell, would hit the pitching wedges—"He had it filed down deeper than anyone else," Jenkins says—while Crenshaw would putt. The colorful Demaret would be his choice for the interview room. As for skins, presses, and other such extracurricular endeavors? Jenkins wants Trevino handling all bets.

Crenshaw, the player-historian, said his perfect Texan would have Hogan's desire and Nelson's precision. Add Burke's competitive spirit, Kite's consistency, Bruce Lietzke's tempo, Marr's wit, and Demaret's foul-weather game and his ability to turn a phrase.

"Nobody was funnier than Jimmy," said Crenshaw. "One year at the Crosby, it snowed overnight. Jimmy woke up, looked out the window, and said, 'I knew I was loaded last night, but how did I end up in Squaw Valley?'"

And while he's at it, Crenshaw would also have the ideal teach like a combination of Jack Burke Sr. and Harvey Penick, gamble like 1946 U.S. Open champ Lloyd Mangrum, and have Stackhouse's legendary temper.

Marr, the former PGA champ who now resides in the television booth, needed just four players for his perfect golfer—Demaret, Hogan, Nelson, and Crenshaw. "Do you know who the smartest player was? Demaret," said Marr. "He was smart whether it was playing golf, running a course, or making money. For all the jolly-guy image he had, when he stepped onto the course, he never had any doubt what club to hit or how to play a hole.

"I'd want Demaret's confidence, Hogan's determination, Nelson's golf game—which I think was better than Hogan's—and Crenshaw's putting."

Ever the rebel, Lietzke, who grew up in Beaumont, played at the University of Houston, and never met a U.S. Open he wanted to play in, didn't even mention Hogan in his description. Instead, he went with a sum total of a dozen parts—Wadkins's aggressiveness, Couples's demeanor, Kite's course management, Crenshaw's putting and short game, Don January's slow, long-gaited walk, and Miller Barber's iron play. He would also add big Phil Blackmar's distance off the tee, Doug Sanders's wind game, tight-fisted Charlie Coody's "long-range financial planning," Bill Rogers's personality, Abilene native Billy Maxwell's colorful—not one expletive was ever deleted—vocabulary, and Scott Verplank's heart.

Duke Butler, the longtime Houston Open tournament director who played at Texas A&M and now works for the PGA Tour, used seventeen different players on his laundry list. In addition to the obvious, Butler wanted Guldahl's U.S. Open record (he won back-to-back in 1937–38), Fort Stockton native Blaine McCallister's good looks, Verplank's amateur record (he won almost everything), Marr's "ability to adjust to the business world," Burke's attitude "that amateurs make the game," and Betsy Rawls's accent. Kite said Nelson, Hogan, Mahaffey, and Wadkins all could have been the perfect golfer, period, had it not been for a few factors. "Nelson if he'd had longevity, Hogan with an earlier start, and Lanny or John Mahaffey if they'd stayed healthy."

And former Houston Cougar Steve Elkington, who moved to Houston eight years ago and hasn't left? "How about Trevino driving the ball, Demaret hitting the short irons, Kite around the green, and Crenshaw putting?" he said. "The only thing wrong is Kite would never get to play."

But you can't beat Houstonian Ed Fiori for brevity: "Tom Kite who putts like Ben Crenshaw. You'd never beat him."

Old Tom

Dan Jenkins

Fairways and Greens, *June 1994*

At a golf tournament many years ago, I was inspired to make the brilliant joke in a Texas newspaper that if Tommy Bolt had not become a touring pro, he would, in all probability, have been married to Bonnie Parker. The following day when I saw Bolt at Colonial Country Club in Fort Worth, he asked me who Bonnie Parker was. I guess I got about two sentences deep into the history of Clyde Barrow and Bonnie Parker—ever smiling, naturally, alert for the orbiting wedge—when Bolt said, "Well, son, why don't you just go out and round up them two, and Old Tom'll play their low ball."

As a journalist, I loved Tommy Bolt. Talk about good copy. But Tommy Bolt the golfer, the stylish shotmaker, was an artist I was often tempted to put up there with Ben Hogan. Those of us who knew him and watched him compete in his prime recognized that when Thomas Henry Bolt was right—confident, calm, and not blaming Arnold Palmer or the Lord for any short putts that curled away from the cup—no other human being could strike a prettier variety of shots, or land them more softly on the targets, other than Hogan, of course.

On the subject of Hogan, whom Tommy always credited with "weakening" his grip, curing his terminal hook, Bolt once said, "Now lookie here at all these baby-faced young mullets on the tour. They come out here dressed up in their Ben Hogan blues and grays. They ought to come to Old Tom, and let him show 'em how to match their reds with their pinks and their fuchsias."

It was at Southern Hills in Tulsa where Bolt strung together some of his—and history's—finest golf. This was the 1958 U.S. Open, the first major to be held at Southern Hills, and Southern Hills was determined to make an impression on the field.

The course presented an arrangement of fairways as narrow as Bolt's four-wood and a Bermuda rough that was not only calf-deep, but as gnarled as Tommy's temper could be. But he finessed the layout, led all the way and won, laughing, by four strokes.

I must tell you how good that was. Of the game's other big stars in that era, only Julius Boros and Gene Littler were heard from at Southern Hills. And Boros and Littler finished six and seven strokes behind Bolt. Sam Snead missed the cut. Jimmy Demaret withdrew. Cary Middlecoff was seventeen strokes back, and Ben Hogan, his wrist slightly sprained after a bout with the rough, wound up in a tie for tenth.

The most dangerous and torturous hole at Southern Hills is the twelfth, a par-four requiring a straight drive and a cautious iron shot, or else you have to deal with rough, trees, and water. Bolt birdied the twelfth the first three rounds and parred it on the last eighteen. He was three under on the hole that took everyone else virtually out of contention.

This was the Open that furnished Tommy Bolt Story No. 1,032. When Tommy entered the press tent after the second round as the sole owner of the Open lead, he pretended to be angry with a Tulsa writer. There had been a misprint in the morning paper. Old Tom was 40 years old at the time, but the paper had said he was 49. The Tulsa writer apologized for the typographical error.

"Typographical error, hell," said Bolt. "It was a perfect four and a perfect nine."

None of us who were privileged to be near him inside the ropes—it was still permitted then—would be likely to forget some of the dialogue that took place over the last few holes as Old Tom closed in on his victory at Southern Hills.

Three of us actually walked along in the middle of the fairways with him. With me were Bud Shrake, a newspaper cohort and old friend, and Jimmy Breslin, who was then with the NEA feature service in New York. This was before Shrake and Breslin had become successful book authors.

"Ain't this somethin'?" Bolt said, mostly to me. "Old Tom's gonna win hisself a Ben Hogan type of tournament. How 'bout that, pard?"

Going up the eighteenth fairway now, the last hole of the championship, after Bolt had put a glorious four-wood on the green, Breslin said to him, "You're going to win it, you ought to throw a club."

Bolt mumbled something about a book he had been reading, a book that had given him "inner peace."

"Inner peace don't sell newspapers," Breslin said. "You don't throw a club, how come you got the name?"

Tommy replied, "If I threw as many clubs as everybody says, the manufacturers would have nothing to do but manufacture Tommy Bolt golf clubs."

"You could throw a little one," said Jimmy. "Something you don't need."

Bolt looked at Shrake and me, as if to ask how Jimmy Breslin ever got admitted to a golf tournament.

Jimmy dropped back a few paces and said, "The story don't work."

Old Tom's reputation as terrible-tempered, tempestuous Tommy (Thunder) Bolt was enhanced by the wire services, of course, just as they made Hogan a lifetime bantamweight, kept Cary Middlecoff a Dr., and insisted Byron Nelson was both a British lord and a mechanical man.

What Bolt did best as a shotmaker was turn the tee shot in any direction he wanted—he could play doglegs like a violin—strike better fairway woods than anybody, and flirt with the flagsticks on his short irons.

He seemed to make the ball land more softly than anyone else, and there was no explaining it, except that his feeling for the shots must have had something to do with it. As he often said, "Son, I can poop one into the water and it don't even splash."

That Bolt did not win more than fifteen tournaments during his ten good years on the PGA Tour was probably a result of timing, as in career timing. His early good years were also some of Hogan's and Snead's best, and then later on his career ran into the rise of Arnold Palmer.

Perhaps Old Tom knew he was never destiny's child, and maybe that is why, now and then after blowing a short putt, he would look up at the sky and say, "Why don't You come on down here and play me one time?"

Not that a few putts here and there could not have changed the record of the man who came out of Haworth, Oklahoma, moved through Louisiana, and settled in Texas to learn the game. He was very close in a few other Opens, as well as the Masters twice, and a couple of times he reached the semifinals in the old match-play PGA. In that tournament he would go around whipping your Sam Sneads (twice), Gene Littlers, Jack Flecks, Lew Worshams, but he would lose to a Claude Harmon, a Jackson Bradley, or a Charles Prentice.

All of which prompted Old Tom to say at one point, "Well, who wants to win some kind of tournament that ain't got nobody in it but mother geese?"

Tommy Bolt Story No. 5,689:

One day Bolt was trying to line up a putt during a round at a tour event—it doesn't matter where—and slowly he backed away, looking irritated. From the gallery behind him, it seems, a spectator's shadow had inadvertently obscured Tommy's view. Characteristically, Tommy's chin jutted out, and he said to no one in particular, "Well, I never could read *Poa annua* in the dark!"

When terrible-tempered, tempestuous Tommy (Thunder) Bolt won the U.S. Open at Southern Hills in 1958, a fellow named Tom Watson was eight years old. Ben Crenshaw was six years old and so was Bruce Lietzke. Jerry Pate, the defending champion this week, was four years old. Thus, it was both startling and sad for me to realize that a whole generation of golfers on the tour has missed Tommy Bolt.

This, I suppose, was for them.

Bolt's Life Is His Curse

David Casstevens

Dallas Morning News, *April 25, 1982*

AUSTIN—Tommy Bolt bought a ranch north of Little Rock, Arkansas, last year with the hope of finally getting away from the curse of his existence.

Golf.

Blankety-blank golf.

He's threatened to quit the bleep-bleeping game countless times, but it's a habit a man of his pride can't seem to break. Bolt's competitive fire and the bitterness simmering within simply won't allow him to surrender and put away the clubs for good.

So here he was late Saturday afternoon, a sixty-four-year-old man complaining of an aching back and tormented by his famous temper, putting himself through sheer hell under the oyster-gray rain clouds at Onion Creek.

The Legends of Golf is intended to be a happy affair. A time for some of the greats of the game, now in their sundown years, to renew fraternal acquaintances and play a little golf. They've earned the right to ride down the fairways. Many of them do, too, waving to the gallery from E-Z-Go electric carts.

The Legends is a time to celebrate their contributions to the sport. A time to relive lost glories. A time to sit around at day's end and swap stories that grow richer with the retelling.

But while the Demarets and Sarazens sipped on gin-and-tonics in the intimacy of the locker room, Tommy Bolt was alone with himself in his private purgatory. He stood on the muddy practice tee and beat ball after ball after ball. The exercise was sheer agony. After each shot, his eyes narrowed like a gunslinger's. His prominent jut-jaw tightened a little more.

"(. . .)," Bolt said, turning the air blue after hitting his last ball. "I hate to end with a (. . .) shot like that!"

Bolt wanted to walk away, but something wouldn't let him. He angrily summoned his caddy to fetch him another bucket of balls.

"I'm sixty-four years old," Bolt muttered. "What the (. . .) am I doing out here? What the (. . .) am I trying to prove?"

Tommy Bolt is a legend, in his own way. History will remember him as something of a tragic hero. He possessed a beautifully sweet swing; a long, sweeping, picture-book swing that hasn't worn down under the grindstone of time. Unfortunately, his temper was his worst enemy. It overshadowed and undermined his outstanding golfing skills.

Bolt won fifteen tour events, including the 1958 U.S. Open and the 1958 Colonial Invitation at Forth Worth. But those who followed his career through the '50s and early '60s suggest he should have won a lot more. He had all the tools. If only he could have harnessed his volcanic temperament.

Terrible Tommy. Tempestuous Tommy. Thunder Bolt, they called him. He spoke two languages: English and Profanity. He elevated cussing to an art form.

At the 1956 Tournament of Champions, Bolt kicked his ball off the green after missing a putt. His club-throwing tirade at the 1957 Flint Open cost him $100 in fines.

One year at Colonial, Bolt went on a tear unrivaled in golfing lore. Upset with the way he was playing, he threw his ball into the water at No. 9, pitched his putter over the crowd at No. 12, hurled his driver at No. 14, and finally broke his four-iron against a tree at No. 15.

According to legend, after lipping out six straight putts in one tournament, Bolt shook his first at the heavens and shouted, "Why don't You come down and fight like a man?"

He reportedly enlivened a clinic one time by asking his fourteen-year-old son to "show the nice folks what I taught you." Bolt's son playfully hurled a nine-iron into the sky.

"Aw, that's all (. . .)," Bolt insisted as he sat in the locker room.

If the Legends selected its Seven Dwarfs, Bolt would be Grumpy.

It's not that he's impolite to strangers. On the contrary; he warms up to anyone who shows an inquring interest in his colorful career. He can be quite amusing. He begins most of his answers with, "Son . . ." As in, "Son, I never was a politician. I never kissed anyone's (. . .). Hell, I'd (. . .) go on (. . .) welfare before I'd do that."

But grumpy best describes the man paired with gentlemanly Art Wall in this year's Legends. The more you question Bolt about his place in golf history, the more he reveals the grievances he's refused to bury. Grievances that have simmered within him all these years. Grievances that have corroded his inner spirit.

Bolt came up the hard way. He quit school after the ninth grade. He worked awhile as a carpenter and later as a golf hustler at Memorial Park in Houston. Reminded that he won "only" fifteen tour events, Bolt screwed up his face and boomed, "Son, I served in the (. . .) war. Not like these kids now. Hell, I was over thirty when I joined the tour."

During his prime, he played in the long shadows of Hogan and Snead, and later Player and Palmer. He believes the public never appreciated him for his skills. They followed him, he insisted, not to watch his shot-making but in hopes of seeing him blow his cool. He hasn't forgotten the golf fans who taunted him and baited him.

Bolt also believes the PGA "downplayed" his record. "I was pretty outspoken," he said. "They never gave me my due. It would have been different if I had been somebody else. Maybe Billy Graham."

Bolt looked tired. He said his bleeping back was killing him, not that any of these other (. . .) in the locker room cared.

If the truth were known, Thunder Bolt probably was right.

A Perfect Swing Carried Nelson on a Magical Ride

Larry Dorman

New York Times, *May 14, 1995*

ROANOKE, Texas, May 6—In the airy sitting room of the ranch house where he has lived for forty-eight years, Byron Nelson holds a picture in his rugged hands and peers back through time. In the frame, a lean young man is in the perfect golf position, his arms extended and the shaft of his club bowed, head behind the ball, body in absolute balance.

Nelson's gaze lingers on the frame, and the deep lines of his face are reflected in the glass. He is the man with the tie and the starched shirt in the old black-and-white photo, swinging with a tensile strength that fairly leaps through the decades and out of the picture; he is the man with the bad hip sitting with his cane at arm's length. He shakes his head slowly, puts a finger to his lips and smiles.

"I don't know about you," he says in a voice strong and full of Texas, "but I don't see anything at all wrong with that swing."

Not that Byron Nelson is bragging, mind you. No, that is the last thing this eighty-three-year-old man would do. It's not his style. This is about substance. This is the golf swing that inspired the United States Golf Association to name its driving robot "Iron Byron." It is the swing that produced fifty-two United States tournament victories in an abbreviated career. And it is the swing that, fifty years ago, launched Nelson on the most remarkable streak in the history of this, and perhaps any other, sport.

With this swing, Byron Nelson won eleven straight golf tournaments in 1945. Eleven straight. It has never been approached. The closest any golfer has come was Jackie Burke Jr., who won four straight back in 1952. And with this golden anniversary of Nelson's unprecedented achievement, the spotlight once again has focused on this quiet man from Fort Worth. During the months and weeks leading up to this weekend's GTE Byron Nelson Classic at the Four Seasons Resort at Las Colinas, Nelson figures he has done many more interviews than he did during all of that marvelous 1945.

"Not that I'm complaining," he said. "It still amazes me. Can you imagine? All this about something a man did fifty years ago? But I've enjoyed it, enjoyed thinking about it and talking about it."

Nelson's eyes are clear and his hands—those huge, callused hands that made golf grips look like pencils—are steady. People used to say the hands are what gave him so much control, what enabled him to keep the club on line longer than anyone before or since. No telling. But during one day recently, he signed 1,520 advance copies of his *Little Black Book,* a fascinating compendium of his notes beginning with the 1935 season, and the signature never varied.

Consistency has always been Nelson's hallmark. Some of the numbers from his career seem unreal. During one stretch in the 1940s, he made 113 straight cuts round the world, a record that still stands. His career lasted just eleven years, but only four players in history exceeded his fifty-two victories. They are Sam Snead (eighty-one), Jack Nicklaus (seventy), Ben Hogan (sixty-three), and Arnold Palmer (sixty). And only Nicklaus was able to approach the number of tournament victories in the United States during his first eleven years on tour. Nicklaus won fifty-one in that stretch.

As impressive as those figures are, they pale next to those from the Streak. That year, Nelson not only won eleven straight. He won eighteen of the thirty tournaments he entered. He finished second seven times and was out of the top five just once. His stroke average for the year was 68.33, an all-time record and nearly a full stroke better than Snead's second-place total of 69.23. Maybe the most mind-boggling number of all is Nelson's final-round stroke average. In crunch time, he shot an average score of 67.45.

"The final-round stroke average, that's really the reason why I won so much as I did," he said. "And I got some good breaks, too. What Snead did at Charlotte, when he bogeyed the last hole and then I won the playoff, that was a break. He could have scrambled around, gotten a par at the last hole and then that would have been the end of it. The whole streak would have stopped at one."

It all began uneventfully enough, with Byron and his running mate Jug McSpaden, the Gold Dust Twins, winning the Miami Four Ball by beating Denny Shute and Sam Byrd, 8 and 6. Nothing unusual there. Nelson and McSpaden were a formidable team and played a lot of golf together since they both were rejected by the military during the war, Nelson for a blood problem and McSpaden for severe sinusitis.

One of the things to note about the first victory is the presence of Hogan in the field. Critics of Nelson's accomplishments often point to what they say were war-depleted fields during the 1945 season. While it's obviously true that some good players were off to war, the facts are that Snead played in twenty-six tournaments that year and Hogan played in eighteen.

"All of that talk about no competition never really bothered me," Byron said, "because, you see, I know how I played. Maybe I wouldn't have won eighteen tournaments, or eleven in a row, but I played wonderfully well."

He surely did. During the eleven victories that stretched from early March through early August, Nelson won by an average of seven strokes. There were only three real scares. The first was during tournament No. 2 at Charlotte, when Snead's three-putt bogey at the last hole allowed Nelson to tie him at 272 and then defeat him after two eighteen-hole playoff rounds, 69–69 to 69–73. The second scare came during victory No. 7, in June at the Philadelphia Inquirer Invitation, when Nelson had to birdie five of the last six holes to shoot 63 and beat McSpaden by two strokes.

The third came in the second round of match play during the PGA Championship. That was when Mike Turnesa of White Plains lost to Nelson and uttered the phrase that summed up the entire year. With just four holes to play at Moraine Country Club in Dayton, Ohio, Turnesa was two-up on Nelson. His shot to the fifteenth hole was ten feet from the hole, and he barely missed his birdie attempt. Nelson, whose shot was inside Turnesa's, made his putt. Nelson then squared the match with a birdie at sixteen, eagled the seventeenth to go one up, and parred the last hole to protect his lead.

"I was seven under and still lost," is what Turnesa said. "How the hell are you supposed to beat this man?"

Five decades later, Nelson leans back in his chair and chuckles at that. He recalls that two weeks later, at Tam O'Shanter, he shot 269 to beat Hogan and Gene Sarazen by eleven strokes for his tenth straight victory.

"I look back on it now, and it just seems like a good long dream," he said. "I don't know, I must have played over my head for a period of a year and a half or so. But you know, the thing was, I consistently drove the ball in the fairway, and when you're doing that, you've got to be swinging well enough to put the ball on the green with your irons."

Always in the fairway. That was part of it. He has not been out of it since. After the following season, he retired from golf, at the age of thirty-four, because he had done everything he set out to do and he had made enough money to buy the ranch, 740 acres in the town about fifteen miles outside Dallas. He and his first wife, Louise, who died in 1985, had always wanted a place like that. He named it "Fairway Ranch" and he still lives there.

Byron Nelson tells you that he has no regrets about golf, and you believe him, because everything about his demeanor tells you so. Sure, he would have liked to win the British Open to complete the career Grand Slam, but in those days it just cost too much to make the trip and he would have had to take a month off from his club job. He only made the crossing twice. No regret. Sure, if he had stayed in the game longer he would have won a lot more tournaments, "but maybe then I wouldn't have gotten into television, wouldn't have had my name associated with my Byron Nelson Classic, you just never know." No regrets.

The only thing Nelson will admit to regretting is associating his name with a cigarette company back in 1936. A devout man who to this day attends prayer meetings and church at the Hilltop Church of Christ, he never smoked, drank, chased women, or stayed out late, something Snead still ribs him about. But he needed the money, and he took a $500 fee for endorsing a cigarette called 20 Grand. When the ads came out, the letters came in.

Pain still creases his face when he talks about it. "None of us realizes how many people we influence," he said, "and there had been a lot of nice articles written about me, about how I was a nice Christian man who didn't smoke or drink or do this or that, and suddenly this ad comes out and I started getting some of the most terrible letters from schoolteachers and Sunday-school teachers. They said, 'Well, there you are, just like everybody else, letting the almighty dollar get to you.' Five hundred dollars. I was sick about that. It was the worst thing I've ever done."

He tried to give the money back, but the company refused. He says now he prayed about it "many, many times, brought it to the good Lord and said I'd never do anything again as long as I lived to influence people the wrong way."

Money has never been that important to Nelson. "If I had made $10 million, I might not be as well off as I am right now," he said. And he means it. It amuses him to think of how much money he would have made winning eighteen tournaments last year—it would have been somewhere in the $8-million range—and he chuckles at the notion.

"I could not be happier than I am," he said, and as he stands to put the photo on a nearby table, his major concession to age is evident. His walk is painfully slow, the result of hip-replacement surgery several years ago. He doesn't get to play much golf anymore, but he will tell you, at the urging of his second wife, Peggy, whom he married in 1986, about the 83 he shot a few weeks ago. The only thing troubling Nelson these days is the illness of Hogan, who is in a Fort Worth hospital recovering from colon surgery.

Although the two men grew up together, caddied together, competed and traveled together and had many meals together, Nelson hasn't seen much of Hogan in recent years. He says he knows that Hogan doesn't want company, and he respects his wishes. It still seems to pain him, though.

"We are good friends and I understand the way he is," Nelson said. "He has never been outgoing. I've always respected his wishes about people leaving him alone. I'm very concerned that he's ill."

Nelson moves slowly into the family room of the ranch, where many of his trophies and memorabilia are displayed. He can't move like he once did, but his eye-hand coordination is still there. He is using a Cleveland Classic copy of his old MacGregor driver as a cane, and as he walks he spots an ant scurrying across the floor. He gets it with the butt of the club on his first try.

Less than a week from this day, on the eve of the tournament that bears his name, Byron Nelson would stand in the Ben Crenshaw Suite at the Four Seasons, announcing the formation of the new Byron Nelson Golf School that will open at the resort in September and admiring the new Byron Nelson Eleven Straight Tournament Trophy, a silver loving cup designed by Tiffany & Co. He was worn out, but enormously proud.

"I feel like I'm the luckiest man in golf," he would say. "Not just because I have a few records attached to my name or anything like that. Just because of the way people have accepted me, wherever I've gone, welcomed me. It has been a wonderful year, a wonderful year."

That it has. All because of a wonderful year, fifty years ago, a year that framed a feat that will never be duplicated and one that even the jaded golf professionals of today and the legions of golf fans recognize as something cosmic, otherworldly. As the sun sets over Texas and the cool of the evening comes to the Dallas suburbs, a pair of tourists sit at the feet of the giant Byron Nelson statue near the first tee and pose for pictures.

As one man stands to leave, he stops and turns to the copper image of Nelson. He salutes. It is a gesture that comes from generations of golfers, from all across time.

(Editor's note: Nelson has, in many ways, been overshadowed by Hogan and Demaret, but it was simply because his streak—and some of his best years—came during World War II, when the nation's eyes weren't on sports, but rather Europe and Japan. In fact, when Nelson won his eleventh straight, both Dallas newspa-

pers ran small wire stories—the Times Herald*'s was six paragraphs; the one in the* News *five. Compare that to one win by Tiger Woods today. It wasn't that the city wasn't proud of Nelson's accomplishment, it was simply a sign of those times. Four days after Nelson's eleventh triumph, the second atomic bomb was dropped on Nagasaki.)*

Jimmy's Raiment, Voice, and Swing Lead Grantland Rice to Pen Poetry

Grantland Rice

North American Newspaper Alliance, March 10, 1947

The rainbow ducks behind a cloud and hides its face in shame.
The redbird, bluebird and thrush look sordid, dull and tame.
The pelican, with startled look, deserts the fish at sea,
When J. Demaret takes his stand upon the starting tee.

Green, blue and crimson, pink and gold, with purple on the side,
He makes surrounding flower growth look drab, and even snide,
In one quick look at blazing flame, the rosebuds fade and fall,
But better still above the rest—the guy can hit that ball.

ST. PETERSBURG, Florida—It is pleasant news to report that Jimmy Demaret, the singing Texan, is once more the swinging Texan and back around the top again. As early as the new season is, Demaret already has won two big open tournaments and has finished second twice. In addition to this, he paired with Ben Hogan to win the International four-ball championship in Miami Sunday.

Just seven years ago the ever-smiling Demaret won nine tournaments and practically wrecked the Winter and Spring League from California on through the Masters at Augusta. During his two-year shift in the navy he missed major competition.

Out of the navy and back on the long circuit again, Demaret decided that his happy, carefree prewar days were over and that it would be strictly business from then on. Being a good-looking, colorful fellow, in order to offset the drabness of training and hard work, Jimmy laid in a supply of green, blue, purple, crimson, and orange golf caps that looked like young balloons. He also added a supply of yellow, green, and crimson coats and sweaters, plus multicolored trousers to keep the ensemble in proper order.

He was the only fellow on the golf course you could recognize two miles away, a human rainbow in action.

"After being away from golf for so long," Demaret says, "it took me some time to get my swing going. I found my timing way off. I also found it hard to keep concentrating. I might be all right for eighteen holes and turn in a sixty-seven or a sixty-eight, but I couldn't keep it up for seventy-two holes. This happened to most of the golfers who had been in the service. My judgment of distance was bad or spotty. But I had made up my mind to work and train and practice. As a result, I now am hitting the ball as well as I ever did, even during the year I won nine tournaments out of eleven starts. It has taken me more than a year to get my confidence back, but I feel much better about things now."

Demaret has now moved up with Hogan in the money-winning class for 1947, and he will be a rough entry to shake loose in any tournament, including the Masters and the Open.

Demaret happens to hail from a rather expensive commonwealth that has given golf Ben Hogan, Byron Nelson, Lloyd and Ray Mangrum, and around ten or twelve others who live in birdie and eagle land. Said commonwealth is Texas, the city Houston.

Jimmy's additional claim to fame is that he has a singing voice that has drawn high praise from Bing Crosby and Bob Hope. He could make an easy living singing but he likes golf better. Being a genial soul, surrounding friends and admirers would keep him up most of the night, which was no great help to his golf game next day.

He found that too much warbling could lead to wobbling. Those nights of music and melody now belong to the past.

Well-built, a trifle on the stocky side like the Hagen of other years, Demaret also has a pair of powerful hands that know how to swing a clubhead. He is not the longest hitter in golf but he is long enough, up with the longer ones. The ease and smoothness of his swing impress you at first sight. In addition to being a skilled handler of the woods, he is as fine an iron player as you'll find in golf, with exceptional control in the wind.

Too many spectators forget to look at Demaret's fine swing when they see a big, deep purple cap, a shiny yellow shirt, and a pair of bright crimson trousers. The next day, it may be a yellow cap, a green shirt, and blue or orange trousers.

It is reported that cardinals, bluebirds, and mockingbirds follow him around the course to get the latest in attire and voice. I would not know about that. For as gaudy as his raiment is, I'd rather watch his swing. There certainly isn't another fellow in golf who is better liked, both by players and galleries.

A Tribute to Demaret's Greatness

Peter Dobreiner

Golf World, *December 1993*

T. S. Eliot nailed the ball flush off the screws when he wrote "friendship should be more than biting time can sever." When a friend dies, a little bit of you dies, too. But time is supposed to be the great healer. You get over your loss. New friends fill the emptiness. So how is it, ten years after his death, that Jimmy Demaret's friends are still aware of this great hole in their lives?

The answer is that he was a colossus, although you would never guess so from the history books. In his *Story of American Golf,* Herb Warren Wind refers to Demaret as "The Wardrobe." Charles Price was probably too close to Demaret to do his friend justice in *The World of Golf.* Demaret gets even shorter shrift in Mark McCormack's *World of Professional Golf* as "that cheerful Texas clothes-horse."

The difficulty about putting Demaret into proper perspective is that certain words in the golfing lexicon have taken on a voodoo power. "Par" is one of them. We sit transfixed by terror like rabbits in the beam of powerful headlights at the sight of par. We castigate ourselves as failures when we take five strokes on a 440-yard hole, steeply uphill and playing into a gale, because the Demon Par, lying through his teeth, insists the proper score should be four.

Another mesmeric word is "major." Demaret won three (1940, '47, '50), all of them early Masters, so not even fully fledged majors at that. So many assume he must have been at best a first-class second-rater. If that is the judgment of history, then history is talking through its hat. At his best Demaret was the best, and especially so in high winds. Yes, even better than Ben Hogan, and we have Hogan's word for it. "He was the most underrated golfer in history. This man played shots I hadn't even dreamed of. I learned them. But it was Jimmy who showed them to me first."

Demaret's progress in golf was essentially the same as Hogan's and Byron Nelson's. His father was a carpenter-painter and Jimmy was the fifth of nine children. At nine he started to caddie at a sand-green course in Houston and he played golf barefoot until he was fifteen. By that time he had won the Houston scholastic tournament.

At seventeen he was taken on by Jack Burke Sr., as an assistant at River Oaks. One of his duties was to baby-sit for the infant who was to become his partner in the creation of the Champions Club. He liked to announce: "I've been baby-sitting Jackie Burke now for fifty years."

A year later Jimmy decided he was ready to play the California circuit. He bought an old Model-T Ford and set off with a friend, Johnny McMillan. At El Paso they crossed the border and in a bar came across two Mexicans who liked to bet on shooting pool and did not look too proficient at the game. In short order Johnny lost $35, all the money they had. They hocked Jimmy's clubs for $13 and the Model-T for $30, and Johnny lost that, too.

Now they had to caddie at a local club to raise enough cash to get Jimmy's clubs out of hock. Cold, hungry, miserable, and considerably wiser in the matter of snap judgments about Mexicans with unorthodox methods of wielding sporting implements, they rode a freight train home.

Tournament golf was a paradox during the depressed '30s. They were all pros but played what was virtually amateur golf because the money was negligible. Demaret concentrated on his club job and his second string as a nightclub singer for the next three years.

It was not until 1940, when tour prize funds were increasing, that Demaret returned to the circuit. He won six tournaments in succession and then scurried home, $8,625 to the good, because he was afraid of losing his singing job.

Now he could put some of his ideas into practice. The drab uniformity of golf dress was anathema to his effervescent personality, as was the dour solemnity of the players' deportment. He found a New York importer of colorful cloth intended for the women's haute couture market and had clothes made up. He involved the galleries, chatting and joking with spectators. The Demaret style was born and it was a revelation. It was also revolutionary, as it changed both the appearance and attitudes of professional golf.

After the war Demaret picked up his mercurial career with renewed flair and panache. Two more Masters, some thirty regular tournaments, six of them four-ball events in partnership with Hogan. In three Ryder Cup matches Demaret set a unique record of winning every encounter.

So why didn't he win more majors and set the official stamp of approval on his exceptional talents? The reason lies in the word "dedication," which implies a lifestyle as rigid and committed in its way as that of a Trappist monk. For Demaret there was much, much more to life than golf. His real vocation was to make people happy, and to make them laugh. Bob Hope called him the funniest amateur comedian in the world. Charlie Price wrote: "Jimmy Demaret is the nicest, kindest, most thoughtful human being I know." That's why he didn't win more majors. More to the point, that's why the void he left has never been filled. It is unfillable.

Lord, How This Man Could Play

Charles Price

Golf Magazine, *August 1973*

When Lloyd Mangrum was elected to the PGA Hall of Fame some years ago, it was an occasion for yawning. The choice was that obvious. But it may today call for an explanation among those who think golf began with Arnold Palmer and is going to end with Jack Nicklaus.

At that time—which was approximately when Ben Crenshaw was born—Mangrum had won fifty-two major tournaments, forty-three of them on the PGA Tour. One of them was the National Open, which he won by birdieing three of the last six holes and then beating, first, Vic Ghezzi and, later, Byron Nelson in a playoff that took thirty-six holes. Another was the old World's Championship, then by far the richest tournament in golf. This he won by defeating Sam Snead in a playoff after tying him by the dramatic expedient of chipping in on the last hole.

Mangrum first came on the national golf scene in 1940, when he established the course record at Augusta National during the Masters tournament with an eight-under-par 64. He finished second to another youngster, Jimmy Demaret. He then lost perhaps the best years of his golfing life while serving as a corporal in the Army, spending twenty-six months fighting in Europe, where he was wounded three times.

In the postwar days, Mangrum returned to the tour sporting a moustache, this at a period in American vanity when nobody wore one unless you were an old lady or a man trying to cover up a harelip.

He stood erect to the point where he appeared taller than he was, and his eyes shone like the blue blades Gillette then put out. He strode the fairways in short, unhurried, positive steps—as though he were playing a game he had personally thought up. When he stepped to the first tee, lean as a one-iron, he glanced coldly at his playing partners, the officials, and the gallery as though he were a faro shark casing a bust-out joint in New Orleans. Then, casual as the riverboat gambler he was so often likened to, he'd pluck his driver out of his bag, remove the head cover, and then stroll to the tee. "Look out, you bastards!" his eyes would say. "Ol' Lloyd has come to play."

And, Lord, how this man could play! He competed against some of the roughest professionals this game has ever known, who grew up tough as Kro-Flites in a semipoverty that meant working for nickels instead of going to school. College was not their dream; they would have settled for high school. Boyhood meant peddling newspapers or shining shoes or toting a golf bag weighing half as much as you did. As a Class A caddie, you made eighty-five cents, seventy-five if you were Class B, and no more than half a dollar if you were Class C. Most of this you turned in to a redneck caddie master, rough as rawhide, who ran the lunch concession, where you could buy a cream soda and a baloney sandwich made out of week-old bread for a percentage of what you had made that day, usually fifty. You gave him this as a kind of honorarium because he had kept you, as a juvenile, from being cheated at cards, knifed because some wino thought you had stolen his fat bag, or because three guys a foot taller than you thought it might make fun to take turns beating you purple.

They came out of everywhere, these pros: from the mountains of West Virginia, the mud farms of Texas, the sun-blazoned vineyards of California, the hill country of the Carolinas, the exurbs of the East. Their names were Snead and Demaret and Hogan and Nelson and Guldahl and Heafner and Oliver and Harrison, to name just a few who come quickly to mind. And they'd play you for your brains. Of them all, Lloyd Mangrum was probably the most worldly. "This guy was so mean," an old pro once told me admiringly, "he'd play you on the hottest day in August wearing tweed slacks and no underwear."

Lloyd doesn't get around much anymore. In the last twenty years he has had ten heart attacks—ten, mind you—and three seizures. When President Eisenhower had his third attack, Lloyd, whose friendship with the general had dated from clear back to the battlefields and who by then had had his sixth attack, sent him a telegram. DEAR IKE, it read, I'M THREE UP ON YOU.

As a result of his not unexpected lack of stamina, Lloyd now spends most of his time sitting around the clubhouse at Apple Valley in California, a club he has represented for years, where he plays gin with the men and bridge with the ladies, cards being a game that fascinates him almost as much as golf. "Why not?" he says. "Cards and golf are pretty much the same. You play both of them with your head. The only difference is that in golf you gotta get up and walk."

A Firm Hand on a Carefree Cat

Myron Cope

Sports Illustrated, *June 17, 1968*

"I could give him fifteen thousand dollars," says Claudia Trevino, fixing her husband with a gaze you could hang wash on, "and he'd blow it in a week. Money means nothing to him."

Lee Buck Trevino lets out a roosterish cackle, delighted by the rebuke. He has been averaging roughly $2,200 a tournament since joining the pro golf tour last June, but still has trouble finding a dime to mark his ball. "Until lately, I never had any money," he says. "It's like pieces of paper to me."

The Trevinos are sipping soft drinks at a table in the Horizon Hills Country Club, which lies twenty miles southeast of El Paso in the desert. Lee is the club pro, a grinning, copper-colored Mexican, twenty-eight years old who at five-foot-ten and 180 pounds is built like a paunchy bulldog. Though he was born and raised in the countryside near Dallas, newspaper columnists almost invariably invite their readers to imagine him standing at Pancho Villa's right hand, with a bandolier tossed over his shoulder. The name Ann is tattooed on his right forearm. Ann, he explains, was a sweetheart who wrote him a Dear John letter when he served in the Marines, but, as matters turned out, the tattoo regained its usefulness. Claudia's middle name is Ann.

"We can go out to shop for a pair of socks," Claudia is saying, "and he'll spend five hundred dollars."

"I never spend nothin'," Lee grumbles, toughening.

"Because I never give you anything."

A lithe, blond cutie from Dallas, Claudia administers the family fortune and is the Wilbur Mills of Lee's existence. The savings and checking accounts are in her name, an arrangement that Lee recognizes as prudent, because any money he can lay his hands on is as good as gone. Deadbeats melt his heart with hard-luck stories. Across the Rio Grande, waiters at the Juarez racetrack find their hands stuffed with Lee's five-dollar tips. Gambling men keep a chair open for him at the table. "If there's a little poker game nearby and if I got five hundred dollars I'll blow it," he says genially. "Or if I got five dollars I'll blow that. I got to bust that poker game or it got to bust me. Unfortunately, I don't bust many poker games."

"He never comes home with a dime in his pocket," Claudia sighs.

"You only live once. Why not have some fun? I'll tell you, this is the most money-hungriest woman I ever seen."

There is no acrimony, only affection, in Lee's tone, for it was Claudia who last summer launched him on a tournament career that already has netted them upward of $60,000 in winnings. There he was, an El Paso nobody, an old Mex of twenty-seven, a golfer who had never had a lesson—who had mastered the game in the Marines on Okinawa. The local qualifier for the 1967 U.S. Open was drawing near at Odessa, but Lee did not regard himself as Open material. Claudia, however, sent in his twenty-dollar entry fee and ordered him to Odessa.

He shot 69-67–136, the lowest local qualifier score in the nation. Next, he finished second in the sectional at Dallas, proceeding from there, on borrowed money, to the Open at plush Baltusrol in New Jersey. "Jack Duffy!" the caddie master called through a microphone to the caddie yard. "You've been drawn. Your professional is here, and he wants you immediately."

Duffy shuffled into view, a fortyish, tournament-hardened veteran. He looked over Trevino as if to say, "Well, there goes my chance for a piece of the money."

Listlessly, wordlessly, Duffy trailed Lee through a practice-round two-over-par 72, confidently expecting to see an 80 before long. But in the next three days of practice he saw instead a 68, a 71, and a 70. By daily stages Duffy quickened his pace, first drawing closer to his professional's heels, then abreast of him and finally out front, authoritatively leading the way. At last he spoke. "Kid," he announced as Lee concluded his last practice round, "I'll tell you something. These guys can have Nicklaus, Palmer, and Casper. I'm ready to go with you."

Lee did not share Duffy's optimism. He phoned Claudia in El Paso and said, "Honey, I've just blown the Open, I shot a 281, and I'm going so good that I can't have anything left for the tournament." Baloney, said Claudia. She ordered him to shoot another 281. Lee went out swinging, sustaining himself each day on peaches and plums, eaten in his motel room. He finished with a 283 for fifth place and $6,000. Back at Horizon Hills, the members tossed down drinks on the house. Meanwhile, Lee handed Duffy $250 that he had hoarded for that purpose; he then ate another peach, endorsed his check, and mailed it to Claudia, who opened a bank account for herself. Later, he would pry $100 from Claudia and send it to Duffy as final payment.

From Baltusrol, Lee flew to the Cleveland Open, arriving with $15 in his pocket. "Can I pay you Thursday?" he asked the lady registrar collecting $50 entry fees.

"You just won six thousand dollars," she reminded him.

"I know," Lee said, "but my wife's got it all, and she's promised to send me a little."

In his heart, Lee yearned to be back at Horizon Hills, knowing the members stood waiting to throw a party in his honor. Distracted by his thoughts, he arrived at the thirty-sixth hole, where he three-putted from six feet away and missed the cutoff by a stroke. He flew home and got joyously drunk.

Except for the Cleveland Open and the American Golf Classic, Lee Trevino finished in the money in each of the thirteen PGA tournaments he played last year, closing the season with $28,700 in winnings. His face creased by a broad smile, enjoying every moment of tournament golf, he has brought to the tour a breezy presence that already has created a Trevino cult. The press tent clamors for his ingenuous interviews. Last August at the Westchester Classic, where he had a 67 rained out yet won $8,125 in seventh-place money, a band of Connecticut Italians more or less adopted him—and have continued to follow him around the country even after discovering he is not a *paisano.* Lee's Fleas, they call themselves.

"Nobody enjoys playing golf like I do," Trevino insists, and he's probably right. On his first day at the scene of the Masters this year, he put in thirty-six holes of practice, then played nine holes on a pitch-and-putt course. After a shower and an evening of cards with a few of his Fleas, he wound up at midnight on a par-three course, going nine holes in a sports jacket and alligator shoes.

The Masters galleries soon found themselves cocking their ears for the whimsical reflections that Lee uttered as he made his way around sedate Augusta National. In the opening round, for example, he stood in the frog hair and chipped far past the hole. "I didn't know no way to play it," he innocently announced. At eighteen, his tee shot seemed headed straight for a distant bunker. "Sit down! Sit down!" he cried to the ball. The drive sat down—a full twenty yards short of the bunker. "Who do I think I am, Jack Nicklaus?" Lee mused. Going into the final round, he lay only two strokes off the lead, but he became involved in a series of naval expeditions in the Augusta National waters. Finally he arrived on the eighteenth green, where he informed the surrounding throng, "I gotta two-putt this for an eighty." Having two-putted, Lee then piped, "It ain't the eighty I'm worried about. Why I'm worried is when I get home my wife is gonna kick me all over the golf course."

Curiously, Trevino has yet to win an official PGA tournament, possibly because of a paradox in his makeup. Though a compulsive gambler off the course, he decided from the beginning to play it scrupulously safe on the tour. Having been penniless the greatest part of his life, he regarded $2,000, say, as a bonanza and preferred to move cautiously, keeping his ball in play, rather than risk chancy shots that might bring him a $20,000 first prize. A spectator once called to him on the practice green, "Pretend you have to make this to tie." Lee turned to the man and bluntly replied, "I'd lay up and settle for second place."

But in May at the Houston Champions International, the voice that at card tables tells Lee to go for broke won out. One stroke off the lead going into the final round, he promised himself, "I'm going after the twenty grand." Shooting for the pins, disdaining the middle of the greens, he seized the lead, then fell into a tie with Roberto De Vicenzo. On the final green he succumbed to pressure. "I couldn't even see that cup," he admitted after blowing a four-foot putt that dropped him to second-place money of $12,000.

Today, there are those who, for a good reason, rate him a serious dark horse wherever major tournaments are played on tight courses. The reason certainly is not his swing, which can be found in none of the instructional books. "I got a wide-open stance," Lee says, "and hell, I got my feet pointed sixty yards to the left of the green. I aim to the left and throw the club out to the right. I try to push the ball to the green. It's the way I learned to play. I don't know any other way. Say, it's worked for a while, hasn't it?"

Somehow it has, and the drives that whistle off Lee's woods are the reason why he's a threat on narrow fairways. Though only of average distance, his tee shots behave beautifully, rarely carrying him into the rough. They travel at a height that almost would enable a fairly rangy first baseman to reach up and stab them. On Lee's El Paso training grounds, you see, there is no other way to play, for an ordinary day in April or May finds the wind blowing at thirty-five miles per hour, which means that the golfer who puts his ball high in the air is a loser. "I've played in sixty-mile winds," Lee says. And why not, when Horizon Hills members are standing by with wallets waiting to be tapped?

Horizon Hills, situated like a lost drifter in a country that is sand, rock, and mesquite, is not precisely the sort of club where one would expect to find a successful tournament pro. For the past four years it has been operated as a business enterprise by Jesse Whittenton, a rawboned former Green Bay Packer defensive back, and his cousin Donny Whittington, a handsome, debonair man who explains that he and Jesse have spelled their surnames differently ever since their fathers had an argument years ago. "Jesse's dad changed the spelling," Donny says. "Hey, Jesse, what was that argument about anyhow?" Jesse says damned if he knows. Anyhow, for a $250 initiation fee and $20 monthly dues, anybody can join Horizon Hills and take a crack at defeating its fairways, which slowly are yielding grass but in the meantime offer an experience somewhat akin to golfing on broken pavement. The greens, however, are excellent and management is pouring a million gallons of water a day into the fairways, conceding that before long Horizon Hills will be an emerald in the desert. . . .

Now it is a fine spring day, with gusts up to forty miles per hour, Lee Trevino is charging across the course in a cart that flies over humps and out of gullies at teeth-jarring speed. He is playing in a fivesome, which for Horizon Hills is rather a small group. Each man pilots his own death machine, followed by a gallery of ten who have made do with seven carts.

"In the winter, when the course isn't as crowded," says Donny Whittington, chopping along in his cart, "there'll be fifteen or eighteen of 'em playing in one group. Well, actually, they'll start out in two groups, but they'll join together at number ten in order to increase the action. Most I've ever seen go eighteen holes is a twelvesome."

Lee's fivesome, known around the club as F Troop, is a motley but receiving group. Martin Lettunich, for example, is a rough-hewn, unshaven man who wears a red leather hunting cap and a cheap blue golf shirt that billows over his beer belly, exposing his flesh at times. He farms cotton and is said to be worth millions. None of the others are hurting either. At any rate, a great deal of cussing fills the air, and everyone makes sure that Lee tees off forty to one hundred yards behind the others, depending on the hole. At No. 4, he stands knee deep in desert brush, teeing off from behind a hill that lies on the far side of a pond. Thus far in the round, he has been playing poorly because, he explains, "I had too much giggle juice before I went out."

The bets mount, in presses and double presses, and before long Lee is standing in the eighteenth fairway, 210 yards from the pin, facing head on into a gale. He needs a strong finish to make the day a substantial success. With a one-iron he drills the ball under the wind. It strikes thirty yards from the pin, skitters up to the green, and comes to rest five feet below the cup. "Goin' to Juarez tonight," Lee chirps. "Need some money for the dog track. Man, I hit that sunnabitch quail high." Stepping briskly up to his putt, he rifles it into the cup for an eagle three. He then throws a burlesque-queen bump at his victims and walks off $140 richer. . . .

Donny Whittington is sitting at the bar, explaining that he originally hired Lee at a salary of $30 a week, plus whatever he could earn from giving lessons. Last year Donny and Cousin Jesse became Lee's backers on the pro tour and wound up selling him a one-third interest in the club under an arrangement that pays him a salary of $1,000 a month and temporarily provides him with a furnished apartment on the grounds. Also they set up a fund that now enables Lee, while on tour, to write checks. "I always write checks for two hundred dollars," Lee says, "because it's a nice round figure." Where, asks Donny, could they find another pro capable of blending so well with Horizon's peculiar membership?

"Hey Lee!" a distinguished, gray-haired gentleman calls from a table. "You goin' down to Houston next week, ain't you? My wife says she's goin' down to Houston."

Professional protocol toward members being somewhat informal at Horizon Hills, Lee responds, "Maybe she got somethin' goin' for her."

Lee arrived at Horizon Hills dead broke, having traveled a trail that was hardly calculated to lead him to alpaca sweaters and sirloin steak. Along with two sisters, he was raised by his mother and grandfather, the latter a gravedigger, in a four-room frame house that had neither electricity nor inside plumbing. It stood in a hayfield by the Glen Lakes Country Club, outside of Dallas. Lee's first exposure to golf came when, at the age of six, he found a left-handed iron that had been thrown into a hayfield. Being right-handed, he simply turned the club around, hitting with the tip of the blade in the fashion of the great trick-shot artist, Paul Hahn. A bit later Lee stumbled upon a right-handed iron in the hayfield. "In those days," he says, "if you could afford to play golf, you could afford to throw away clubs. I made me a two-hole course in the pasture, and when they cut the hay in summer I had me the plushest course you ever seen."

Though he caddied at Glen Lakes and sneaked in a few holes at dusk, Lee took no serious interest in the game, being compelled to quit school after the seventh grade and go to work. But when he was nineteen and already serving the second of two hitches in the Marines, he glanced at a bulletin-board notice announcing tryouts for the Third Marine Division golf team. "Shucks, I know a little about the game," he told himself. His executive officer, weighing Lee's request for permission to try out, challenged him to a round in order to evaluate his game. "I waxed him," says Lee.

In time he waxed the entire division team, and two years later emerged from the Marines a skillful, if not especially stylish, golfer. In Dallas, Lee went to work as a pro at a par-three course. Presently he married Claudia, and to make ends meet he began enticing lesser golfers into irresistible matches. He could agree to use left-handed clubs, or, if given half a stoke a hole, he would play the entire par-three course equipped only with an empty Dr. Pepper bottle—the one-quart family size. "I can hit a ball a hundred yards with a Dr. Pepper bottle," Lee says. "I can control it fairly well, too. In fact, I never lost a bet using that bottle. I once won ninety dollars playing two holes. A fella said, 'I'll play you a hole for forty-five dollars,' and then he insisted on one more hole. I think Claudia and me blew the whole ninety dollars that night."

The pro tour, in the meantime, seemed but a faraway dream. Young golfers cannot obtain a place on the tour simply by showing up with a bagful of clubs. Lee learned to his dismay that in order to make the big time he first would have to attend the tournament players' school at Palm Beach Gardens, Florida, and show a minimum of $6,500 available to pay his way on the tour. He lacked the wherewithal to do either. But PGA rules offered him another, though slower, way. By putting in four years as a course pro and matriculating at the PGA's business school in Dallas, Lee could qualify for the precious Class A card that automatically admits a player to the tour. At last he fulfilled both of those requirements and asked his employer to sign a form verifying his four years of service on the par-three course.

"I'm not going to sign it," the man replied. "I don't think you're ready for that Class A card." Lee supposed his boss simply did not want to lose his services, but he lost them anyhow. Enraged, Lee quit.

Tycoons and wealthy playboys across America were lining up to back hotshot college golfers, and now a Dallas man named Bill Gray came forward willing to sponsor Lee in scattered tournaments that did not require a Class A card. The only trouble was that Lee's sponsor needed a sponsor. Bill Gray held a modest government job that barely enabled him to foot Lee's expenses to the 1965 Texas State Open at Houston and the Mexico Open. Happily, Lee won the State Open and $1,000, and in Mexico City won second-place money, $2,280. "So we were in business," Lee says.

By now Bill Gray had become so enchanted with tournament golf that he quit his job. This turn of events dictated that certain expenditures—airplane tickets, for example—be eliminated, so to reach the

Panama Open, the dauntless sponsor drove seven-and-a-half days through Central America, sleeping in Gray's car and, at one stop in El Salvador, in a fifty-cent hotel room that they shared with a large bat. The southern portion of Costa Rica, the last leg on their journey, proved arduous.

"The reason was," Lee says, "there was no road. We drove on a riverbed. It was all boulders. The fastest we could go was fifteen miles an hour. Then we went up through mountains on a horse trail, and finally, in the middle of the night, we find a little road. But now we see there's a truck parked sideways across the road, and there's four guys waiting for us. One of them is wearing a big straw hat and no shirt, and he's got a carbine. Bill Gray says, 'It's all over. They're fixin' to kill us.' Well, the guy with the carbine says to us in Spanish, 'Hey, you got a cigarette?" And in Spanish, I tell him, 'Here. Take the whole pack.' So they moved the truck. Till we got to Panama, I like to suffocated. We had the doors locked and the windows rolled up tight all the way." In Panama City, Lee won fifth-place money, $716.67, and Gray sold his car, making it possible for them to fly back to Dallas and unemployment.

Enter Martin Lettunich, the millionaire cotton farmer. Lettunich had observed Lee's performance in the State Open, and now he was phoning from El Paso with a proposition. He wanted to put Lee against a hot local golfer in El Paso. "Fly over here," Lettunich said to Lee, "and I'll pay your expenses and three hundred dollars, win or lose."

"I shot a sixty-five and a sixty-seven," Lee says of the match, "and beat the guy like a tom-tom. I turned him every way but loose."

What's more, Lee persuaded Donny Whittington to make him the Horizon Hills pro. He worked furiously to improve his game. "I saw him break five clubs over his knee, one after the other, on the *practice* tee," says Claudia. Last year, still wondering how to get a Class A card, Lee had a brainstorm. "What would happen," he asked himself, "if a pro worked for a guy for four years and the guy dropped dead before signing the verification? Would the pro lose credit for those four years?" He put the analogy to Texas PGA officials. It was common knowledge that he had worked four years in Dallas and, that being the case, was it really necessary that his former boss verify it? Sympathetic, the PGA handed him a card. The next thing he knew, Claudia was hurling him into the U.S. Open. "I went up there and beat the big shots, and that's how it all started," says Lee.

On the fringe of Horizon Hills, a residential development known as Horizon City is springing up. The builders have just about completed a five-bedroom adobe villa with a walled courtyard and a private putting green. Lee and Claudia, their three-year-old daughter Lesley, a dachshund named Bogey, and a Doberman named Judy will move in any day now. Lee surely is getting to be a man of stature. In nightclubs, headline performers join his table, as did singer Robert Cameron at the posh Camino Real in Juarez not long ago. Over coffee in the Horizon Hills breakfast room the next morning, Claudia said to Lee, "Did you see how those two beautiful girls moved right in at the table when Robert Cameron sat down?"

"Whaddaya mean, Cameron!" Lee protested. "I was the star, the celebrity. Cameron ain't nothin'."

"Aw," said Claudia, "you make me sick."

For Merry Mex, the Laughter Only Hides the Tears

Skip Bayless

Dallas Morning News, *June 13, 1980*

SPRINGFIELD, New Jersey—Nicklaus and Weiskopf belong here. The Mexican knows he never did and never will.

Nicklaus and Weiskopf were born in Ohio WASP nests all too similar to Baltusrol Golf Club. They feel at home in the men-only mansion of a clubhouse, black attendants asking, "Shine, Mr. Nicklaus? Shine, Mr. Weiskopf?" They had the best teachers money can't buy. They learned at clubs blue blood, not bucks, gets you in. They were bred to tie the U.S. Open record of 63, as they did on glorious Thursday.

The Mexican was born to pick up empty baskets at Hardy's driving range on Lovers Lane in Dallas, Texas. He does not belong in this moneyed suburb, Manhattan's World Trade Center looming twenty miles in the distance. Neither do Calvin Peete, a black, or Isao Aoki, a Japanese. Peete, born of Florida migrant workers, shot 67 Thursday. Aoki had 68. Neither was asked into the press-tent interview room.

But the Mexican was. The Mexican, the one with "Ann" tattooed on his forearm, laughed all the way to a 68. He stole the show on the course and in the interview room.

He didn't laugh with them, but at them.

At age forty, Lee Trevino is rubbing their upturned noses in hallowed tradition. His swing is too flat, his stance and mouth too open. Doesn't he call this place Baltustrol, with an extra "t"?

But you watch. Come Sunday, when the wind swirls and the fairways are baked and nerves melt, Trevino still will be making jokes and birdies. Watch: Tom Weiskopf will lose concentration and strokes. Jack Nicklaus will lose putting stroke and ground. This Open no longer will look like the Joe Garagiola–Tucson, birdies flying.

And the Mexican will be right there to sweep up. *Sí, señor.*

"I take nothin' from nobody," Trevino said recently. "Nicklaus—Jack Grout taught him how to play. [Tom] Watson—Stan Thirsk taught him how to play. *I* taught me how to play. I come from a long line of striped [range] balls.

"When you do it by yourself, you owe nobody nothin'. It's a sweet feeling."

There are two Trevinos, the Merry and the not-so-Merry. There is the gifted showman and the shotmaker—the Refried Piper more gifted than we *gringos* may realize. And there is the "wetback"—the surly loner who trusts no one but himself.

Beneath the twenty-four-hour fiesta lives a bitter man. But, then, doesn't he have a right to be?

It's amazing what a lovable public image Trevino has talked his way into. It's even more amazing how he can click his *Sunday Afternoon Live* personality on and off. Jose Jimenez one second, Pancho Villa the next. The Mexican knows when he has to perform and when he doesn't. When he has to wear the hat with the sombrero logo and when he doesn't. When he has to play Merry Mexican, make America chuckle, and when he doesn't.

Word is, Trevino and Watson now command the highest Monday appearance fee, an average of $20,000. Word is, Trevino demanded—and got—$50,000 for a recent exhibition. The Mexican hasn't won some $2 million on the course—and made some $2 million off it—by saying, *"No hablo inglés."*

He began Thursday's mass interview by telling another one of his made-for-newspaper tales. He said some new putting aid—he carefully mentioned the company name—had shown him he was striking the ball with a hooded blade. His habitual forward press, he said, had putter catching ball off-solid, high on the face. So late Wednesday night, he slipped into the garage of the home where he's staying—"that's Dr. Craig Wilson's"—found a hammer and pounded some loft into his putter. The Mexican can read. He could see the headlines: *Merry Mex "Hammers" Out 68.*

Like any good comedian, he left 'em laughing. He was talking about how good his back is feeling. He injured it moving a planter in '75 and had it operated on in '76. "Now I don't lift nothin'. Nothin' but a twelve-ounce Coors. And if they give me a case, I sit on the curb and drink it all."

What beverage is he now advertising? Coors, of course.

Then the not-so-Merry Mex strode out of the tent toward the clubhouse. At the door, a woman tried to stop him. "Lee," she said, "I'm from *Home* magazine and I wonder if I could do an interview with you."

"Nobody writes anything about *my* home," Trevino snapped over his shoulder at the cowering correspondent. "My home is private."

She hadn't learned the rules. Trevino talks to audiences, not individuals. Unless, of course, the individual writes for the audience Trevino wants to reach.

Recently, at the Kemper Open in Washington, *Star* columnist Tom Callahan decided to stake out Trevino's locker and, one-on-one, try to talk to the Merry Mex about his not-so-Merry side.

"He almost blanched when he saw me waiting for him," Callahan says. "He's got to have a crowd."

Callahan tried to warm him up by saying, "What do you think of this weather?"

"I ain't no weatherman," Trevino replied, lacing his shoes.

Callahan asked about his "serious" side. Trevino was quiet for the longest moment, then shot back: "Look, nobody knows me. I don't *want* anybody to know me. I have no friends . . ."

"Well," he added, "I have one or two. That's all a man needs."

Callahan asked about his fairway act. (Example: When Trevino punched a hundred-yard wedge shot to within eighteen feet on No. 17 Thursday, the applause was faint. "Maybe they don't give a damn about it, but I did," Trevino cracked in his stage voice. Hundreds laughed. When you think about it, maybe Trevino wasn't trying to be funny.)

Trevino answered Callahan, "I can't concentrate five hours out there. Can you concentrate five hours straight at the typewriter? All I need is five seconds. I take my stance, tap my foot, and for the next five seconds, I'm deadly serious.

"Hey, we're delivered to you (bleeps [the press]). We give you birdies and bogeys and one-liners. I say, Columbus went around the world in 1492, which ain't a lot of strokes, considering the course,' and you guys write about Columbus."

Much has been written about how Trevino's name first went up in leader-board lights when the Open last was played here in '67. Thursday afternoon, with just a couple of writers listening, Trevino said,

"Everybody makes a big deal how that was my first Open, but it wasn't. I played at Olympic Fields back in '66."

It made legendary copy. But do you think Trevino likes to talk about his back-of-the-bus days? About those '67 nights he stayed at some fleabag motel and walked across a killer highway to some Chinese restaurant? In laughing at himself, he laughs at us.

The Mex's court-jester act has made him many pesos. But has it cost him some respect? How many think of him as a surgeon of a shotmaker? How many know he carries specific clubs for specific courses? This week, he feels he can't reach the par-fives. So instead of two- and three-woods, he carries a more lofted and accurate six-wood and a one-iron.

How many know Trevino, not Nicklaus, has the best per-round stroke average over the last decade? Who thinks of him as the Nicklaus slayer? In the early '70s, the Mexican was the only one who wasn't afraid of the big bad Bear. If it hadn't been for Trevino winning the '72 British Open, it's likely Nicklaus would have hit a Grand Slam.

Lately how often has it been written Nicklaus might be "over the hill"? But who remembers Trevino is six weeks older? Who knows Trevino works as hard as any pro in this, or any, country?

Mostly, we know only Merry Mex, who jokes away the pressure and occasionally shoots pretty good with that funny swing. That, it seems, is the way the Mexican wants it. Merry Mex sells more enchiladas and soft drinks and beer.

The next three days, it will be different. Thursday, the wet fairways slowed the hooks and slices. Perfectly manicured, they afforded nothing but perfect lies. The wind seldom bothered the mandatory long-iron shots.

"Baltustrol has its guard down," Trevino said. Then predicted: "But she'll knock most of us out in the end."

Most, probably, except the Mexican. He has survived darker alleys. Maybe he'll win again, as he did at Oak Hill in '68. Afterward, he was asked about all the free shoes he'd get from different companies.

"Where were the free-shoe men when I needed them?" Trevino said, not to merrily.

Moody's March at the Top Was Brief

David Casstevens

Dallas Morning News, *May 11, 1984*

Nobody wins the U.S. Open. It wins you. —Cary Middlecoff

In 1969, the U.S. Open tapped Orville Moody on the shoulder and whispered, "Hey, Sarge. Yeah, you. Listen up. I'm about to make you rich and famous."

Like Claude Rains in *Angel on My Shoulder,* Moody didn't recognize the voice in his ear. Why should he?

Sure, he was playing well, very well, in fact, for a thirty-five-year-old ex-Army sergeant with a PX beer belly and a cross-handed putting grip. But this was the U.S. Open, not the All-Army Championships. In 1968, his first year on the tour, Moody had finished 103rd on the money list.

Except for friend Lee Trevino, everybody figured that down the stretch, Ol' Sarge's nerves, along with his game, would go AWOL.

But in the final round, while the favorites wilted around him—Miller Barber, the third-round leader, blew to a 78—Moody refused to unravel under the pressure. He kept driving the ball long and straight and knocking in putts with that goofy-looking grip and steadying himself by reciting a verse from the Bible: "I can do all things."

The U.S. Open won Orville Moody. As a result, he became the most famous sergeant since Alvin York.

President Nixon called and offered his congratulations. Promoter Bucky Woy, who reportedly made $1 million for Trevino, the 1968 Open champ, proclaimed, "With his Army background, Moody's signature golf clubs ought to make a fortune in PX's alone."

Killeen, home of Fort Hood, gave Sarge a hero's welcome. When the mayor presented him with a key to the city, Moody smiled and said, "I hope this unlocks the door to the bank."

"Over the years, if you count everything, I guess the Open was worth a million dollars to me," Moody says now, fifteen years later.

After the Open, the money dried up, along with his instant fame. Half his earnings, he says, went to his sponsors; the other half to his Uncle Sam.

He invested in a golf course in Denver and lost his shirt. He tried the restaurant business. That deal soured, too. The way Moody's luck ran, had he bought a pumpkin farm, they probably would have canceled Halloween. "I listened to too many people. I trusted the wrong fellows."

Stock in Moody fell, too. He went from nobody to somebody and back to nobody almost overnight. Sarge became the answer to a trivia question: Name the guy whose only PGA victory was the 1969 Open.

He won the 1971 Hong Kong Open and the Morocco Grand Prix. Then he didn't win again until 1977, and again it wasn't the Crosby or the Doral, but something called the International Caribbean Open. Between 1974 and 1976, Sarge's earnings on the PGA money list dropped from 130th to 185th to 190th.

Putting is an art that comes and goes. During the Masters, someone asked Larry Nelson why he carries an extra putter in his bag. Nelson explained it "was to let the other one know it could be replaced."

Moody blames his touch around the green, or lack of it, for his drought on the PGA Tour. Listening to him, one gets the idea that during the late '70s, Sarge could have putted about as well with an M1 rifle.

His story gets worse. In April 1977, Moody and his family were asleep at their home in Lago Vista, Texas. Sarge awakened at four A.M. to find his house in flames. Luckily, Moody, wife Beverly, and their two small children escaped through a window.

Many of his golf trophies and plaques he had received during his fourteen years in the Army were lost in the fire. His U.S. Open trophy was damaged.

But there is a happy ending here. Perhaps a happy ending is more appropriate.

Moody, now fifty, joined the PGA Senior Tour this year. He's already won three tournaments and $70,200. Before he teed off Thursday at the Byron Nelson Classic, Sarge was all smiles. As the runaway winner in last week's Senior Tournament of Champions, he received $30,000. That's the same amount he got for winning the U.S. Open.

"Where's your Open trophy?" someone asked.

"In the attic," Moody replied.

Sarge spoke like a man who, for the first time in a long time, is happier talking about the future than he is reliving the past.

America's Most Wanted Match Player: Lanny

Tim Rosaforte

Golf Illustrated, *September 1991*

The six-footer was for birdie. PGA Tour qualifying. The Regionals. Tanglewood Park, Winston-Salem, North Carolina. The cocky little guy from Wake Forest University stalked the putt and stroked it. And missed. It was inexcusable.

It happened at the seventeenth hole, the thirty-fifth of thirty-six. Lanny Wadkins needed a birdie–birdie finish to shoot 62 and break 130. He was already a lock to advance, so he'd made that his goal. It wasn't him against the field anymore, it was him against a number. When he missed that putt—well, he just wasn't going to stand for it. So he backhanded the second putt. Not into the hole, but back to the vicinity of the six-footer for birdie. This time he made it. He walked off the green with a bogey.

There is no in-between with Lanny Wadkins. There never has been. The backhand stab after a missed putt is an expression of his personality. It's either/or. Yes or no. He should have made the damn putt in the first place. Yeah, he may miss the backhander and throw away some money, maybe even a tournament. But so what? That's the way you have to think in this game. *So what?* I don't care what anybody thinks. I'm Lanny Wadkins, and I'm better than you, and I'm going to beat you anyway, so what's the difference? Now get out of the way, because I'm playing through.

Early in his career, he was paired in the Crosby with Jim Simons, a former teammate at Wake Forest. Playing the back nine first, Wadkins rifled a three-iron over the green and into the rough. The green was running away from him, and Wadkins hit a good chip that somehow stopped short. He missed the putt and went into a rage. As the ball was going by the hole, he reached out as if to rake it back in. His amateur partner yelled. Wadkins waited until the ball stopped. He walked off the green with a quadruple-bogey seven. "Five putts," Simons says. "One normal and four backhand."

But that wasn't enough self-punishment. At the eighteenth, he aimed out over the ocean and deliberately drove into the surf. He then made birdie with his second ball for a net bogey, and went on to birdie five of the first seven holes on the front.

"The thing that gets him out of control is the thing that got him where he is," says Jesse Haddock, his coach at Wake Forest.

Wadkins always seems to be burning about something. His character is essentially no different today at forty-one from what it was at twenty-one or when he was throwing high heat as a Little League pitcher. He is to golf what Nolan Ryan is to baseball. He can still bring it with a vengeance.

"Lanny's going to challenge you with nothing but fastballs," says Paul Azinger. "Lanny's saying, 'I'm shooting at the flag. If it goes in the bunker, that's just the way it is."

The arrogance Wadkins wears when patrolling the golf course comes from years of seeking perfection. When he's rolling his shoulders and wagging his head and strutting after a shot, you know he's on his game. This is a guy who tries so hard that he gets headaches. You see more of the scowl than you do of the smile. He's always been trying to prove himself to himself.

Wadkins didn't have much while growing up. His father drove a truck for a warehouse. His mother was a grammar-school principal. They didn't give him a dime to mark his ball. The money he made on the golf course was spending money. One year at Wake Forest, he never lost a match to Jim Simons. If Simons shot 66, Lanny shot 65. If Simons shot 65, Lanny shot 64. Wadkins birdied the last three holes to beat him. He was just hungrier.

"If I made six bucks off Simons, I could eat at McDonald's for lunch and the chicken place for dinner," Wadkins says. "That was my existence."

Now he treats himself to nothing but the best, whether it be meals, accommodations, or transportation. And what he doesn't spend on himself he gives back to several charities, including a shelter ministry in Dallas, the Alzheimer's Foundation, and a $125,000 scholarship fund he set up at Wake Forest. Unfortunately, most people don't hear about those things, because quiet philanthropy is a gentle side that might ruin the gunslinger image.

Friends say you don't really know him unless you know him. "He's not totally understood," Haddock says. Wadkins casts a don't-approach-me image, but break through that and he isn't intimidating at all. That may explain why he is the way he is. He can keep distractions at arm's length and opponents wary. Anything to stay one up.

One on one, he's the man feared most on the PGA Tour. He and Curtis Strange (when Curtis had it going good) are the Green Berets. If they could snap the shaft in two, stick the jagged end into an opponent, and twist it to make sure he was dead, they would.

That's why Wadkins is especially nasty in match play. They say the Europeans have an advantage in match-play situations because they play more of it than American players. But that's not true in Wadkins's case. Match play is all he played growing up at Meadowbrook Country Club in Richmond, Virginia. Thirty-six in the morning. Swim for an hour after lunch. Maybe thirty-six more after that. His fast play is an old habit. The more holes he could get in, the more bets he could win. It's no different now against the bandits at Preston Trail in Dallas, his home course, where he needs to shoot 65 to win any money. That's why he's so good in the Ryder Cup.

The Ryder Cup match that pleases him most is one that he eventually lost. He and Larry Nelson were four down with five to play against Sandy Lyle and Bernhard Langer at Muirfield Village in 1987. They birdied fourteen, fifteen, sixteen, and seventeen, and then Lanny hit a seven-iron stiff at eighteen. It looked like the greatest comeback in Ryder Cup history until Langer stiffed it. They had to give him the putt. Even Langer would have made it.

But what Wadkins will probably be best remembered for is the shot he hit at PGA National in 1983 to nail down the most recent United States victory. From ninety-three yards, Wadkins hit a sand wedge to eighteen inches to win the hole and secure a half against José Maria Canizares of Spain. Jack Nicklaus, the relieved U.S. captain, cried and kissed the divot.

His last singles match may have been his best. Paired with Nick Faldo at The Belfry in 1989, Wadkins was two up standing on the tenth tee. His caddie wanted him to lay up and let Faldo make the mistake. Wadkins reached for the three-wood. "Let's try to bury him," he said, and stuck it six feet from the hole. He went on to win the match and improve his Ryder Cup record to 15–9–1.

"Maybe it's a touch of little man's syndrome," says Johnny Miller. "He floors it around every turn. If he can make it, he'll beat you. Sometimes he spins out."

In major championships, a pedal-to-the-metal approach is not always the best strategy. Majors are tests of patience, something that Wadkins is short of. In part, that explains why his only victory in a Grand Slam event came in the 1977 PGA at Pebble Beach, where he won in sudden death against Gene Littler.

He lost a playoff in the 1987 PGA to Larry Nelson, and had the lead with nine holes to go in the 1984 PGA at Shoal Creek, until Lee

Trevino out-putted him down the stretch. In the 1986 U.S. Open at Shinnecock, his final-round 65 put him two strokes back of Raymond Floyd, but he was never a factor. This year's Masters was the most recent close call.

"I've got too many seconds," he says. "When you've got a chance, you've got to put it over the top, and I haven't."

Sober self-analysis for the second-most prolific winner of his era. Other than Tom Watson, nobody of Wadkins's vintage has more career victories. Wadkins won his twentieth in this year's Hawaiian Open by shooting 65 in the final round to come from six strokes back. He said he didn't miss a shot.

Over the past two years, Wadkins has been playing some of the best and most consistent golf of his career. The curves on the mood chart aren't as abrupt anymore. There has been less streakiness and more intuition. Turning forty may have tempered him—a little.

"He has natural talent," says Johnny Miller. "He's a lot like Sam Snead, Byron Nelson, and Jimmy Demaret. I think he's finally learned to play aggressive-smart."

When Wadkins was an amateur, he and Miller played a practice round before the 1971 Heritage Classic. Miller remembers looking at Wadkins's swing and wondering how he made contact. His action is a contradiction of physics and tempo. You'll never see it on an instructional video. But when he's on, there is no purer striker of a golf ball, no better shotmaker in the world. And with the exception of some recent fine-tuning by Dick Harmon, it's all self-taught. He's always had the ability to head for a practice tee and work out his swing problems on his own.

At Doral in 1987, he had an opening-round 75 that included three missed backhanders. The next two days he went 66–66, came out on the windy Sunday, hit it "quail high," and won by two shots. At Riviera in 1985, when the conditions were ideal, he averaged 66 strokes a round and transformed Hogan's Alley into Lanny's Lane.

He can be savage, always trying to extend his lead. "If I'm four ahead, I want to be five ahead," he says. "The last thing I want to do is give one back."

Wadkins is no less brutal playing for a ten-dollar Nassau at Preston Trail. Wadkins plays off a plus-seven, but gives no more than three strokes over his opponents' handicaps. "He's hard to outmaneuver on the first tee," says Bill Hooton, one of his playing companions. "It seems like he's always the one getting paid at the end of the day."

It was always that way for Wadkins. No reason to think it would be any different now that he's got money to pay off his bets. And, by the way, Wadkins has never missed a backhand putt at Preston Trail.

"We give him those," says Hooton.

What You See Is What You Get

Melanie Hauser

On Tour, September 1994

As he put the finishing touches on the easiest little 67 you'll ever see at Doral's Blue Monster, Fred Couples allowed himself the slightest grin.

The feel was back.

No more bending his swing just slightly to carve a path for the ball to bore through the blustery winds. No more bracing himself over every shot so he could have a chance to hit the green or the back of the cup.

The breeze was rustling softly through the tops of those stately palm trees instead of whipping them into a hurricane frenzy the way it had a few days earlier. Bright sunshine and cool temperatures had replaced driving rain.

Couples had launched his rainbows at the flags all day, then watched as they landed with a soft thud. The course was just where he wanted it. So was his swing. So was his confidence.

Forget that he had just missed a ten-footer for what would have been his third birdie in a row. Couples had.

It didn't matter.

There was no need to head to the range to beat balls. There was even less need to fiddle with his putting. He had slipped back into his comfort zone.

Back in his room, Couples kicked off his shoes, pulled out his shirttail and flopped on the bed with a soft pillow and the television remote.

He channel-surfed his way to the golf so he could watch what was happening a hundred yards—and a huge crowd—away at the eighteenth green of the Doral Ryder Open. His fiancée Tawnya Dodd was beside him; caddie Joe LaCava and close friend and swing guru Paul Marchand were crashed on the sofa.

Couples delivered several punches to the pillow, then folded, tucked, and twisted it just so before letting his head fall against it. Too soft. He tucked it again and this time his dark hair sank to the perfect depth.

You wonder which came easier for Couples—his to-die-for swing or the art of getting comfortable. Both fit him like a well-worn pair of jeans and are Gap basic when it comes to understanding him.

What you see is what you get with Couples—a booming, silky-smooth arc suited for winning major titles, a quiet confidence, and an unassuming, unflappable thirty-four-year-old who is amused by all the ruckus he seems to cause.

He'll tell you straight out he's no big deal, just another guy who loves sports and happens to play golf the way Bobby Jones, Ben Hogan, and the boys used to. There's no hidden agenda, no secret to his success.

So don't try to figure him out. The more complicated you try to make him, the colder you'll get.

"What really makes me tick is playing good golf," he said, rolling to one side as he added a little commentary on the player putting out on the screen. "Not a whole lot else. It doesn't matter what people write or say."

And they've said a lot.

He's lazy. He doesn't care. He needs a kick in his shorts. He doesn't have the fire to win. He's a flake, a genuine, certified, channel-surfing couch potato.

Couples grins. Sure, he likes to get away. Who doesn't? But as for the rest?

Well, this is a man, after all, who once said he doesn't answer the phone when he's home because someone might be on the other end. Then again, he also said he didn't read much either because he couldn't.

Can't we take a joke without looking for a hidden meaning?

"People seem to dig for some sophisticated agenda with Fred, as if it's tough to figure him out," Marchand said. "It's not. He loves to play golf. He loves to play golf well, he likes to be liked, and he wants to fit in well.

"He's not trying to be anything he isn't. He's always been that way."

Always will.

Couples doesn't care about swing mechanics or making official commitments to tournaments or having a garage full of Ferraris and a helicopter at his disposal. Give him a nice house, a golf course to play, a place to get away with his friends, the hot sports topic of the week to chew on, and he's as content as a puppy lying at your feet.

"I'm very boring," he said matter-of-factly. "I think the people around me make my life more exciting. I like to be around people, but I like to choose the people. I like to feel comfortable."

Couples isn't unlike the pillow sandwiched between his head and the bed. No matter how many times you plump and punch and twist it, it always seeks its own level. It will never be as rock-hard as a two-by-four, nor will it be as flat.

"Fred," said Gary McCord, "is like a Lava lamp on a hot day. Give him a space and he'll bend and twist until he finds his comfort zone. Not yours."

"Fred will do it his own way and get there in his own time," Marchand said. "Fred will never be Jack Nicklaus or Greg Norman or Fuzzy Zoeller. He'll never make brash predictions or sulk over tournaments he tossed away. Look long and hard. You'll never see even a glimmer of your basic superstar ego."

Imagine Norman or Nicklaus or Magic or Michael or Emmitt Smith taking a twenty-four-hour road trip to the Final Four to hang out with the boys, talk hoops, and run Cokes to Jim Nantz. They'd be in a luxury suite with a security entourage, not on the floor cheering like your basic hoop junkie.

"He does everything but go to the bathroom for us," Nantz said. "A lot of guys would skip it, but Fred is serious about doing what he's down there for. There's a break, and here he comes balancing two Cokes and two popcorns."

Couples's now-annual detours to the Final Four on his way to the Masters in Augusta, Georgia, have become legendary. In 1992, for example, he seemed to get more tube time than Nike.

The hottest player in golf running popcorn and hanging in the CBS-TV hospitality room? Oh, please. Golf gods play their way to the Masters in New Orleans or, at the very least, spend the weekend fine-tuning on the range of their choice.

"If I had a nickel for every time someone wore me out about that in the last two days," Couples said on the plane from Houston to Augusta, "I'd be a millionaire."

Nantz, Couples's suitemate and teammate at the University of Houston and confidant since, understood the headlines and thirty-second clips. He also understands Fred.

"He can't believe people make such a fuss over him," Nantz said. "He sits and laughs at how everyone analyzes what he does. He doesn't think he's that big a deal."

He certainly didn't in 1992 when he drove down Magnolia Lane with every finger pointing directly at him. He didn't stride into the clubhouse. He ambled.

He hadn't been contemplating Amen Corner or a green jacket on that flight to Augusta. His focus had been on a trip to the grocery store when he landed. After all, he said in a voice that would make advertising executives stand in line, what's the NCAA Final without chips and salsa?

That week, Couples wore pressure as easily as one of his over-sized sweatshirts. He played it cool. He was, as always, unflappable. His game was flawless.

The pieces were finally fitting together and nothing could stop him. Not even the demonic par-three twelfth hole. When he flirted with the banks of Rae's Creek, his ball turned into Velcro. When the other contenders were wilting, he was heavy-on-the-starch crisp. Did someone mention stress? Just try to find a pulse.

The irony of it all was that in the midst of his coming of age, Couples's personal life was coming unraveled faster than a tightly wound balata golf ball.

Outside the ropes, his soon-to-be former wife, Deborah, was catching eyes in an azalea-pink blazer. She oohed and aahed and courted the media. She told them what Fred had for breakfast. But when someone mentioned how great it must be to see Fred relax, kick back, and watch videos with his close buddies each night, the smile faded.

"Don't even get me started," she snapped.

Three months later, the two split for good at the British Open. Fred simply moved on.

To this day, Couples doesn't publicly criticize Deborah. Nor does he talk much about their eleven-year marriage. There isn't really much point. It's done. He skated those divorce bumps, bruises, and newsmagazine specials as best he could in 1993. He wants to concentrate on 1994.

"For me, '93 was not a low year at all," Couples said. "I knew I was going forward. It was not a problem. The only problem was getting it over. For me, it was distracting. But it wasn't like I turned into a mental midget."

Instead, he packed up, moved to a new home just north of Dallas, and settled into a new life that centers around Dodd and her twelve-year-old son and Couples's new sidekick, Derek. If that's not enough, he's a mere fifty-minute plane ride away from Marchand's watchful eye and, as always, a phone call from Nantz's well-worn ear.

Those couch-potato afternoons have been replaced by letting the kid in him come out with Derek. They play everything from video games to archery. And, if Couples has his way, there will be a few more children in his future.

Kids, after all, are his idols.

Give him a few weeks off and Couples is content to sit home. He doesn't need a whirlwind vacation to an exotic destination or a week deep-sea fishing. The highlight of his day may be taking the car down to the service station to have the oil changed. Or driving one of his three classic Mustangs.

He loves it when he gets the chance to hang out with the likes of George Brett and Michael Jordan because he can't wait to hear their stories. But he's not about to pick up the phone just to set up eighteen holes or dinner.

"I can't imagine calling up Michael Jordan to shoot the breeze," he said. "Or, when I'm in town, calling him for dinner. That's just not me."

In the past few months, Couples has had far too much time on his hands. He injured his lower back while warming up for the final round of the Doral Ryder Open and was forced to withdraw. The original diagnosis was that he tore the outer layer (annulus) of a disk and he returned to Dallas to rehabilitate it. Later, doctors found more extensive problems, and he was forced to the sidelines.

When everyone first tried to wedge him into the superstar mold, Couples rebelled. But as the years have gone by, he's grown more comfortable with his status as one of the game's best players and accepted his role, as always, on his own terms.

Couples is as unassuming as he was the day he showed up at the University of Houston to play for Dave Williams. He didn't have a driver's license back then, let alone a girlfriend. He didn't want to stand out. He wanted to fit in. But he kept standing out.

Like the day Williams got his freshmen and junior-college transfers together. "We kept looking back, and this guy kept knocking down the flagstick," Nantz said. "We knew this guy could really play."

Couples shot 70. Nantz shot 81.

There was no mistaking the raw talent and power in Couples's swing. There was no way to ignore his casual approach to the game. And life. While others were grinding their way through college and PGA Tour qualifying, Couples was on cruise control. As long as he played his best, whatever he shot was good enough. So was second or third.

We viewed it as not caring. His friends saw it as Fred.

"He doesn't seem to care and doesn't act like he wants to win, but he does," Marchand said. "Just because a guy doesn't tell you he's going to beat everyone doesn't mean he doesn't care. Fred's just not all caught up in how great he is. One of his strengths is he's not going to tell you how great he is."

On or off the course.

A year ago, Nantz was honored by his alma mater at a black-tie function in Houston. Couples flew in for the bash and they—plus Marchand—warmed up with eighteen holes at Houston Country Club.

"We were on the eighth tee, and I said, 'Fred, you do realize this is black tie. You gotta wear a tux,'" Nantz said. "He said, 'I know, I know. I've got it under control.'"

Nantz still had his doubts until Couples walked through the door looking Oscar-night fabulous. But as with everything Couples does, the best part was the story behind the fashion statement.

It seems Couples went to rent the tuxedo and, after taking his measurements, the saleswoman handed him a suit. It fit perfectly, but he noticed it was a bit too well-worn. Threads were hanging off the sleeve.

"It's thirty-six dollars if you have it back by tomorrow," she said.

"That's nice," Couples replied, but did she have something a little bit nicer?

"We have more expensive tuxes," she said, "but you just struck me as a guy who's on a budget."

"That's Fred," Nantz said. "There's no air of bigness about him. He's a normal guy."

Couples feels the same way about Nantz.

"When you get around Jimmy, he's always working," Couples said. "He's so good at what he does. You can't affect him. "He'll be goofing around thirty seconds before he goes on the air and he'll say, 'Excuse me,' then go do the opening lead."

Couples, Nantz, and Marchand have remained close since those long nights in Taub Hall when they'd sit around dreaming of the future. Couples wanted to win the Masters. Nantz wanted to be seated in Butler Cabin beside him.

On a spring day in 1992, those dreams came true. When the credits started to roll that afternoon, Couples and Nantz stood up from their chairs, took one look at each other, and started to cry. Couples threw his arms around Nantz and bawled.

It was a side Couples only lets close friends and family see, a side that comes out more often than we'll ever really know. Yet, the only time we saw Couples cry publicly was in 1989 when, in one swing at The Belfry's eighteenth hole, he went from Ryder Cup hero to goat. He's made up for that tenfold in the past five years.

Couples will never be as outwardly intense as Ray Floyd, whose stare throws fear into men half his age. But there is a drive, a churning inside. And Couples is capable of more than just tip-of-the-visor emotions, as evidenced in early 1994 when he let a few expletives fly at a tournament. It wasn't the first time he's cut loose, and likely won't be the last.

Couples was fined for the incident and took it on the chin with fans, too. He got sacks of indignant mail. He took the time to write a few people back.

"I told them what happened, how it happened, and that I was sorry it happened," he said. "I told them, 'I'm a normal person. I'm not up on some pedestal. I made a mistake. If you haven't made a mistake, then please write me back."

He didn't get a single letter.

Now that, we understand.

Paying Attention to Details

Melanie Hauser

On Tour, *July 1996*

A bumblebee the size of a quarter is buzzing around the soft lavender wisteria blossoms that wind slowly up the old pine tree. A sidewalk flows through the gardens and past the tree, its destination the wide white steps of an airy Southern veranda.

There's a screened-in breakfast nook on one side, a screened-in guest bedroom on the other. The facade is the soft white of a magnolia, the shutters the soft, deep green of the leaves that cradle that flower. Today, the huge ceiling fans lining the porch are silent. It's one of those rare crisp spring days in Houston when the locals can open their doors and windows and let the breeze blow through. The oversized wicker chairs invite you to come up and sit a spell. Rock for a while. Watch the sun filter across the gardens and the porch and dance along the corrugated roof of the sprawling plantation-style home. . . .

At last count, Steve Elkington had 112 species of plants packed into a delightful smorgasbord of Texas garden. Everything from Double-wing Silverbell to Australian bottlebrush to rosemary and basil have their place under the sprawling live oaks, pines, and pecans that offer a canopy to shade both the gardens and house.

Elkington has just recited the garden inventory as though it were a litany.He walks through it, pointing out each plant and adding a few asterisks along the way. The object of his attention right now? That Japanese wisteria.

"Don't you love it?" he said, pointing to the spirals around the tree trunk. "Don't you think it gives a lazy look coming up the walk?"

As Elkington rattles on in that fast-forward Australian accent of his, you realize this house really does reflect its owner. The detail is as impeccable as Elkington's wardrobe, the design as meticulous as one of his pencil-and-watercolor drawings. It flows as gracefully as the owner's swing and is filled with the richness and warmth of well-worn, functional antiques that allow year-old daughter Annie to steady herself as she learns to walk, but at the same time set the tone for a night at the Elks' where everyone's got a beer in one hand, barbecue in the other, and a story rolling off his tongue.

The mini-estate, just two minutes from Champions Golf Club, is pure Elkington—half elegance and classic swing, half whoop-it-up, blue-collar lad from Wagga Wagga, a small town that borders the Australian outback. The house itself was designed after Magnolia Mound, a 1791 Baton Rouge plantation, but it's got just enough Aussie in it—the corrugated roof—that it could just as well have sprung from a ranch in Queensland. It's warm and elegant, yet a bit rough and rowdy. There are touches of Down Under splashed around a true Texas feel; a little whimsy tossed in here and there to balance out the serious lines. . . .

The last year has brought so many changes Elkington doesn't know where to begin. Annie. A major title. A Vardon Trophy. A real place in the game.

A year that started with a victory at the Mercedes Championship ended with the PGA Championship and a major-championship record for seventy-two holes; a career that began with so much promise and has been nurtured as meticulously as his garden has finally begun to blossom the way everyone thought it would. No longer known simply as the great dresser with a velvet swing and a penchant for missing chances and crucial putts, Elkington has stepped up and become one of the more powerful players in the game. At thirty-three, he is just hitting his stride. Just where does he see himself fitting in?

"Too early to tell," he said. "But the nice thing is I'll be ranked somewhere in there. I'll be one of the best Australian players in there. I've already got the tag of the great swing."

And he is already taking his place among his country's greats. He grew up watching the likes of Peter Thomson, Kel Nagle, Bruce Devlin, and David Graham, and has labored in the shadow of countryman Greg Norman, eight years his senior. But now he stands by their sides.

In the past few years, Elkington has added some twenty pounds of muscle to his six-foot-two frame. He works out daily when he's home, pedaling and pumping to the news of the day on CNBC or a new CD. The strength—he can leg-press five hundred pounds—has given his game a new consistency and made him not just another golfer, but a presence.

A few weeks after Annie was born, Elkington floated his way through the Masters. His mind was back home with his wife and daughter, not in Augusta. Yet he finished tied for fifth. At the British Open, a bogey at the Road Hole cost him a chance at the playoff; he finished third. And, at the Grand Slam of Golf, it took Ben Crenshaw's eighty-yard hole-out from the fairway to beat him. Then, at the PGA at Riviera, the man with the to-die-for swing finally finished a major, beating Colin Montgomerie in a playoff.

"I maxed out," Elkington said. "And to be honest with you, I don't know how I could organize myself to do it again. I think it just happened. I maxed out everything—hitting, putting, mental. That's what you have to do to win a major. I don't know anyone other than Jack Nicklaus or Ben Hogan who didn't have to."

In ten seasons, Elkington has won six tournaments and nearly $5 million, yet he is one of the least visible stars. You see him on the course, but not plastered across your television screen. A putt here or there the past few years and he might be another Greg Norman right now; instead, he can enjoy being the middle-class kind of guy he really is—and work on being the great player he wants to be.

Everything about Elkington is built to last. The swing, the body, the attitude, the determination, the style. He wears clothes with an elegance about them—pleats, drapes, lightweight wools, cashmere, and soft cottons. He carries himself with grace, strolling the fairways and addressing his ball not with bells, whistles, and waggles, but rather simple economy. The swing is Sam Snead fluid and efficient; the determination and attitude, Jack Burke crusty and cantankerous.

There isn't an eighteen-hole game he doesn't take seriously. Just ask him about the 1978 Wagga Wagga club championship. Steve was sixteen then and came to the last hole leading his older brother Robert by one.

"My brother hit a great shot with a four-iron in there about four feet," Steve said with a grin. "And I made an ace on top of him. My mom and dad didn't know what to say."

A year later, he caught Dave Williams's eye at the Doug Sanders Junior World Championship and Williams offered him a scholarship at the University of Houston. Elkington turned his back on an art scholarship to the University of Sydney and set out for Houston, Texas. Save a visit back home each year, he has never left.

The new kid on the block moved into Fred Couples's old UH suite—101 at Taub Hall—and, despite qualifying for the first few tournaments, was left at home. "Coach didn't take me," Elkington said. "He didn't know if I could handle it. And, I think some of the players were concerned when I came in because I looked like I was going to be on the team."

He won the first tournament he played in and had a good season, but at the end of the year Elkington passed on the chance to play at the NCAA championships. He was homesick and told Williams to take senior Mark Fuller instead. UH won the team title with then-freshman Billy Ray Brown winning medalist and Fuller finishing third.

"At that time, I didn't know how big the NCAA was," Elkington said. "It was really a blessing because Mark got a national championship ring."

Elkington didn't leave UH empty-handed, though. The Cougars won titles his last two seasons and he fell in love twice—with his wife Lisa and with Texas.

The swing has always been graceful and athletic. Alex Mercer saw the gift years ago when the backswing was long, loose, and "a bit flicky at the top." But as the years went on under Mercer's watchful eye, it became more connected and synchronized. Now, through weight training in his home gym, he has built a physique that complements the powerful arc.

"I accept that people like to watch it, but I work at it all the time," Elkington said. "I'm always trying to perfect it. I never think I've got it. I never feel like I'm under control with everything."

But he is. Always has been.

Elkington was fourteen when he and Robert began to take the ten-hour train ride to Sydney each Friday to spend the weekend working with Mercer on their games. The train left Wagga Wagga at ten P.M. and pulled in at eight A.M., whereupon they would embark for Royal Sydney Golf Club. Often the brothers would stay up all night, but they were always scrubbed up and ready for the no-nonsense, spit-and-polish Mercer.

"When they first arrived I think they got a shock because I sent one boy back to the clubhouse to clean his shoes and clean his gear so I could get himself into a position so I could teach him," Mercer said. "I told the boys, 'Can you see a mark on my shoes? Are my trousers perfectly ironed? Have I shaved? I don't want anyone to turn up for a lesson who doesn't look in order because I won't teach you.' That was always my policy and I think Steve didn't mind that one bit because that was his idea too."

To this day, Elkington is a perfectionist. He dresses in subtle tones that evoke the grand old days of Hogan and Nelson, and his closet is immaculate; his clothes always custom-tailored and neatly pressed. When he wanted to have the pleats lay softly from the waistband, he learned about fabrics. When he and Gary McCord heard about a guy in Fort Worth who has slacks with one percent mink in the fabric, they each grabbed a pair—just to say they had them.

But the details don't stop there. It took Elkington two years to build his dream house, in part because of his penchant for perfection. Everything had to be exact—from the period rosettes on the doorjambs to the fixtures and the floors. . . .

When he's at home, Elkington gets up before the sun rises, pulls on his hiking boots and shorts, and spends three hours or so in his garden.

"It's his downtime," said Lisa. "His time to think."

And, it's yet another place where everything is perfect, where everything fits a niche—the Azalea Garden, the Cottage Garden, the Native Texas Garden, the Hummingbird and Butterfly Garden, and the Courtyard Garden. He started stockpiling plants while the house was being built, storing them on extra acreage at Champions. . . .

"Half the fun of gardening is walking around and seeing everything grow," he said. "Right now I'm fine-tuning it. Can you imagine what it will look like in five or ten years?"

Perhaps the best-kept secret in the Elkington house isn't in the garden. It's tucked in the antique secretary in the master bedroom. Flip it open and there it is—a small, leather-bound book Elkington started the day Annie was born. There are pages about her birth, a sketch of her first shoes, and another of a koala. He'll give it to her when she's old enough—maybe at eighteen.

"I just write to her," he said. "I write what's going on; things I think she'd like to know about. I wrote her a Christmas poem. I'm going to fill it with notes and pictures."

Since Annie was born last March—he had to withdraw from The Players Championship when Lisa had an emergency cesarean—Elkington has settled down a bit. He's looking more toward the future—and a brother or sister for Annie. Yet there's still the rough-and-tumble side of him that can't live without those spur-of-the-moment celebrations and "guy" kind of days.

Being a semi-nervous guy off the course, Elkington fidgets; he doesn't always finish sentences and he hates like the dickens to be interviewed for more than fifteen or twenty minutes. But the restlessness is never more evident than when he wins a tournament. He always celebrates by staying up all night. The reason? He can't sleep. So he calls every person he knows. No matter what time zone they're in.

After the PGA, he called buddy Derrick Carr, a hairdresser in Ayr, Scotland, at four A.M. "I had given him a bottle of single-malt Scotch whisky, and he was going to keep it until I won a major," Elkington said. "When I called him, I couldn't even understand him. He'd drunk the whole bottle of single malt. He was crying."

He once celebrated a birthday in South Africa by singing bare-chested onstage with John Daly and Ian Woosnam. And, a few months after the PGA, he celebrated again, this time after the three-hundred-man Champions Locker Room Rhubarb, a match-play event pitting the south side of the locker room against the north. Afterward, Elkington grabbed the Wanamaker Trophy and filled it with beer—thirty-seven of them. Then he and about one hundred club members drained the cup dry.

Elkington is one of the boys from way back. That's just the way it was in Wagga Wagga, an aboriginal saying that means the river forks here and reforks on the other side of the town. He hung out with his mates, telling stories and talking golf. There was always something nearby to cut the thirst. . . .

A talented artist, he used to sketch things around the locker room all the time, but when the demand got too high for his witty sketches, he stopped. Eventually, he would like to try his hand at golf-course architecture, but for the moment he's busy with his new golf-course landscape company—Major Landscaping—which is working on a project in McAllen. After all, he has the drawing and landscape background.

"And," he said, "I can see things out there."

That above all, says Mercer, is why Elkington may one day make it to the top spot in the world rankings.

"Golf has always been an art, not a science," Mercer said. "That's why Steve's so successful and Norman's such a great player. They have that kind of artistry. They can produce the picture they see, and that takes an unbelievable artistic quality apart from the athleticism and technicalities of the swing. It's an imagination that some people have more than others."

And a drive for perfection. The same one it takes to design a house. Or a garden.

But most of all, a career.

Holy Cow

Franz Lidz

Sports Illustrated, *December 5, 1994*

It's one thing for a golfer to be booed by the gallery, quite another to be mooed. But there was Robert Landers swinging a sand wedge in the pasture behind his house to a bovine ovation. Landers's Legion—five heifers and a calf—chewed over his follow-through with contented countenances. "Out here, a ball that lands on a cowpatty is not an unplayable lie," said Landers as he hit from a dung heap. "You can tell when your ball hits one 'cause it won't bounce a bit." Has there ever been a more unorthodox chip shot?

Landers was uncowed and unbowed during the Senior PGA Tour qualifying tournament last month in Lutz, Florida. Wearing sneakers, lugging a garage-sale carry bag, and wielding a set of glue-and-go clubs he'd bought from his cousin Steven Sosebee for $70, Landers, a hardscrabble Texas farmer, shot a 73 in the final round. His four-over-par 288 tied him for sixth place, earning him $4,270. Even better, it earned him a berth on next year's Senior tour, where he'll be competing against the likes of Ray Floyd and Dave Stockton for $1-million purses.

"Just eight of the one hundred and eleven entrants won full exemptions," says Steve Champion, a club pro who first met Landers last year. "Seven of the eight were either playing pros or solid club pros. Robert is the only one who will need the purse money to play on the tour."

Of the handful of steelworkers, mechanics, and insurance salesmen to have qualified for the senior circuit since its inception in 1980, none have followed a more unlikely path than Landers, who has been trying to eke out a living on his farm since the clothing store he managed went bust two years ago. Since then, he has spent much of his free time—and there has been lots of it—chopping wood, raising cattle, and honing his game with constant practice in his pasture. "The cows come in handy," Landers says. "They keep the grass down."

As plain and solid as an oak plank, Landers is a simple, practical man who may be slow to act but is unswerving when he does. Before Lutz, the most Landers had won in a tournament was $700, at the Texoma Senior Open earlier this year. "Imagine, seven hundred dollars!" he says guilelessly. "I was so happy, I didn't sleep for a week."

At fifty he is about to see his life changed by the lavish Senior tour, mostly in ways he doesn't care to think about. "How we're gonna deal with this deal I got us into, I don't know," Landers says. "I don't even know how to get to those tournament cities, or where they are."

He hates planes and hasn't flown since 1981. "Truth is, I haven't even had time to consider what I've done," says Landers. "The whole thing's like a fairy tale. *Cinderella,* maybe."

His wife, Freddie, demurs. "Except that Cinderella knew her stepsisters had fine things and that she was entitled to fine things," she says. "Whereas we were contented where we was at. In our wildest dreams, if we was gonna dream a dream, it wouldn't be this big.

"Until now, our dream was that we weren't gonna get any worse off. We were just a couple of nobodies from nowhere."

Nowhere is about eighteen miles northwest of Fort Worth. It's called Azle, and you could clear downtown with a seven-iron. "I lived in Fort Worth for ten years, but it was too fast for me," Landers says. "Being out here with the trees, the birds, the creek, and the dirt is the best life I could ever imagine having."

He moves around his dung-dotted practice range, pointing out the landmarks. Large plywood cutout cows are nailed to the sheds and scattered over the pasture. "Over that way is Dino's Cliff," Landers says, indicating the short precipice off which a calf named Dino once slid into a ditch. "There's Jenn's Gulley," he says, wagging a finger at the culvert Jenn the heifer plunged into. "Want to see Willie's Corner?" Poor Willie was his beloved dog, who met his end between the blades of a mower and was replaced by a mutt named Oleo.

"Why did you bring another dog home?" demanded Freddie.

"Reason is," Robert said, "if I'm out cuttin' wood and a tree falls and kills me, I need something to say goodbye to."

Robert and Freddie met twenty years ago at Mitchell's department store in Azle. He was the manager; she was a clerk. "I was dustin' some purses when I first laid eyes on Robert," recalls Freddie. "I thought, 'Oh, he is so good-lookin'. He's gonna be hung up on himself.' Of course, we were married to different people then."

They became friends but not intimates. Then Freddie's son died in a car crash, and her husband left her for a younger woman. Robert says his own wife "hated golf, hated guns, hated me." He would skulk around town, digging his hands deeply enough into his pockets to scratch his knees. "Freddie and I realized we had a lot in common," he says. "We were both thrown-away people."

Tears formed in Landers's eyes as he related all this at the farmhouse dinner table. Freddie had set out steaming bowls of corn, peas, and mashed potatoes. Robert jabbed a fork into a heap of brisket. "This is Gus," he tells a visitor. "He was an ornery little calf, so he's probably tough."

The kitchen is decorated in Early Holstein, festooned with cow clocks, cow cookie jars, cow pot holders, cow soap dispensers, cow teapots, cow planters, cow refrigerator magnets—even cow bowling pins. Since Freddie lost her assembly-line job a few months back, she has carved out a slender living painting cows on old tenpins. "I sell them at flea markets every Monday," says Robert. "In these parts, everybody collects cows."

Their collection of live cows runs to forty-five. Robert and Freddie bought their first calves seven years ago at Smelley's Dairy in nearby Springtown. "Freddie and I didn't know anything about milking them," says Robert. "So I'd milk the right side, and she'd milk the left."

Freddie christened each calf. "If they didn't have names," Robert says, "we wouldn't know who we was talkin' about." There was Spooky, Daisy, Rocky, Dino, and Hope. "Hope was sick," says Freddie, "and we hoped she'd live."

In fact, the only one that wasn't sickly was Rocky. "One morning we went out to feed them," says Robert, "and Rocky was lying out there, and he was dead."

"We tried to make his eyes move," says Freddie.

"They didn't," says Robert with heavy finality.

The herd grew with the addition of Sundance and Teensy and Wobbles and Peekaboo and Dirtsy. "Another's called Moolah, because we're gonna have some money now," says Freddie, who thinks up names faster than a bad-check artist at a teller's window.

As a kid Robert couldn't afford to play golf. He was twenty-two when his uncle Foster taught him the basics. "I improvised from there," Landers says. He scraped together enough for a driver, a sand wedge, and a Patty Berg eight-iron. A year later he got his first putter.

He started to play seriously six years later, in 1972, though always on municipal courses. He qualified for the U.S. Open and the U.S. Amateur in 1980, missing the cut in both, and twice was the low amateur at the Texas Open. However, a pinched sciatic nerve curtailed his career, and he stopped playing competitively in '81 to ease the pain that made his left leg go numb. The move to the country in '87 proved salubrious. "Farm life strengthened me," he says. "After building fences, hauling hay, and splitting logs, golf does not hurt."

Landers got to thinking about the Senior tour in 1991 and prepared for it with a sense of sacrifice and stern calling. He played the Texas Barbecue Circuit, a series of two-round tournaments run by civic groups in small towns. Most other days he would whack balls in the pasture, walk after them, and whack them back. Sixty thousand practice balls a year. Finally Freddie said, "Either you're gonna play, or you're gonna get a job."

So Robert composed a letter to friends and local business people about backing him in his effort to join the Senior tour. The prospective said, in part, "I will work hard, and there will be winnings."

But he never sent the letter out. "Forget everybody," Freddie told him. "You're gonna do it on your own."

To cover the $2,000 entry fee for the Senior tour qualifying tournament, Robert cashed in an IRA. Also, some buddies at a nine-hole muni where he plays put out a jug. "We raised fifty bucks," says Champion, who owns and teaches at the Casino Beach Golf Academy in Fort Worth. "Robert graciously accepted."

After successfully competing at the regional qualifier in San Antonio, Landers advanced to the finals. Or more precisely, puttered. He and Freddie made the 1,300-mile trip to Lutz in their 1989 Chevy.

Playing in his muddy Reeboks, Landers cut an unimposing figure. He wouldn't wear the new Foot-Joy golf shoes that Freddie made him buy, because he hadn't worn spikes in more than five years and thought he would scuff the greens if he dragged his feet. "Everybody in Lutz knew us as the 'Farmers from Azle,'" says Freddie, who rode in the cart with Robert wearing a bandage on her nose because Sundance had kicked her in the face. "We looked plenty pitiful, but nobody treated us ugly."

Fighting head winds up to forty miles per hour that were the result of tropical storm Gordon, Landers shot an opening-round 72, which put him in a tie for fourth. "Gordon helped me a lot," he says. "I can keep the ball down and control it. Some golfers shot themselves out. They couldn't handle the weather."

Much less the competition. "Q school is the toughest event I've ever played in," says veteran Senior Tour player Rocky Thompson, a thirty-year pro. "If a man is good enough to get one of the eight spots, he should succeed. On the other hand, I've seen some talented qualifiers not play to their capabilities when they're upside the Trevinos, the Stocktons, and the Floyds. They get too excited. You've got to be pretty sure of your game."

Which Landers is. "I've always been very insecure," he says. "Golf gave me greater self-esteem. I'm now to the point where I feel equal to the next guy."

In this case, equal is more steady than exciting. "I'm not much into risk," Landers says. Nor is he much into sand or water. Over seventy-two holes in Lutz, Landers hit into only two bunkers and two ponds.

He relied on a reconditioned three-wood, which has a graphite shaft he found in a garbage can. "Robert spent twelve dollars on that club," says his friend Jerry Hamilton. "That's really extravagant for him."

Landers wasn't being cheap, just frugal. He used a coupon that got him and Freddie into a Ramada Inn for $34 a night. During the entire ten-day trip, they spent $69.35 on gas, $4.59 on Advil, and $147.75 on food and other necessities. "We would have spent less," says Landers, apologetically, "but we had to buy a couple of pillows for my back."

In Lutz he used only seven balls over four rounds. "I would have used fewer," he says, "if the two hadn't landed in the drink." He had intended to use the same ball the entire final round but reconsidered when he double-bogeyed the fifteenth. "By golly, using a new ball turned out to be a good move," he says. "I parred the last three holes."

After Robert qualified for the tour with a short putt on eighteen, he and Freddie embraced. And cried. And embraced. And cried. But they didn't futz around Lutz. "I had to get back to Azle to chop firewood," Robert says. "I had promised some folks I would have it for them by Thanksgiving."

So how did Robert and Freddie celebrate? "On the drive home," says Robert, "we stopped at a Waffle House instead of a McDonald's."

"And Robert left the waitress a two-dollar tip," says Freddie.

Call Him "Lucky"

Jim Murray

Los Angeles Times, *July 18, 1963*

Even if he were not the only non-Caucasian in the field, you could recognize Charlie Sifford in a golf tournament by the cigar clenched in his teeth. You could almost keep score by the trail of butts. He chain-smokes them but, on the days when he's on his stick and the birdies fall, he barely gets time to light more than three or four.

Charlie Sifford has won only one tournament—a three-round affair at Long Beach in 1957. His swing is nothing to go home and press in the leaves of the family Bible. There are days when he could putt better with a rake.

Yet he is as big a cinch to go into golfing's Hall of Fame as Sam Snead. This is because Charlie is the only Negro ever to win a PGA Tour tournament and in one month will become only the second of his race to become an official paid-up member of the Professional Golfers Association. The only other one is seventy-four years old.

Golf did a better job for years than the government of Alabama in pretending the Negro wasn't there. A colored man on a golf course was either handing you a stick or picking up paper cups with one.

To become a member of the PGA, you have to play for five years, show up with a shave, and not throw clubs or drink out of your bag where the public could see you. People with jail records made it. Kids who didn't need to shave regularly made it. But not even if you brought a letter from your chaplain could you make it if you weren't white.

Sifford was raised in North Carolina, where he caddied by day and practiced by moonlight. It wasn't the golfers who were prejudiced, it was golf. The game is too tough for anyone who plays it regularly to fear someone is going to come along and surround it. A man who has just missed a four-foot putt would gladly hand the club to a Martian and burst into wild applause if he thought he could make it.

Charlie played with the likes of Skip Alexander and Clayton Heafner, a massive man who once kept his PGA standing intact by not dropping his clubs in a lake, but dropping Charlie instead. Charlie didn't complain. He was slow in coming up with the five-dollar Nassau. To tell the truth, he didn't have the money. But a study of the fast backswing of one of his partners encouraged him to think he would in a few holes. Heafner couldn't wait. He had a pigeon of his own whose feathers were showing.

Charlie took his methodical backswing and box of cigars to Philadelphia, where his artistry in arranging first-tee bets earned him the nom du course of "Philadelphia Shorty." A chunk of a man who looks more as if he was quarried than born, Charlie runs five-foot-seven and 180 pounds. He once dropped a donkey with a single punch in the Philippines to win a bet from Willie Hunter Jr. "It was ten dollars 'Do or Don't,'" explains Charlie. The donkey went down, shortly followed by Willie and Charlie as half of Manila set upon them. "There were several jackasses on the floor before the evening was over," Charlie recalls.

Charlie didn't start out on the tour under prodding of the NAACP but under the prodding of money. He won respect with his sticks, not a court order. He still thinks it's the best way, although his independence has earned him an occasional sneer as an "Uncle Tom." But like the original, his methods pricked the conscience of the white community, in this case, golf. And it stirred the attorney general of California into action on at least one important occasion, when he ran the PGA tournament right out of Los Angeles and the "Caucasians Only" clause right out of the PGA because of Sifford. There was no way golf could contend Charlie didn't belong. The scoreboard contradicted them.

Charlie didn't get an "approved player" status until he was almost at the bifocal stage. The best way to describe Charlie's age is "somewhere between forty and forty-five, mostly the latter."

But he began showing up at tournaments, cigar and all. He had to qualify for every tournament. PGA-ers and "approved players" get a rash of exemptions, but Charlie could even finish second (which he did once in the Canadian Open) and have to hustle to the next town to qualify.

He used to drive Mike Souchak's or Bo Wininger's or Frank Stranahan's car from tourney to tourney whenever they wanted to fly to the next stop.

For Charlie, the tour stopped at the Mason-Dixon line on the South and the Mississippi River on the East. "When the tour left the United States, I left the tour," he used to explain. But he was the first Negro ever to tee up in an open in North Carolina. He led it after the opening round.

He has since played in other Southern tourneys. He dast not drink, chew, swear, cuss out the customers, or bury his putter in the skull of a green or a caddie. He has to have a haircut and a shave. His clothes must not be loud, even when his buddy Joe Campbell shows up in gold shoes and orchid pants. The difference is Joe also shows up in blond hair.

He has to keep his counsel even when, as has happened, someone kicks his ball out of bounds. He has to pretend it hit a rock. " I think," said Jay Hebert carefully once, "that Charlie's the greatest player out here. If we had his problems not one of us would shoot the way he does."

Putting is just as tough for a colored man as any other man. Charlie gets the yips the same way Sam Snead does. He has left a ball in a sand trap occasionally, has hit a tree and the ocean. For years, he couldn't play in enough tourneys to get on the complicated ladder of golf that means Ryder and Cup trips, mass exemptions, the Masters, the big money.

But now he has signed on as public-relations counselor with a beer company whose slogan is "It's Lucky When You Live in America." Charlie has seen the day when there was more poetry than truth in that, but now he drives his own car, which Buick gives him. He occasionally bunks in with his good friend Mike Souchak, and Charlie is looking forward to the day when *he* can turn to Mike and ask *him* if he'd mind driving the convertible to the next town while he, Charlie, takes the plane.

(Editor's note: Charlie Sifford moved around a lot, but even though he had it rough south of the Mason-Dixon line when he was playing, he settled in Texas when he was playing on the Senior Tour. He and his wife reside in Houston.)

Morris Williams

Dan Jenkins

Excerpt from "A Semi-Tough Return to Golf," Fairways and Greens, *June 1994*

Ben Hogan witnessed the best shot I ever hit in competition, but let me set it up properly.

It was in 1950, my sophomore year at Texas Christian University, a thrilling time in the annals of Horned Frog golf, for I was the team's No. 1 player.

Somehow that spring, our team won enough matches and tied enough matches against Bears, Owls, Aggies, Mustangs, and Razorbacks that we came down to the final match against the University of Texas at Colonial with the Southwest Conference championship on the line.

I, of course, knew the championship wasn't on the line. There was no living way we could beat Texas—Texas had Morris Williams Jr.!

The son of an Austin sportswriter, Morris was a slender, wiry, supple, good-looking guy who never hit a crooked drive, never struck an iron that didn't sound pure and wasn't clotheslined to the flag, and never missed a putt he needed to make. He had a quick smile and a friendly nature, but on the golf course there was an ax murderer struggling to climb out of his heart. He had a beautiful upright swing and played along in the quick-hitting style of a Lanny Wadkins or Tom Watson. He had become a friend, through the Texas amateur circuit, but I was in helpless awe of his talent.

Morris Williams Jr. was invincible, unbeatable, incomparable, and otherwise stupendous—the Ben Crenshaw of his day.

That I knew of, the only match he had ever lost was to North Carolina's Harvie Ward, one down in the thirty-six-hole final of the 1949 NCAA championship, which was no great embarrassment if you knew anything about Harvie Ward.

This was during a more romantic time in our history, when prominent members of TCU's varsity football team would come out to Colonial to caddie for us in college matches. School-spirit deal, they said. It was a flattering thing, though very few of the gridiron heroes knew anything about golf.

The caddie for my match against Morris Williams Jr. that day was a burly, maniacal defensive end from Odessa named Billy Moorman.

As we were all fooling around on the putting green before the matches started, Billy quietly said to me, "We're gonna mop up on them teasippers today."

"Speak for yourself," I said.

"Naw, really," he said. "Look how skinny they are."

I figured there were two things that might help keep me from being totally humiliated by Morris. One, he had never played Colonial before, and two, Ben Hogan would be following us in a golf cart. Ben had read about this celebrated kid from Austin and wanted to take a look at him.

We played the back nine first to avoid a collision with some of Colonial's grumpiest members, and through fifteen holes, rather miraculously, I was all square with Morris and we were both even par. Quite frankly, I was playing my career round. I might even have been one up or two up if God had been wearing the purple of TCU instead of the orange of Texas.

But now we were at Colonial's par-four seventh hole—our sixteenth—which back then called for a one-iron or four-wood off the tee and a six-, seven-, or eight-iron to the green unless you wanted to try to thread a needle with the driver, in which case you'd have a pitching wedge to the green, the green being one of those shadowy throw rugs sheltered by tall, overhanging trees.

Smart money usually played it safe, but I was never known for that. So I sky-sliced a driver into the right rough behind a tall cluster of oaks.

I looked over at Hogan, who was sitting in the golf cart with Marvin Leonard, his old friend and the man who built Colonial. I put my hand to my throat and smiled weakly. Ben shook his head sadly. Meanwhile, Morris nailed it down the gut with a four-wood.

I had a remote chance to reach the green on my second shot if I could get a six-iron out of the Bermuda rough and up quickly over the trees and then down quickly over some more trees, which, curiously, is what happened. Don't ask me to write an instruction article on it. All I did was swing the club, and mostly out of anger at my tee shot. The ball barely cleared the trees going up, and barely cleared a front bunker coming down, and bit into the green and stopped about six inches from the cup.

"Gosh, Dan, great shot," said Morris from out in the fairway.

I said thanks, and tried to act like the shot was merely a part of my normal repertoire.

The defensive end, my caddie, said, "There you go, son—nothin' two more of those won't cure."

I looked at him incredulously.

For the next long moment, while I waited for my opponent to spray his own approach out of shell shock, I entertained some wonderful thoughts. I had a gimme birdie, thus I was going to be one up on Morris Williams Jr. with only two holes to play. I was going to beat Morris Williams Jr. I was going to win the individual championship in the conference tournament next month. I was going to turn pro, go on the tour, wear beltless slacks, and complain about courtesy-car drivers the rest of my life. I was . . .

This is about the time that Morris holed out his seven-iron for an eagle two.

Yeah. Holed it out. Hit a seven-iron in there about ten feet short of the flag. The ball took a gash out of the bent grass and rolled slowly past my six-inch birdie and died in the cup—a deuce.

All I could do was laugh. All Morris could do was laugh, though apologetically.

Still laughing, I looked over at Ben Hogan. He was shaking his head again as he turned the cart around and headed for the clubhouse. I guess he knew the match was over.

Needless to say, it was. We both parred the last two holes, so with the lowest round I ever had on old Colonial, a one-under-par 69 from the tips, I lost one up, didn't win the conference the next month, never won the conference, didn't turn pro, and only went out on the tour with a typewriter.

(Although I'm not generally fond of parenthetical information, it would be incorrect for me not to mention here that Morris Williams Jr., one of the nicest guys I ever knew and one of the best golfers I ever saw, was tragically killed in the crash of an Air Force jet in 1953. He had planned to go on the PGA Tour when he got out of the service. I don't have any doubt that he would have been a big star out there and would have given Arnold Palmer a run for his charisma.)

Part Five

Babe and the Girls

On Awe, the Babe, and Making Money Playing Golf

Blackie Sherrod

Program, 1991 U.S. Women's Open

In the press-box business, there are three stages of awe. At least there used to be, back when Damon and Granny and the rest of us graduated from Harvard with honors and took our great literary talent to the ballyards.

Three stages of awe. When you started as a sportswriter, there was the complete absence of awe. You refused to be impressed by anyone, no matter the neon involved. You wore confidence like a chip on the shoulder. You were brimming with assurance. You would give Joe DiMaggio a hotfoot, or you would slap Jack Dempsey on the back and ask what's good on the menu today. Armed with your pad and pencil, you knew it was only a matter of time before you wrote the great definitive American treatise on world peace or world war or maybe even the infield-fly rule. You didn't know enough to be timid.

Then there was the second stage, when you had been around a few years and realized this really was Ted Williams you were talking to, or Vince Lombardi or Ben Hogan. These were great celebrities who lived in the headlines, and if you wrote a hundred novels and won seven

Pulitzers, you still would never be recognized by one-zillionth of folk who doted on these subjects.

You were overwhelmed by the weight of these personages. And you became rather in awe of them; you memorized your questions in advance and straightened your tie and cleared the frog from your throat and prayed to the journalistic gods that somehow you would escape the role of complete idiot.

Of course, there is the inevitable third stage. This condition is immediately identified by the gray in the beard, the totter in the walk, the cough in the morning. Press-box years have erased awe from anything—moon shots, earthquakes, no-hitters, Bo Jackson, Madonna, or whatever. Awe goes the way of the dodo bird and the Hula-Hoop.

Anyway, I was in the fell clutch of the first stage the first time I met Babe Didrikson Zaharias. This would have been around 1948, when Pop Boone, the sports editor of the old *Fort Worth Press,* suggested I take myself out to River Crest Country Club where the Texas Women's Open was being played.

And so, there on the brick terrace (I think it was brick) of the country club, I strode purposefully to this person, ignored formalities, called her Babe, and asked if I could bend her ear.

"Sure, pal," said the person, "if I can bum a cigarette from you."

By then of course, Babe had already established women's professional golf. She had help, surely, from Patty Berg and Fred Corcoran, the master promoter, and Wilson Sporting Goods. But it was Babe Didrikson who donated immediate credibility to the circuit when it was launched a dozen years before. Credibility and merchandising.

"No question about it," says Polly Riley, the illustrious amateur contemporary. "Babe sold the LPGA."

But there on that brick terrace at River Crest, perched on a railing, Babe did not look nor act the part of a founder or a benefactor. It was in October and Babe had just won her semifinal match. (Polly Riley would defeat her in the final by a remarkable 10 and 9 margin.) Babe wore a long brown tweed skirt, I remember, and she was rather broad and flat across the beam. Not plump. Broad and flat. She wore hose and anklets both, for goodness sakes, and some forgettable sort of blouse and beret.

Babe was not a comely woman. Her nose was hawk, her lips were thin, her complexion was spotty with freckles and weather. She was a bit bowlegged (and I have never seen a great natural athlete who wasn't). But she was charming in her looseness and relaxed naturalness and great good nature.

Most sports celebrities, some without realizing, immediately assume some sort of pose when speaking with media, even if it's a wet-eared kid from a small paper who doesn't know women's golf from polo. But not Babe. Loose and easy. In forty years of this dodge, I've seen only a handful of jocks with that freewheeling ease in interviews. Abe Lemons, the basketball coach, was one. Roy Campanella, the catcher, was another. Don Meredith came close. Johnny Miller, the golfer, and Magic Johnson. But Ms. Babe wrote the book.

Goodness knows what the interview was all about. Smithsonian has lost its copy. But that first impression of Babe was indelible. And the awe came shortly afterward, after I had time to reflect and appreciate the enormity of her naturalness. Not her accomplishments, not her reputation nor her history, but her down-home personality.

I had watched her play several holes that day. Once she was six yards in the rough, stymied by a small sapling. She barely glanced at the situation, jerked a mid-iron from her bag, and whanged the ball away. Uh-oh, she will be far, far left, I thought from my expertise. But out over the River Crest grass, Babe's ball began to slice, a great curving arc that found the green like one of those heat-seeking missiles we have today.

It was also later that I realized Babe was doing just what came naturally. Her track accomplishments are legends, of course. In the 1932 AAU in Evanston, Illinois, she won five of her eight events, everything from shot put to hurdles. She took two golds and a silver (because of disqualification) in the Olympics that year. Heck, she was a baseball pitcher; she toured with a semipro basketball team. She played volleyball and pitched horseshoes and swung a racquet. The first full game of golf she ever played, with three sportswriters (Grantland Rice, Braven Dyer, and Paul Gallico) at Brentwood in Los Angeles, she shot an 86.

But the reason she was there on the River Crest patio is because she could make a living at golf. Hell, if Babe could have made the same money flinging the javelin, she'd have done that, too.

In this respect, she reminds me of another great natural athlete. Doak Walker, the immortal footballer at SMU and Detroit, once abandoned his usual modesty to admit that he never tried a sport that after thirty minutes he couldn't play better than average. Except golf, Doak said. He never fully conquered golf.

Babe did. She worked at it. For all of her easygoing nature on the course, she was serious enough to practice until blisters fumed bloody. She didn't give that impression.

"Aw, I just loosen my girdle and take a whack at it," was her favorite expression.

"Babe wasn't limited to athletics. She was a wonderful pool player. She was a great card player; she could beat your ears off at bridge or gin. She had marvelous ability to focus on whatever she was doing at the moment," says Polly Riley.

Women's golf, both amateur and professional, past and future, is fortunate that economics led Babe to focus on that particular activity. She was still playing amateur in 1925, in the Texas Women's Amateur incidentally, when complaints from Dallas women golfers led the USGA to rescind Babe's amateur standing. She was so important to the game that the Texas Women's Open was then started, and subsequently the LPGA and the tour. What Red Grange meant for the NFL, what Babe Ruth did for the Yankees, what Bill Tilden did for tennis and Arnold Palmer for the modern PGA, Mildred Zaharias did for women's golf.

"Babe would call up some friend in Seattle or someplace," said Polly Riley. "She'd say, 'Hey, I got thirty women golfers and we need a tournament.' And she'd get it."

But, of course, all that's in the history books. In my own personal album, however, was the afternoon Babe Didrikson Zaharias, in her tweed skirt and anklets there on River Crest bricks, completely disarmed a cocky kid reporter and installed therein an awe that, against all odds and all years, remains to this day.

Babe Could Play

Curt Sampson

Golf Journal, *January–February 1991*

It's a sultry Sunday evening in August 1953. Ike is in the White House, the Cleveland Indians are in first place, and, on your television set, live and in black-and-white, is *The Ed Sullivan Show.* Among Ed's guests are singer Frankie Laine, twelve-year-old singer Little Jimmy Boyd, a circus act from Bulgaria, and Babe Didrikson Zaharias, regarded by some as the greatest athlete and woman golfer of all time.

"Those of us who follow the exploits in sports of Babe Didrikson, Babe Didrikson Zaharias, we all of us felt just the same, we just felt beaten up, when we heard she'd been afflicted with the malignant growth that was to end her career," says the cadaverous-looking Sullivan, in his trademark cadence. "Then, in this most recent Tam O'Shanter tournament out in Chicago, she turned in the most amazing expedition. Exhibition. Ladies and gentlemen, Babe Didrikson Zaharias."

It is difficult today to overestimate Mrs. Zaharias's celebrity. The star of the 1932 Los Angeles Olympics, she finished first and set world records in all three events she entered, the high jump, high hurdles, and javelin. [*Editor's note: Zaharias won only two gold medals. She finished second in the high jump due to a technicality.*] Extroverted and uninhibited, Mrs. Zaharias helped cure the U.S. of its Depression depression. After the Olympics, she seemingly tried every sport and won in every game she tried, especially golf. When the WPGA was reorganized into the LPGA, in 1950, she won five of the eleven tournaments held that year.

Even more endearing was the courage she showed in coming back from cancer surgery, in 1953. Her recovery was followed breathlessly: VEGETABLES NEXT, ran a headline in the Houston paper after her surgery; under that, BABE WALKS, EATS FIRST SOLID FOOD. And later, BABE TAKES RIDE, NOW FEELS BETTER. She finished third in her first tournament (the Tam O'Shanter, referred to by Sullivan) just four months after her first operation; she would win the U.S. Women's Open the next year, in 1954—by twelve strokes.

So the Sullivan show audience was surely hoping for nothing more than just to see the Babe and hear her twang, "Howdy, and thanks for the get-well wishes." Instead, they witnessed her national debut as a musician. Now here was something else Mrs. Zaharias could play—the harmonica.

Holding her inexpensive M. Hohner Marine Band Model #1896 (key of C) in her left hand, she blows out a peppy version of "Begin the Beguine." With considerable flair, she cups her right hand over the mouth organ to produce "wah-wah" and tremolo effects. The audience is impressed, and Sullivan asks for an encore, this time with vocal and guitar accompaniment from Betty Dodd, Babe's golf and music protégée, and a vocal from Little Jimmy Boyd. Little Jimmy is a Howdy Doody look-alike, a kid with freckles, a flannel shirt, and a hit—"I Saw Mommy Kissing Santa Claus." The trio performs "Little Train A-Chuggin'."

After the show, a representative from Chicago-based Mercury Records approaches Mrs. Zaharias and Miss Dodd. Would you two like to cut a record for us? Without hesitation, the two budding country-music stars say yes, we sure would.

"Babe really had a lot of talent on that harmonica," says Miss Dodd, now a teaching professional at the Fort Sam Houston Golf Course in San Antonio, her hometown. "She had her own style. Played her own sharps and flats. But we had to keep buying her new harmonicas. She'd blow 'em out." The Babe, in other words, was such a powerful harmonica player, the reeds inside her Hohner would collapse after only a few tunes.

The Babe began playing harmonica when she was growing up in Beaumont, Texas. She became good at it because she never did anything casually. "All my life, I've always had the urge to do things better than anyone else," she wrote in her autobiography, *This Life I've Led.* She first entertained an audience soon after her Olympic triumph as the headliner in a short-lived but successful vaudeville-style stage show in Chicago. Babe sang a song or two, played the harmonica, told a few jokes, and ran on a treadmill. "I love a gallery," she said. But she quit the stage after a week—she wanted to play golf.

"Right after the Sullivan show we went to Chicago," Betty Dodd recalls. "But they [Mercury] didn't want us to do anything we knew. They wanted us to pick from a list of amateur recordings. We listened to dozens of them over several days.

"Babe finally said, 'I'm playing "Detour" on one side.' And she did."

BABE EMBARKS ON HILL-BILLY MUSICAL CAREER, reported UPI the next day: "The professional golf queen from Texas made her 'country tune' recordings for Mercury Records yesterday on a 60-cent mouth organ . . . Babe played the harmonica while Betty Dodd sang 'I Felt a Little Teardrop' . . ."

The Zaharias-Dodd single wasn't a Top Ten hit—"I only heard it once on a San Antonio country-western station," Miss Dodd says—but it wasn't their last recording. They cut another disk in Los Angeles some months later "for no purpose other than we wanted to, and someone could do it." Babe and Betty did "Begin the Beguine" and "Detour" this time. A bored musician/technician assigned to help in the recording session suddenly perked up when he heard Babe play, Betty remembers. "So you know this woman is playing a cheap harmonica and making her own sharps and flats?" he said.

Babe and Betty appeared on *The George Jessel Show* in 1954—"Babe did a few numbers with Jerry Murad and the Harmonicats,"

Miss Dodd remembers—and that was the end of their career together as musicians. But it was not the end of music in their lives.

Babe Zaharias won her last tournament, the Peach Blossom Classic, in Spartanburg, South Carolina, on May 1, 1955. Her illness came back; she needed more surgery in 1956. Over a period of more than year when she was largely bedridden, Miss Dodd—and her guitar—were the Babe's constant companions. "We got closer, closer, and closer," Betty says. "Ninety percent of the time she was in the hospital, George [Babe's husband] wasn't there. He didn't want to fool with it.

"I used to play for her. I didn't necessarily want to play . . . she wanted to hear a lot of ballads, like 'I Gave My Love a Cherry.'

"The last time I played for her, I played some rock 'n' roll, some Elvis stuff. 'Blue Suede Shoes.' She loved it."

The Babe died on September 27, 1956.

Wrong Image But the Right Touch

Barry McDermott

Sports Illustrated, *July 25, 1983*

On the bus, cutting across the lower midsection of the United States, the mother and daughter were awed as the land changed from flat, dry Texas plains into the lush spring landscape of Louisiana and Mississippi. The journey was full of magic. It was also scary, because it led to an uncertain future. Forty-two hours on a Greyhound bus. Round-trip fare: $62.40. Odessa, Texas, to the Titleholders Championship in Augusta, Georgia.

When the Whitworths, Dama and her eighteen-year-old daughter, Kathy, arrived in Augusta on that March day in 1958, they caught their breath and then hailed a cab for the old Bon Air Hotel, a huge white structure that to these visitors from Jal, New Mexico, seemed the biggest, swankiest place in the world. Later they would discover the heat wasn't working. After registering, they walked out back. There stood Betsy Rawls and Mickey Wright, two giants of women's professional golf who had played an exhibition against Kathy and didn't regard her as pro material. "What in the world are you doing here?" Wright exclaimed. Kathy Whitworth wondered the same thing.

Now, a quarter of a century later, Whitworth will, in all likelihood, do something one of these weeks that will put her name in the record book in bigger type than those of Rawls or Wright. She'll win a tournament somewhere, and it will be the eighty-fifth victory of her pro career, tops for any woman, or man, in history. At present the forty-three-year-old Whitworth's eighty-four titles tie her with Sam Snead, another hero from rural-route America, for the most wins regardless of sex. She almost got No. 85 in early June, when she was in a playoff at the Rochester Invitational in Pittsford, New York, but she was beaten on the third extra hole.

Whitworth turned pro in 1959 during the dark ages of the LPGA; she was a small-town girl in a small-time sport. Now she's a small-town lady in a big-time sport. Golf has changed, but Whitworth hasn't. She's still Dama and Morris's girl from Jal, a community of 2,675 in a bleak landscape. In Jal the back of a man's neck pretty much reflects whether he does an honest day's work.

Golf fans don't hear a whole lot about Whitworth these days. In the jazzed-up LPGA of the '80s, she has the wrong image. She's not willowy, or young, or colorful. Black-and-white is her favorite color scheme. She doesn't have bizarre love affairs or throw tantrums. But she still wins: four victories and $415,572 in the last two-and-a-half years. She's fourth on the LPGA's 1983 money list with $143,937. "Back in the old days, it took ten years for someone to know your name," says Whitworth. "You could win twenty-five tournaments and nobody cared. Now, if you win the right one, you can be an instant star."

Whitworth has always had the stats for stardom but has managed to avoid the role for a lot of reasons: because no one was watching back when she joined the LPGA, because she was shy, because she does what she does for motives dear only to her. She never has excited the public.

She has a matter-of-fact way—her vocabulary is laced with country expressions like "sashay," "I reckon," and "mosey." The only endorsement she ever did was a Colgate-Palmolive television commercial promoting the detergent Axion. But with her down-home twang, it kept coming out "Ass-eon." Says Judy Rankin, another LPGA veteran, "Some people are never meant for stardom, even if they are the star type."

And Whitworth was the star type out on the course. When she was good, she was very, very good. Only Wright could touch her. In eight of nine years from '65 to '73, Whitworth was the tour's leading money-winner. But some other good players, for example, Marlene Hagge, were also lucky. They were pretty. Every year Hagge would win something called the Best Dressed Award, a euphemism for most beautiful, and get a lot more attention than Whitworth.

"It's not necessary for people to know you," Whitworth says. "The record itself speaks. That's all that really matters. Anyway, I don't know of any other thing I'd like to do or enjoy as much."

There have been two major disappointments in Whitworth's life. One she can do something about: Just as Snead somehow never won the U.S. Open, Whitworth has never been the U.S. Women's Open champion. The other item is tougher: Whitworth always wanted to be married and have kids, but that's a course she never could handle. "Back when I had my chances, it was something you just didn't do," she recalls. "I wanted to be a golfer, the best I could be, and marriage and golf didn't mix."

Whitworth is on the practice tee, down at the end, where distractions are fewer. To stay one up on golf over the years, she has put in the hours, and a spectator can see the rhythmic, exact results. Whitworth still hits the ball as well as ever. Only occasionally does an odd hook creep in. When it does, she gives a little jump, as if she has seen a snake.

One hand on her hip, the other leaning on her driver, Whitworth waits. She's out of balls, but walking toward her down the line of golfers is a young attendant carrying a huge basket of them. Whitworth is at last April's CPC International at Hilton Head Island, South Carolina, and up near the lead as usual.

Halfway down the line, the boy pauses by a young player. She has that up-to-date LPGA look: cute, with silky hair. The boy asks her if she needs any practice balls and they begin a little flirting. Whitworth waits, watching. After a minute or so, the boy picks up his basket. Whitworth raises her hand, beckoning, and her mouth opens, probably to say "Thank you" to him. But the boy turns and walks the other way.

Whitworth is standing there, arm up, mouth agape. Someone else might have started screaming, "Hey, stupid, can't you see that I need some balls? I've only won more tournaments than the rest of the people here put together, and the bimbo you've been talking to is never going to win even one." Instead, Whitworth gives an imperceptible sigh and then sashays over to another pile of balls about twenty yards away, scoops them up, and carries them back to her workbench.

A moment later, an old caddie walks up and watches her swing. "Kathy," he says, "you got where you are through hard work." Says Whitworth, "Yeah, but after all these years, you'd think it would be easier."

Harvey Penick wears a hearing aid and walks with a cane. His skin is mottled, an angry combination of red, brown, and white patches, the result of being out in a searing Texas sun for all of his seventy-eight years. And he's bent into a question mark because of a back that simply wore out, probably from teeing up too many golf balls. Penick started as a caddie at the Country Club of Austin when he was six. His mother made him wait until then. Later he became the golf pro, and his record as a teacher has made him a legend. Ben Crenshaw and Tom Kite grew up "taking" from him, and he wears a watch the back of which is inscribed BETSY-MICKEY-BETSY, as in Rawls, Wright, and Cullen. Penick says he has seen more golf balls hit than anyone. Until '75, he charged $5 for a lesson. His current rate: $15.

Penick has been Whitworth's teacher since she was a teenager. Hardy Loudermilk, the pro in Jal, realized he had a potential champion and called Penick. "I've taken her as far as I can," he said. "Will you work with her?" Dama and her daughter would drive the 420 miles to Austin. Kathy was a lot different back then. She was a big, heavyset girl, strong as could be. Penick liked several things about her. She was a terrific putter. "The ball would die true," he recalls. And she worked. Dama sat patiently and copied down what Penick said. Then they would drive back to Jal and the little nine-hole course hacked out of the mesquite and sand dunes, and Kathy would get down to business. Says Wright, "Probably the smartest thing she ever did was stick with Harvey. He always could tell her the word or phrase that would snap her out of a slump." Penick says, "She's been mighty faithful."

That's an apt word for Whitworth—faithful. To her family, to her town, to her coach, and to her game. She's had the same putter for twenty-one years—and most of her friends just as long. They don't seem to wear out. But most of all, Whitworth is true to a set of principles: Be gracious but guard your time; it's more precious than money. Don't forget your roots. Remember favors, and pay them back. Be generous. And let your clubs do your talking.

Asked what it is that has made Kathy so successful, the parents have different answers. "Luck," says Morris. But Dama sets her jaw. "Determination," says she. When Kathy, who started playing golf at fifteen, using a set of clubs that had belonged to her deceased grandfather, won her first amateur tournament at seventeen, officials offered her a choice: a beautiful turquoise necklace or a trophy. "I'll take the trophy," said Kathy.

Actually, neither mother nor father thinks it extraordinary that the youngest of their three daughters would come out of a small frame house at 629 S. Fourth Street, learn the game on a primitive nine-hole course where the rain shelters are lime-green fiberglass sheds and where the ground is baked hard by June and is almost barren by August—and then go on to dominate a sport in which the best player wins only sometimes. "We always have a pretty positive attitude when we start something," Morris says. "It's hard not to make it with a positive attitude. You can't walk on water with one foot on the bank."

Kathy won the '57 women's state tournament, and the following spring an invitation to the Titleholders Championship in Augusta arrived. The tournament then was the equivalent of the women's Masters, right down to a green jacket for the champion, although it was played not at the Augusta National Golf Club but at the Augusta Country Club next door. Neither Kathy nor Dama had any clue what the Titleholders was, but an invitation was an invitation. "We thought it meant you had to go," Dama recalls.

Two things stick in Dama's mind from that tournament. No caddie wanted to carry Kathy's golf bag, a pitiful, scrawny plaid model from her father's store. And her daughter finished almost last. A few years later, when Kathy returned to the tournament as a pro, she employed the same caddie she had used in her debut in Augusta. Faithful. "She went on to win that green jacket twice, in '65 and '66," says Dama. "And I treasure those jackets more than any other trophies."

When Whitworth joined the tour, fresh from dropping out of Odessa (Texas) Junior College, she wasn't much of a golfer. Her credentials included a couple of New Mexico state titles, and Wright gently advised her to remain an amateur and go on with college.

During a rookie season in which her scoring average was a big fat 80 and her earnings were $1,217 in twenty-six tournaments, Whitworth went home and said she wanted to quit. She was testing her support. Dama, Morris, and Loudermilk, who had kicked in with financial backing, sat around the kitchen table and talked sense into her. Said Morris, "Save yourself those tears."

"When I came back to the tour later that season," Kathy remembers, "I said, 'Well, self-pity isn't going to get it. If you're going to be out here, you might as well start working at it and see what you can do.' I practiced and I watched. I'd go to the practice tee and sit and study Patty Berg and Louise Suggs and Mickey Wright, watch 'em like a hawk." About that time she gave her parents a bottle of champagne. "We'll open this when I win my first tournament," she said.

It wasn't until 1962 that she popped the cork, upon winning on the last hole of a tournament in Baltimore. The following year Whitworth won eight tournaments, and she got to feeling pretty good about herself. She had dropped about fifty pounds. She had money to spend. And she had proved herself in golf and no longer was a hick nobody.

But in 1964 she suddenly lost it. By the time the tour reached San Antonio toward the end of the year, she hadn't won a tournament. Berg had a saying: "It's not how fast you get there, it's how long you stay." Whitworth, it seemed, was a flash in the pan.

Loudermilk had by then moved to San Antonio, and Whitworth had dinner with him and moaned to him about her season of bad luck. Her old pro looked her in the eye. "Did it ever occur to you that you have the big head?" he asked.

"Well, I was destroyed," Whitworth recalls. "But of course he was right. It was one of the great lessons of my life."

Whitworth won the tournament in San Antonio. And in the next five years she won forty-two more, assumed a leadership role in the LPGA and became its president in 1971, and twice was named the Associated Press Woman Athlete of the Year. She also was influential in the making of one of the LPGA's biggest decisions. In 1969 the players ousted executive director Leonard Wirtz, a strong-willed man who ran the organization, more or less, from the trunk of his car. Wirtz was good for the tour. He gave it backbone, but his autocratic style terrified most of the players.

By dismissing Wirtz, many of the players probably were standing up to a man for the first time. "It taught us a lesson," Whitworth says. "No one is indispensable." Aided by corporate money from firms such as Colgate and an infusion of young talent from the colleges, where Title IX was taking effect, women's golf took off during the 1970s, but Whitworth receded into the background.

In 1973 she decided that she just didn't want to push anymore. "My nerves were completely shot," she says. "I shook so bad in the last tournament of the year that I couldn't sign my scorecard. I knew then that if I didn't back off, I'd burn out. That was hard to face."

So Whitworth eased off on herself, but even operating at a kind of mental half-throttle, she continued to be a power on the tour, picking up an occasional win, though '73 was her last year as No. 1 on the money list. Then in '79 and '80 she hit a real slump—two years without a victory, two years of snap-hook ground balls into the left rough. If there was a time to quit, it was then. Whitworth finished thirtieth, then twenty-fourth, on the money list. "I was fighting for my life," she says. "I got real depressed. Scared might be a better word to use." Finally, she went back to Austin to see the old man with the cane. Penick just shook his head. Whitworth's swing looked okay—until she hit the ball. "Let's try and get back to your old swing," said Penick. "It never was classical, but it was sound. Purty is as purty does."

Whitworth went home and practiced for two months. Slowly, the old feeling returned. And in the middle of 1981 in the Coca-Cola Classic in Ridgewood, New Jersey, she birdied three of the last four holes, then birdied the second hole of a playoff to win the tournament. It was victory No. 81, and the thrill was the same as it always had been. That week she received a letter from Wright, who had eighty-two career victories. It said, "Don't settle for just eighty-one." Nos. 82 and 83 came last year. No. 84 she won this March.

For fifteen years Whitworth has lived in Dallas, where reading and housework—"therapy," she calls it—are her only hobbies, and where she has a closet full of long gowns, which she wears when she goes out to dinner or appears at a charity affair. "I look pretty good all spiffed up," Whitworth says with a smile. She has made only a couple of concessions to the times and her lofty stature in golf. She has incorporated herself, and she's thinking seriously of buying a Mercedes.

There's no question that Whitworth loves the tour life. The other players kid her about playing an orange ball, about her age, and about her hair, a semibouffant style that would stand up well in a New Mexico sandstorm. "No strand ever moves," says Debbie Massey incredulously. Whitworth thinks back to her high-school days when she played the bass drum in the band. During practice each musician would perform singly. "Alone we sounded terrible, but put us all together and it was just great," she says. The tour is like that. It has a sense of community that Whitworth would have a hard time finding elsewhere.

Recently, she was asked why she doesn't want to be an LPGA officer anymore. It's better that way, she said, because it gives the reins of leadership to the younger women. "It's not my tour anymore," she added. Of course, she was wrong about that, but she was right about something else. Someone asked her what she would choose as an epitaph. "I held my age well," she replied with no hesitation at all.

Betsy Rawls

Harvey Penick

from Harvey Penick's Little Red Book

Betsy Rawls came to the University of Texas out of high school with a very strong grip. She was a talented player who loved golf, and I began gradually to change her grip. Betsy improved fast and won the city tournament in Austin, followed by the state championship.

I taught her that she must learn to play on all kinds of courses—good and bad—with all different sorts of people. I learned a lot from Betsy in return. She was a Phi Beta Kappa in physics.

One thing I learned from Betsy was that you don't win a tournament with good golf shots only. There are many more things of importance, and they grow even more important when you start playing against the whole world.

Betsy could choose a club and have confidence it was right with no indecision. The same applied once she decided on the type of shot—pitch or chip, hook or fade, whatever.

She knew the person in the best physical shape had the advantage, especially on the last day of a tournament. She kept herself in top shape, always ate a healthy and correct diet.

Betsy had the ability to walk over and say hello to someone in the gallery and then return to her shot with total concentration. We discussed whether it was best for me as a coach to apply pressure, or just let the player know I was interested in improvement, and I took her advice in relation to other players I coached as well as Betsy herself.

I learned from Betsy not to give a pupil too many things to think about in one lesson. One day I was teaching her two or three things at once. She said, "Harvey, let's learn one or two things this week and save the third thing for next week."

That was a real lesson for me. If a Phi Beta Kappa and talented golfer like Betsy can't concentrate on more than two things at once, what chance would an ordinary student have?

This became a cornerstone of my teaching—one thing at a time.

Betsy won four U.S. Women's Opens and made the Hall of Fame. A major intercollegiate women's tournament, named for her, is played every year in Austin.

She was an ideal pupil. She had good common sense and the willpower to make any shot that was important, whether it was a drive or a putt.

Fading Fame

Ed Hinton and Mark Stewart

Sports Illustrated, *May 6, 1996*

Betty Jameson is standing amid a still life of her past, a lovely clutter of precious things yellowed, brown, brittle—sepia tones in an otherwise sunny living room in Delray Beach, Florida. She was a golf prodigy by age twelve on the sand-greens courses of Texas during the Depression, then twice U.S. Amateur champion with a perfect swing but a fitful putter, then an unabashed pro at twenty-five in a time when the term was frowned on, then a pioneer and glamour girl of the LPGA with ten tour wins, including the 1947 U.S. Open title, then a charter member, at age thirty-two in 1951, of the LPGA Hall of Fame. But Jameson stands now, at seventy-six, perhaps forty pounds thinner than she should be, on the brink of homelessness in a house that is not legally hers but, she says, "is me."

The only semblance of order is by the fireplace, where her seven favorite golf clubs stand. Away from the hearth in all directions is a jumble of photographs, letters, calendars, clippings, books, paintings, sketches, easels, brushes, palettes . . . and, especially, some pottery and pictures and diaries of her late great friend, another early LPGA star, Mary Lena Faulk.

Mary Lena. Jameson does not just say the name, she nearly sings it: "MaryLEENah." For more than thirty years, in this house, "we lived beautifully."

Then last year Faulk suffered a recurrence of lung cancer and fell gravely ill and incoherent with an awful suddenness that caught the two admitted procrastinators unprepared. She died last August 3, at sixty-nine. Faulk was the one who had attended to most of the household financial matters. The house was in her name, and she had not gotten around to revising her will to provide for Jameson. The will, drawn up in 1981, left the house and all of Faulk's financial interests, mainly stocks and bonds, to blood relatives, primarily a niece.

So here stands Bess—"She called me Bess," says Betty—amid this marvelous mess. She could be sent packing any day on short notice to God knows where, should Faulk's relatives invoke the harshest application of Florida law. Her monthly Social Security check is $246, which doesn't even cover the storage bills for her paintings and golf clubs. Since Faulk passed away, Jameson has lost close to forty pounds ("At least," says a friend) off a once athletic five-foot-eight-inch frame—

"My, you're a big girl," Babe Didrikson Zaharias remarked when they met long ago. Jameson's gauntness is due to a lack of interest in food, she says; due to lack of grocery money, friends think.

"When friends say to me, 'Well, Betty, you've got to apply for food stamps. You deserve them,' I say, 'No. I don't want to talk to you anymore.' I won't do that."

At the moment she has, to her name, "forty dollars, I think," the last of the $700 she got for parting with two of her precious paintings. The LPGA has found a way to help—with an advance check on proceeds from the pro-am before this week's Sprint Titleholders Championship.

But none of that promises to secure this house for her, and moving would be devastating: "I can't imagine not living in this house," she says. But she will not think about that now. Besides, "this is a bad dream—the whole thing," she maintains, true to the chronic state of reverie that has never let her take life hard, in nearly seventy-seven years of living it. To have planned and run the household more pragmatically "wouldn't have been us, I guess," she says. "We just lived for the day."

She stops among her paintings to say a lot about herself: "This is my portrait of Samuel Beckett. It reminds me, in ways, of Tommy Armour." Such are the connections in a mind wherein golf imitates art and art, golf; and life is largely an interval for savoring both.

Suddenly she is reading aloud from her beloved T. S. Eliot—specifically from "Burnt Norton," first of the *Four Quartets*—in a volume Eliot personally inscribed for her on April 24, 1958. ("It was," she recalls, "a wet day.") In a voice that is half knowing old woman, half breathless girl, she gasps:

> What might have been and what has been
> Point to one end, which is always present.

This is both admonition and solace ringing down the years to her from her favorite poet. A few lines later he is telling her what is being done to her life, and her voice grasps the meaning with certainty:

But to what purpose
Disturbing the dust on a bowl of rose-leaves
I do not know.

Is that it, Betty? Is that what they are doing to you, these unanticipated intruders so foreign to your reverie: law, finance, inheritance, harsh truths of kindred blood over kindred spirit?

"Yeah, yeah," she says. "Oh, yeah." Thus disturbed, the dust may as well be blown from this lovely clutter, this bowl of rose-leaves, these several thousand memories in photographs and letters and clippings.

Here's a photo of the LPGA Hall of Fame's charter members, previously known as the Big Four—Betty and Babe, Patty Berg, Louise Suggs.

Babe. What a character. Babe and Betty were on a U.S. women's team that went to England in 1951 and defeated not only the British women but also a top team of amateur men. "Babe said to Leonard Crawley, who was both an excellent amateur and a renowned golf journalist, 'I'll play you for your mustache,' " recalls Jameson. "I have no idea what she wagered against it. But his big walrus mustache was all him, all his identity. And their bet was that if he lost, he had to shave it off. She beat him badly, and he was gone—disappeared. Babe never found him. 'Play you for your mustache.' That was Babe. So braggadocious, so entertaining because she always delivered on what she said. She was Muhammad Ali, all the way, many years before.

"Driving between tournaments, she might see a golf course and stop and say, 'Let's go out there and give these guys a treat. Let's play a few holes. Wait'll they learn who stopped here.'

"One Sunday morning, I think it was in Indianapolis, we were sitting around and I said, 'I'm going to church. Would anybody like to join me?' Everybody looked at one another. Babe said, 'Oh, what the hell, let's all go to church.' Off we went. On the way up the steps Babe said, 'Hey, can we smoke in this place?'"

That was the sort of Bette Davis–Lauren Bacall–tweed-slacks world

Jameson lived in. Then, "sometime in the late forties," she happened upon another world entirely, in the deepest South, south Georgia. "Thomasville was an angelic little town," she says. "I went in the spring. The dogwood was in bloom all over town, and of course it was the Rose City, and it was a special little environment, with all the plantation people."

It was the first and last time she would feel welcome there, in the hometown of the Tomboy from Thomasville, as sportswriters dubbed Faulk. At the time, says Jameson, "I was just a fan of hers. You know, you'd pick an amateur, or somebody [up-and-coming] that you were watching."

Their friendship didn't flower until 1961 when Jameson, somewhat impromptu, coached Faulk to the Western Open title.

"Psychologically I helped her," recalls Jameson. "I talked to her every day. And she marched through that tournament, won it. That's when I first got to know her. I don't remember what I said. It was just something." But when Thomasville celebrated Faulk's triumphant homecoming, "they never asked me," says Jameson. "The family never welcomed me. Mr. Faulk [Mary Lena's father] was rather brusque, and Mrs. Faulk was never—I don't know—tolerating."

The Faulk family "thought I was, I guess, maybe too domineering," says Jameson. "I don't know why. But I did not care. I didn't find them that interesting, for one thing. If I'd found them that interesting, I could have had a little set-to: 'Why? What's going on here?' But I had lots of other things on my mind. And certainly Mary Lena, when she got out from under there . . . it would have been very hard for her to live with her family and stay down in Thomasville after she'd been around. She was interested in cultural things, like I was, and that's why I was attracted to her. She was writing poetry when I first met her on the tour."

> But to what purpose
> Disturbing the dust on a bowl of rose-leaves

"We didn't like talking about death," says Jameson, "but over the years Mary Lena assured me I'd be taken care of, that I'd have a place to live and money to live on."

"The estate was opened, and Betty got nothing, despite spending more than thirty years with Mary Lena," says Bill Layton, the attorney who is representing Jameson, on contingency, in civil litigation. "The basis of the litigation is breach of contract. There was an oral agreement. Florida statutes say that sharing a house is evidence of some kind of agreement. As it stands, eviction proceedings could begin on three days' notice, because she has no lease and nothing in writing."

"The heirs offered [Jameson] a settlement to keep her in the house for two years, but she filed a suit to keep what I'd call a widow's portion of the estate," says John Ross Adams, an attorney who represents Jane Watt, who is Faulk's sister and executor of the will, and, indirectly, Kate Sedgwick of Washington, D.C., who is Faulk's niece and the sole beneficiary. "In California, [Jameson] might have a case, but I don't think she does in Florida. California is much more advanced in terms of palimony. I've had no pleasure in handling this case. I don't think the niece wants to evict her, but she doesn't want to support her for the rest of her life, either."

"The Faulk family," Layton alleges, "is basically representing Betty as a housekeeper."

"You've got to be kidding?" says Sally Iglehart, who has known Jameson and Faulk since they moved to Delray Beach in 1964. "No. That's insanity." Iglehart, widow of polo hall of famer Stewart Iglehart, laughs out loud. "I mean, you've been to the house!" The lovely clutter. "If anybody was a semblance of a housekeeper, it had to be Mary Lena. Mary Lena did all the cooking. The farmer and the artist, I always called them. Mary Lena liked to dig up the backyard and plant flowers and vegetables. And Betty was the abstract intellect. Never in my wildest dreams could I ever believe that Mary Lena would have wanted Betty to be left like this."

Here is a photo of Betty at maybe forty-four, but still the glamour girl, blond with the quintessential Pepsodent smile. ("I've had some trouble with my teeth lately, and the dental bills—they called me the other day and said, 'Ms. Jameson, if you could just pay five dollars . . .'") In the photo she is leaning over the shoulder of Mary Lena, who is sitting, legs crossed, maybe thirty-eight at the time but still youthful, wide-eyed. This was circa 1963, when they decided to share a house and settled at first in Southern Pines, North Carolina, where they opened a sportswear shop together and immediately, merrily, failed at it.

When friends offered them a better location at Pinehurst, Jameson recalls, "we said, 'No, thanks, we're going south to Delray Beach.' " There on the sweet spot of the Gold Coast, between Palm Beach and Fort Lauderdale, they settled and went to work as teaching pros. Jameson first worked at Delray Beach Country Club—where Armour, her close friend and guru since 1938, held court and taught, gratis, in his later years—and then at the very exclusive Gulf Stream Golf Club.

So, for a long time the household was two-income, but "I was never as well-versed at making money as Mary Lena," says Jameson. Faulk also had inherited money and left a stock portfolio Jameson estimates at "maybe two hundred thousand dollars, maybe more. I don't know."

She dismisses the matter with a sort of grooved gesture of her left hand, still the one-handed perpetual practice swing of the pro, and still, in her case, the perfect swing. Here's a picture—shot by a friend—of Betty on a practice tee in Texas "four or five years ago." She was in her early seventies, and behind her, by coincidence, Kathy Whitworth was hitting. They happened to hit at the same moment, and both women's finishes were caught in the photo. They are identical, one the mirror of the other.

Here's the little diary Mary Lena kept of her last trip abroad, to Greece. In her meticulous hand, it opens on her day of departure: "Bye, Poppy [her dog]. Bye, house. Bye, flowers. Bye, Bess."

"When she traveled, she would never stay with friends or family—always in a hotel, where she could smoke," says Jameson. After Faulk's illness was first diagnosed as lung cancer ten years ago, the removal of part of one lung appeared to arrest the disease. "She gallantly tried to kick the habit but couldn't," says Jameson.

Here's one of Mary Lena tan-faced, healthy, impish, beaming from beneath the floppy old straw hat she wore while gardening.

"She looked like Mahatma Gandhi at the end," says Jameson. So weak and confused was Faulk that "when they [relatives] asked her, 'Do you want to be buried or cremated?' MaryLEENah . . ." Here Jameson, who is standing, bends double with resounding grief, and gasps, "MaryLEENah said, 'I want to be buried and I want Will Watt [a nephew] to sprinkle my ashes behind the sixth green at Glen Arven [Thomasville's turn-of-the-century course].' And two days later . . . she . . . died. In those last days she was so weak she couldn't talk, only whisper: 'Is this . . . the way . . . it is?'"

And now in the predawn hours, when Betty Jameson indulges in her one luxury of each day, a sausage-biscuit and coffee at McDonald's, she is disturbed by what she sees: "Every morning there is a woman sleeping on a bench outside. I see her and I wonder what she does, where she goes from there."

But she cannot imagine herself in that position, for surely this is all a bad dream, disturbing the dust on a bowl of rose-leaves.

Our Daughter Sandra

Harvey Penick

from For All Who Love the Game

Sandra Palmer is like another daughter to Helen and me. As is the case with a number of my friends and pupils, I met Sandra because of Betsy

Rawls. Sandra was teaching school in Fort Worth when Betsy phoned and asked me if I would take a look.

Sandra drove to Austin every Friday afternoon and back to Fort Worth every Sunday night for a year afterward. She never missed a weekend. Summer vacation she spent with us.

I told her to walk and carry her bag whenever she played golf. She needed to build strength in her legs to create more power and hit the ball farther.

One day, I was giving a lesson to Governor Allan Shivers at our club on Riverside Drive, and we saw little Sandra struggling with her big red leather golf bag on her back.

Governor Shivers said, "That girl needs to be riding in a cart."

I said, "No sir, she needs to be getting stronger."

The governor looked at me and said, "Harvey, would you want your own daughter out there carrying a huge bag like that?"

I said, "No sir, I guess not."

I sent a cart for Sandra. But when she came in after her round, I pulled her aside and said, "Go in the shop and pick out a little carry bag and use that around here from now on. I want you walking, not riding."

After a year with Helen and me, Sandra went on the pro tour. Nowadays most young women join the pro tour after a career of playing in tournaments on their college golf teams. They already know a lot about competition. But Sandra had to learn to play golf on the tour against the best in the game. It was a rough introduction.

Sandra would phone often from tournament sites around the country. I recall once she called and said, "Harvey, help me. I am skying my tee shots."

I asked her, "How many?"

She said, "I did it four times today."

I said, "I bet you missed more putts than you did drives."

That put her mind where it needed to be.

She phoned the night before she won the U.S. Open. She needed reassurance.

I told her, "Are you just wishing to win, or do you really have that desire?"

"I have the desire," she said.

I said, "Then let God's hand rest on your shoulder, and if it's your turn to win, you will."

Those are the swing thoughts to carry with you for a lifetime.

Part Six

Characters, Legends, and Lore

Dave Williams's Houston Dynasty

Mickey Herskowitz

Golf Digest, *May 1987*

Never mind that Dave Williams has dominated his sport more than John Wooden or Bear Bryant did theirs. What makes his record so unusual, aside from the fact that hardly anyone outside the Southwest, or college golf circles, ever heard of him, is the way he did it.

To begin with, no coach ever started later or brought less to a job than Williams and carried it farther. He was twenty-six before he played the sport he coaches. He was never much more than a high-seventies shooter up to the day he put away his clubs, seven years ago, when he says he realized: "My score didn't count."

At a school where longevity is the rule, he has outlasted everybody. You must understand that the University of Houston is to college sports what St. Petersburg, Florida, is to shuffleboard. Bill Yeoman held the football job for twenty-five years. Guy Lewis lasted thirty in basketball. And Dave Williams at sixty-eight, on the job since 1952, is still going strong after thirty-five years.

He has been called "The Father of College Golf" and he may have coined the phrase himself. This smiling, beefy man who teaches Sunday school, likes to pick a guitar, and favors loud shirts and a panama hat may not strike you as intense or driven, but he is both.

Most simply put, Dave Williams is the most successful college golf coach who ever lived. To begin with, there are the sixteen national titles his University of Houston teams have won, the first in 1956. Think of it: The Cougars have averaged a national title every other year for thirty-two years. Of course Dave has been a record-setter since he was a kid back in Hunt County, Texas.

"I was the best cotton-picker the county ever had," he says, proudly. "I was in high school when I set the one-day record. Picked five hundred seventy-nine pounds and ran out of cotton with two hours of daylight left. Always wished we hadn't run out. I could have gotten seven hundred pounds, easy.

"That's still the record, and no one will ever break it. People don't pick cotton anymore."

Over the past thirty-five years, Dave Williams has coached golf the way he picked cotton. No one told him how to load the truck. He just loaded it. And he proceeds as though he's afraid he might run out of light.

If you ever wondered what Rex Baxter, John Mahaffey, Dave Marr, Keith Fergus, Bill Rogers, Kermit Zarley, Jacky Cupit, Homero Blancas, Bruce Lietzke, Phil Rodgers, Jay Sigel, Fuzzy Zoeller, Fred Couples, and Ed Fiori have in common, the answer is a snap: All played college golf at the University of Houston under Dave Williams. They didn't always like it, but they played.

How this program began, how the tradition grew and the sport flourished, is the stuff of only-in-America. Part of it, maybe most of it, has to do with the kind of person Williams is. A superb organizer and motivator, he worries about his players the way some people worry about the hungry orphans of the world.

"Of all the hundreds of players I have coached," he says, "I've only had one—I won't tell you his name—who never has been able to make much of a living. He can't hold a job and he has had dozens of them.

Got a great personality and he's a great young man. Just can't keep a job. I worry about him more than all the rest, I guess."

A sometime lay preacher, Dave can find his orders in the Bible, in the parable of the ninety-nine sheep, and the one that went astray. "The Lord left the ninety-nine," he reminds you, "and went to find the one."

Whatever the perception of the Houston golf program around the country, adversity has always brought out the best in Dave's teams.

When Williams accepted his first teaching job in 1939, the year he graduated from East Texas State, his salary was $1,100 a year. "That was big money," he says. "With my first paycheck I went to Dallas and bought a car and the first three suits I ever owned. The local postman made about sixty-five dollars a month and he could've married anybody in Hunt County."

Today Dave Williams probably runs the only program in America where the golf team has ever contributed money to the football budget. Says Dave: "I don't like to hear that golf is a nonrevenue sport. You can get donations for a golf program, believe me. If I was an athletic director starting a new program, the first sport I'd put in would be golf. You're talking about a small squad. And you're talking about a sport that can bring a school a lot of attention."

The Cougar dynasty in golf has been the greatest in modern collegiate annals, surpassing USC in baseball and UCLA in basketball and . . . well, no one has been even close in football. The figures come at you like marbles falling down a rain pipe: national championships in each of four decades; five in a row from 1956 through 1960; eight individual titles; 393 team championships in twenty-four states; twenty-one Southwest Conference tournaments; seventy-one all-Americans, most recently Steve Elkington and Billy Ray Brown, in 1985.

For a fellow never noted as a teacher, Williams has won in different eras, with different types: rich kids and poor kids, some obedient and respectful, others free spirits and rebellious. Whatever went into the compactor, championship teams kept coming out.

He is a master recruiter who has relied almost entirely on the mails and postal service. Whether anyone believes it or not, he says he has made only about one trip a year to recruit a golfer, and has flown one in for a visit only once.

Although he carries the title "coach," Williams, in common with most college golf team coaches, doesn't teach his charges how to play the game. It is the job of the coach to get the best players on his team and then choose the right players for each tournament.

"I never saw him swing a club," says television commentator Jim Nantz, who was once a marginal member of the Cougars. "But he could qualify as a psychologist. He was great at reading people and knowing which players were just right for certain courses." Adds Ed Fiori: "He never taught us how to play. He just picked us up and made sure we got to the course on time. I always thought he would have made a great prizefight promoter."

Bob Kepler, the late Ohio State coach, once told Dave, "If you had called Jack Nicklaus one more time, he would have played for you instead of for me." The memory brings a grin to Williams's round face. "The thing is," he says, "I didn't *need* Nicklaus." And the truth is, he didn't.

Mike Holder, the Oklahoma State coach, remembers that in 1979 and '80, "Houston had the three best teams in the country. The five guys who made it and the ten who missed." . . .

. . . According to Williams, the frustrations of a golf coach are multiplied by eighteen once the match begins. Unlike his counterparts, there are no substitutions he can make, no time-outs he can call, no signals he can give for a timely maneuver that turns the tide of the game. Says Dave: "No other coach has to sweat as much as a golf coach. A baseball coach sweats for two hours and a football coach sweats for three. But a golf coach has to sweat for four days." . . .

. . . The winning began with Rex Baxter, an Amarillo schoolboy who wanted to attend college in Houston. He wrote three letters without arousing Williams's interest—until Williams overheard two coaches talking about him at the nationals. "He hadn't won anything. But I could tell by the tone of their voices, he was a stud. You get that inflection. That's how you know about a guy, the inflection.

"That summer I saw Rex qualify in Houston for the USGA Junior Amateur, and I never saw anybody hit a ball better, never in my whole life. Straight, never left or right. Wham, like that. I ran to [Houston's athletic director] Harry Fouke and said, 'I got to have Rex Baxter.' We had already used our three scholarships. But I said, 'If he wins the national junior will you give him a scholarship?'

"Fouke said sure, but he didn't think we'd ever get a national junior champion. Nobody from Texas ever won that. But Rex went through those matches like they were child's play. He came to Houston and that was the start of it.

"Rex thought he was the best and it rubbed off. Before a match I'd look at the other teams and they sure looked good to me. But Rex would say, 'These clowns can't play. We'll bring 'em to their knees.'

"In 1956, at Ohio State, he came to the last hole needing a par four to give us a tie for our first championship. On his second shot he was in the frog hair forty feet from the cup. He got out his putter and hit the ball. It looked like it was going to be four feet short, but it kept going and plopped right in the cup for a birdie. We had won a national championship for Houston. I'm telling you, everything broke loose. Richard Parvino jumped all over me. He put spike marks on Jim Hiskey's feet.

"John Brodie, the quarterback, was there playing for Stanford. He just turned and walked away, muttering, 'Those damned lucky Texans.'"

In one of the dozens of team photographs that adorn the office wall of Dave Williams is a group shot of the first of those sixteen national champions. The four players are all wearing light-colored sport coats—Baxter, Parvino, Hiskey, and Frank Wharton. All came from the closet of Rex Baxter. . . .

. . . The Cougar athletic department was flat broke in 1959, when Dave had to fight to save the golf program. "I wasn't going to have any budget at all," he says. "So I said I'd try to raise money through our tournament [the All-American Invitational]. We had to have a tournament that meant something, and it wasn't going to be easy. Dave Marr, Tommy Tyson, Monte Bradley, had all turned pro on me because college golf wasn't big enough for them.

"Well, we found out a funny thing: If you let everyone in free you get five mommas and daddies, but if you charge admission you get seven thousand people."

The Cougars sold sponsorships for $10; each sponsor received three badges and a brochure and a ticket to the banquet. Within five years they were clearing $20,000, more than the team's annual budget, and had the hottest tourney in college golf.

His office walls are so jammed with photographs no one can remember what the original color was. In one frame is a cartoon from *Ripley's Believe It or Not,* featuring a former Cougar star, Homero Blancas, from the 1962 team.

"What a team we had that year," Dave recalls. "Homero, Fred Marti, Kermit Zarley, Wright Garrett, and Mark Hopkins. Fred had a six-stroke lead with eighteen holes to go and shot sixty-six. Homero shot a fifty-five and won by five strokes.

"There it is, believe it or not. A record round of golf. A fifty-five. Didn't see it myself. Didn't have the money to go."

In the early years, Williams often bummed a ride with one of the parents, and whether he got to go depended on whether a baby brother or sister stayed home. For years the Cougars traveled seven to a car, in an old station wagon the players called the Blue Goose. Dave remembers warm, funny times, with the players napping on a mattress in the back or playing cards all the way to west Texas.

At one point, the players refused to let him drive unless he agreed to wear his glasses. This was after an incident in New Mexico, where he stopped to ask directions of one of those yellow wooden signs shaped like a traffic policeman. That was as close to a rebellion as the Cougar golf team has gotten in thirty-five years. . . .

. . . Not everyone enjoyed the Houston experience of playing for a coach who passed a rule forbidding a Cougar from complimenting an opponent on a good shot. "That's not the way I play the game," says Fuzzy Zoeller, who quit the program to make the tour on his own.

You get an unusual sense of Williams's roots, reading a biography of him, published in May 1986, by Kelly Williams, age eight, who happens to be his granddaughter. The opening sentence of the book, entitled *A Coach of Success,* is one of my favorite lines in all of literature: "One day a legend was born . . ."

We learn that Dave starred in football and basketball in high school and entered East Texas State at sixteen. Two years later he entered Texas A&M, supporting himself with five jobs. He returned home when his father died, graduated from East Texas State, earned a naval officer's commission in an accelerated engineering program in Maryland and, after the war, a masters degree from Houston. He was on the faculty there, teaching chemical engineering, when his brother, Noble, found an abandoned set of golf clubs in the attic.

"Noble and I needed some exercise. So I said we ought to take up this game of golf. We went to the Lack's Auto Store and bought two dozen golf balls and played at Glenbrook, which has lots of bayous. What we didn't hit in the water we cut. We lost all two dozen that morning. I said, 'Noble, let's buy another dozen and give it one more try.' We went back after lunch. By the fifth hole we had lost every ball but one, and I told Noble to get his putter out. He putted all the way in and said, 'That's it. Goodbye.' And he never played again.

"I stayed with it. Started playing at Hermann Park, and my first time out there the pro, Robie Williams, gave me a lesson on the tee. Someone said to me, once you learn how to play you won't hack up those balls so much. I said, 'Thank goodness. I didn't think I was going to be able to afford this game.'"

In 1951 Harry Fouke, Houston's athletic director, was also the part-time golf coach. One day Harry shot a 75, a score that beat every player on his team. Fouke decided the time had come to bring in another coach. By then Williams was a regular in one of his foursomes, and Harry—impressed by Dave's good humor and enthusiasm—offered him the job.

There was no salary, no home course, a total of two scholarships, and a losing streak that had reached twenty-five matches. But to Dave Williams this was the American Dream. . . .

. . . They introduced Dave as the new golf coach at Houston's spring sports banquet. "They asked me to say a few words," he recalls, "and I choked. So I said we were going to win the national championship." That prediction fractured them in the very narrow geographical area where Cougar athletics mattered at all. The school had not even competed in intercollegiate sports until 1946. The golf team was not even a member of the NCAA. On the campus, Dave had a derisive new nickname: "National Championship" Williams.

But the onetime sharecropper's son already had a role model. In the early 1950s, Fred Cobb had built a national power at North Texas State, with a team headed by Don January, Joe Conrad, and Billy Maxwell. Cobb had defied the U.S. Golf Association at the time by awarding college scholarships and had made enemies by winning four national titles.

"I was just getting started," recalls Williams, "and I would hear the other coaches running him down. They're saying, He's a sorry this and a sorry that. I thought, Boy, that's all right. He's winning; he's what I want to be. I idolized Fred Cobb. I didn't realize what they were talking about until I started winning myself. If you lose you're a dog, if you win too much you're a hog."

Over the years, Williams has heard all the accusations: The Cougars buy golfers, give them cars, and pass out scholarships as though they were M&M's. "When we started winning, even the people in Houston thought we were paying the players. We had been down among the ROYs—the rest of you's—so long they figured it was the only way possible. Well, I can remember when we slept seven to a room in Athens, Georgia, and one old boy snored so loud he kept half the team awake and we finished sixth. We ate on three dollars a day per boy. Mostly hamburgers. The football players would sneak our kids apples from the training table. Jim Hiskey and Rex Baxter always complained about how tight I was. They thought I was using psychology, trying to keep them hungry."

Every Christmas, Dave sends out a newsletter that brings up to date what each of his former players is doing. A rough count reveals that more than sixty are still either on the PGA Tour, connected with a club, or coaching in high school or college. Williams can flip through the names and on any page find a story or a laugh or a line to lump up the throat. . . .

. . . His standards have changed little in thirty-five years. More than half his players have gotten degrees, which is well above the national average for college sports programs, and the percentage was higher before the prize money exploded on the PGA Tour. Houston is not exactly Harvard in terms of athletics, however. By the time Sigel transferred to Wake Forest, he had accumulated fourteen credits, but Wake Forest would accept only one of them.

Williams was made a full-time member of the athletic department in 1955 and for a few years helped recruit for the football team. The older coaches still tell of the time that Williams prepared the grounds for a visit from Don Meredith, then the state's premier quarterback. Houston's enrollment drew heavily from war veterans and working students, and Quonset huts still served as temporary quarters for married couples on the campus. "Twice," recalled Jack Scott, then the UH sports publicist, "Dave went out and policed the whole area; he cleared a path from the parking lot to the athletic-department offices. He got on his hands and knees and picked up cigarette butts, beer cans, contraceptives. And at the last minute, Meredith canceled.

"But those were probably the only two times all year that the parking lot was clean."

The Trials of Lefty Stackhouse

Curt Sampson

Golf Journal, *July 1991*

Across the earth-toned pages of golf history, there once shone a flash of bright scarlet named Lefty Artist Stackhouse. A small, lean pro from Seguin, Texas, Stackhouse defined the outer limits of golf-course comportment of the 1920s, 1930s, and 1940s professional tour. He swore more, broke and threw more clubs, and partied more than any of his comrades—most of whom were not exactly church mice themselves. Even as a young man, Stackhouse had the haunted, world-weary look of a man who had seen too much. Lefty didn't play golf; golf played him.

When it all became too much for Stackhouse, rage radiated through him, reddening his face, neck, and ears, making his blue eyes bulge. In his fury, he would clench his teeth and mutter, with a strange and frightening sincerity: "Why, you gol-danged idiot, you stupid son of a . . ." What he would do next was often unbelievable.

One extremely credible observer—Ben Hogan, a contemporary on the pro-golf tour during the 1930s and 1940s—recalled the bizarre final stage of a Stackhouse eruption. "After duck-hooking a drive," Hogan told an *Atlanta Journal* reporter, "Lefty walked over to a thorny rosebush and began whipping his right hand back and forth, with the thorns tearing gashes. 'That will teach you to roll on me.' Then he looked at his left hand. 'And don't think you're going to get away with it either,' he said, and whipped that hand back and forth until it was ripped and bleeding, too."

Shelley Mayfield, who later played the tour, witnessed the carnage. Mayfield caddied for Lefty that day and reported, "There was blood spurting everywhere. Another time, I was caddying for Lefty at Starcke Park (in Seguin), and he was four under par after seven holes. He was always fighting a hook, but off the eighth tee, he blew it right, into a lake . . . He took the bag from me and threw it in the lake. Then he took his shoes and socks off, rolled his pants up—being very deliberate—and walked back to the clubhouse, through a two-hundred-fifty-yard field full of bull nettles."

Did Stackhouse really find solace in self-mutilation? He did. Merely throwing and breaking clubs did not provide the necessary release—and he broke more clubs than an airline. After a bad shot, a livid Lefty might grab a tree with both hands and butt it with his head, or kick himself savagely in the shin.

He was not completely without self-control, however. He claimed to be scrupulous about not disturbing his fellow competitors with his outbursts. For instance, Lefty was careful to go to a quiet, semiprivate place in the woods the time he broke every club in his bag over a tree stump. The clubs were borrowed. "I never hurt anyone but myself," he often said. How true that was: Don Cherry, a Walker Cup player in 1953 and 1961, once watched golf's angriest man smash his hand on a hackberry tree after skulling a chip. "Broke every bone in his hand," Cherry said.

For a while, Stackhouse actually punched himself to relieve the rush of adrenaline he felt after his golf ball misbehaved. But he discovered he had knockout power in his left hand, so he stopped.

The causes of Lefty's self-destructiveness and low tolerance of frustration were complex. Perhaps on some deep level he coveted the attention he attracted with his unorthodox behavior. Or maybe it was the booze; Stackhouse was an alcoholic.

"Lefty never brought any prize money home," his son, Wayne, recalls. "If he won, he'd drink to celebrate. If he didn't, he'd drink anyway."

Lefty himself described his drinking strategy in a thirty-page reminiscence Wayne keeps in a scrapbook: "If I had a real bad round and the payoff was heavy, I'd rush into the locker room and tell the bar boy to set up a fifth of 100-proof stuff with a double shot glass handy. Then I'd fill the glass rapidly and drink rapidly. If, on the other hand, the round was good, I'd order a fifth of 86-proof whiskey, plenty of ice, and a small jigger. I'd pour a jigger in the glass, fill it with water, Coke, or 7-Up, and sip it very slowly while gloating like The Chief [Ky Laffoon] did that time on the coast . . ."

Not that Lefty didn't drink before he reached the clubhouse bar. "If anyone has more alcoholic pass-outs on the golf course than I do, I certainly feel sorry for him," he wrote. Once, in Knoxville, in a wartime eighteen-hole tournament, Stackhouse refreshed himself so liberally during the first half of his round that he appeared to be riding an invisible surfboard as he staggered onto the ninth green, struggling to remain upright. He tried to putt—then fell. He rose—and fell again. Watching his performance was World War I hero Sergeant Alvin York, who'd been brought in to hype the gate. "I had no idea golf was so strenuous," said York, who had never seen a golf course—or Lefty Stackhouse—before.

Fred Corcoran, who ran the tour in those days, persuaded Stackhouse to rest in the locker room for a few minutes before he attempted to play the second nine. A few minutes became hours, then a few hours more. He awoke from his nap in the middle of the night, his head throbbing, the place deserted, and although the sponsor had promised a prize to every professional in the small field, Lefty's snooze had caused him to lose even this guaranteed payday.

Sports columnists, golf writers, and several authors of books have found Stackhouse stories irresistible. The tale they tell most often has Lefty leaping into a giant thornbush after a bad round and remaining there, in an attitude of self-crucifixion, refusing all aid. It never happened. "But once he passed out in a century plant in our front yard," Wayne Stackhouse remembers. The century plant, a member of the agave family, has leaves you could shave with. "You see, when Daddy came home [to the family farm in Seguin, about thirty miles east of San Antonio], wherever he fell asleep, that's where he had to stay. My grandfather was very strict about that."

His storytellers never touched some aspects of the Lefty legend. The sadness and emptiness of an alcoholic's home life, for instance, or his brutal early years (the death of his mother, abandonment by his step-mother, and the death of his father, all while he was in his teens). Or how, during a ten-year period of sobriety—roughly in the 1960s—Stackhouse helped found a golf program at Texas Lutheran College. That he also helped coach Seguin High School to five consecutive state championships, built a reputation as a great teacher, and founded the Pan American Golf Association may not make as good copy as his baroque temper, but it's all true.

Wilburn Artist Stackhouse was born near Atoka, Oklahoma, in 1909, the son of an oil-field worker. The family moved to Mexia (pronounced (m'hay uh), Texas, south of Dallas, and little Wilburn quit school to work with his father. He was eleven. "I was what they called a mule skinner," he wrote, "driving two, four, or six mules hauling oil-field machinery. There would be from four to ten wagons in a row, making thirty- and fifty-mile hauls with no sleep." Occasionally, the mule train would pass a golf course. "The skinners would let out with 'Look at those so-and-so's hit a little white ball and chase it down to hit it again and with knee pants on.' To be with the crowd, I would yell the same thing. But deep down, there was a fascination about it to me."

His first wood club was a broom handle attached to a piece of two-by-four. "A piece of flattened three-quarter conduit was the iron," he recalled. Lefty initially played left-handed, as he hit in baseball (thus, his nickname—Stackhouse had a 12-and-2 record as a pitcher for Mexia in 1926). He learned to play by caddying at the local nine-hole sand-green course; there he first saw respected citizens throw clubs and snap shafts in anger.

As the sixteen-year-old city champion, Lefty was chosen to play with Tommy Armour and Bobby Cruickshank when they came to town for an exhibition. Despite "only weighing 120 and using the old hickory-shaft star-face Spalding driver, I was popping the ball past the big boys, sometimes by twenty-five yards," Lefty wrote years later. "Armour offered $25 for old star face—no deal."

Despite the twin handicaps of alcohol and temper, Stackhouse was a good player. He finished sixth and seventh in the Western Open, qualified for the 1941 U.S. Open, and placed fifth in the 1963 PGA Senior.

In the 1930s, he beat Ben Hogan and Byron Nelson in a pro-am, and he beat Nelson in an exhibition. He invented two clubs: a driver with a lightbulb-shaped head—it didn't catch on—and a Y-shaped putter with two grips. The USGA disallowed this putter.

He was also a teacher of note. He provided the first golf instruction for Betty Jameson and Babe Didrikson; Lawson Little also took lessons from Lefty. He was Pro of the Year in his PGA chapter three times, and he was dedicated to introducing youngsters, like his caddie, Shelley Mayfield, to the game.

"People laughed at Stack, at what he did, but he was not a funny man," Mayfield said. "He was a respected man."

Lefty Stackhouse died of a heart attack in December of 1973 while he was watching the Thursday Men's Golf Association at Starcke Park, where he was the pro for the last fifteen years of his life.

"You didn't have to see Lefty to know when he was watching you," recalls Freddy Lewis, a member at the club. "He made the hair on the back of your neck stand up."

Newest Contribution to Golfdom Invented by Houston Golfer

Van

Houston Press, *August 5, 1930*

The niblick from now on will *not* be the most hated club in a golfer's bag, thanks to the ingenuity of E. K. MacClain, Houston's cotton man. For years Mr. MacClain (and millions of other golf enthusiasts) experienced the greatest difficulty in recovering from traps. And all courses are becoming heavily trapped.

The Houston Country Club golfer, with a view toward cutting

strokes from his game accrued in traps, began experimenting on a niblick. He soldered here and there, made changes on the face of the club, and after five years his experiments are a success.

The sand wedge is the newest contribution to golfdom and the only decided change in the face of a club in so many years. The sand wedge differs from the ordinary niblick by having a concave face and is reinforced at the bottom, weighing seventeen ounces.

What a joy to us dubs to be able to swat the pill from a trap successfully, giving no thought to any kind of a lie. The wedge throws the ball out of the sand very easily. In fact, the ball is blasted out, with the curvature of the club face giving perfect backspin. For a trouble club out of heavy grass this new stick is without equal. It is used the same as the regulation niblick, but is easier to handle.

Bobby Jones used a sand wedge presented to him by Mr. MacClain in the British and United States Open tournaments. "One of the greatest trouble clubs I've ever used," was Bobby's comment.

In March, Horton Smith played a round at the Houston Country Club and was shown a model of the club. At once, the popular pro waxed enthusiastic and borrowed the club to use on a tour.

As a result of Smith's visit, the Hagen Company is now manufacturing and marketing the sand wedge. Trick-shot artist Joe Kirkwood, Leo Diegel, Donald Moe, George Voigt, and George Von Elm have all ordered a similar club, which no doubt will be in every golfer's bag all over the country.

Mr. Dub will be the most benefited. Hearing of the new iron, he rushed out to Houston Country Club and borrowed the wedge from MacClain. Willie Maguire, club pro and one of the game's best instructors, joined me for a demonstration. "How does it work, Bill?" he inquired. "Try the club yourself," was Maguire's reply. We buried the ball in a sand trap at the No. 9 green with just the top of the ball showing . . . and dead against the four-foot bunk. "I'll never get it out," Bill wailed. "Blast at it the same as with the regular niblick," Maguire said. Lo and behold, a dub made a perfect shot and with comparative ease. The ball traveled high over the bunker and dropped down on the green ten feet from the pin. Was it luck? Tried several shots from every possible kind of trap lie and concluded that the sand wedge will be the most popular club in the game.

(Editor's note: MacClain's sand wedge was manufactured by Young Co. [which was later bought by Wilson] and marketed as the Walter Hagen Sand Wedge. Hagen popularized it in 1929, but the USGA banned the club in 1931 in favor of today's nonconcave back.)

The Arthritis Special

In the 1940s, there wasn't a better junior player in Houston—and not many in the country better—than Preston Moore Jr. And, although the man who grew up to become the CFO of the Commerce Department under President George Bush lost his game in his twenties, he still managed to become a little part of golf history.

Moore, you see, lived just off the tenth fairway at River Oaks Country Club, where he spent his days and some of his nights. Each afternoon, after he and his friends had worn themselves out playing golf, Moore always took the straightest route home—through the rough lining the south side of the hole—on his Cushman scooter.

One afternoon in 1944 or '45, young Preston—aged thirteen or fourteen, he can't recall—was pulled over. Not by security, but by Dick Jackson, a member at Houston Country Club who, thanks to World War II gas-rationing, had been granted playing privileges at the closer-to-his-house ROCC. It seems Jackson, a Houston car dealer, had severe arthritis and could still play, but had difficulty walking the course. He liked the way Moore was motoring down the hole and wanted a closer look.

The rest, as they say, is history.

After checking out Moore's scooter, Jackson went to Cushman Motors, which was only a few blocks from his own Jackson Motors Chrysler-Plymouth dealership in downtown Houston, bought an industrial maintenance cart, and went to work designing the first golf cart.

Playing off the idea behind Cushman's Package-Kars, which were used for moving airplane equipment, Jackson went to work on what would become the "Arthritis Special." He put a swivel seat behind the wheel, added a seat to carry three people in front, a compartment behind that for the bags, and, behind that, a seat for a caddie.

The gas-powered cart, which was patented in 1948, caused quite a stir at HCC and ROCC, kicking up a trail of smoke as it puttered along. Watson Distributing retrofitted ten more scooters, and the first golf buggies were off and running. One of the early versions was bought by the king of Sweden.

Although players originally had to have a doctor's note to ride a cart, the production line rolled them off for a cost—at the time—of $600. Watson continued to make them after Jackson died in the 1950s and eventually developed a quieter, more ecology-minded electric cart. By 1954, golf carts were becoming more popular and E-Z-Go was founded in Augusta, Georgia.

Today, carts provide a large portion of revenue for most courses, which maintain fleets of the vehicles. They owe it all to Jackson and Moore.

"The only thing I wish I had done when he pulled me aside," said Moore, "was to ask him to let me negotiate the deal. I think they've made a little money over the years."

John Bredemus

Harvey Penick

from Harvey Penick's Little Red Book

John Bredemus was a truly incredible person, and I am proud to say he became a friend of mine. I might have known John as well as anyone ever did. He was a loner who lived frugally in rooms that had more books than furniture. When he died of a heart attack in Abilene in 1946, his family back east would have nothing to do with him. John faced a pauper's grave. Murray Brooks, pro at Brackenridge Park, took up a collection from Texas PGA members to pay for John's funeral.

People came to the funeral and looked into John's casket to see if he was being buried with Jim Thorpe's gold medals. From 1913 until his death, John was known to many only as "the man who got Jim Thorpe's gold medals."

Nobody ever found those gold medals. I may be the only person who knows what happened to them.

It was Bredemus who gave the first lessons in Texas, staged the first Texas tournament, built Corpus Christi Country Club in 1923, and wrote the first golf instructional pieces for Texas newspapers.

Credit for dreaming up and organizing the first Texas Open, won by Bob Macdonald in San Antonio, goes to sportswriter Jack O'Brien of San Antonio. But it was Bredemus who was the genius behind it. The best golfers in the world converged on Texas for that tournament, and it started a golf boom.

In 1922, the Texas PGA had been formed with Willie Maguire as president and Bredemus as secretary. John advocated a "winter tour." He was on hand for the first Shreveport (La.) Open (1922), the first Texas Open (1922), the first Corpus Christi Open (1923), the first Houston Open (1924), and the first Dallas Open (1926).

In 1927 Bredemus landed the National PGA for Cedar Crest in Dallas. To prepare for the tournament he added forty bunkers to the old Tillinghast course and lengthened it several hundred yards.

Golf courses were being built all over the state, and I think John had a hand in about eighty percent of them.

John traveled with just a few clothes, a bag of books, a canvas golf bag of seven clubs, a checkerboard and sockful of checkers. John was often seen to beat Titanic Thompson in their checkers matches in Houston. Taking off across the state by himself, telling no one where he was going or what he was working on, John built golf courses without leaving records. He didn't want fame. Nobody knew what he did with the money he was making. He wasn't spending it on himself.

John's most famous course is Colonial Country Club in Fort Worth, built in 1936. Bredemus had put bent-grass greens in San Angelo in 1928 and Seguin in 1935, but when he used bent grass at Colonial, that course became known as the first bent-grass-greens course in Texas.

One time John took me to the site where he was laying out the second eighteen holes at Fort Worth's Ridglea Country Club. He said, "Here will be a tee and over there a green, Harvey." He could picture all the holes in his head. The main thing I could picture was that we were knee-deep in brush and I was getting covered by chiggers.

John taught me it takes the eyes of an artist to design a course, but the skills of an engineer to build one. John was both. John worked on many famous courses in Texas that are credited to others, as well as many that do bear his name, like Braeburn in Houston, the historic Offat's Bayou in Galveston (sadly destroyed to build an Air Force runway during World War II), Memorial Park in Houston (the best muni in the country at the time), Hermann Park muni in Houston, and others too numerous to name. If he didn't build the course, chances are, he came along later and changed it.

Toward the end of his life John was the head pro at Hermann Park in Houston. He would visit the Burkes at River Oaks and sit under the trees and play checkers with the members. But John wouldn't go into the clubhouse. He said he felt he didn't belong among the people inside.

Not long before he died, John showed me Jim Thorpe's gold medals. He kept them in a cigar box.

"You know what I'm going to do with these things at last?" he asked.

"No. What?" I said.

"I think I'm going to melt them down," he said.

That's what I think happened to Jim Thorpe's gold medals.

Gus Moreland

Curt Sampson

Golfiana, *1992*

It was as if the 1927 Yankees had announced that winning baseball championships had become tiresome and that they were getting out of the business. Bobby Jones, aged twenty-eight, won the Open and Amateur championships of the United States and Great Britain in 1930—the Grand Slam—and retired from competitive golf. Jones left no heir apparent. Who would take over the throne? Sarazen or Hagen? Horton Smith or Lawson Little? Perhaps one of those kids from Texas, Nelson, Hogan, or Guldahl, would play his way to the top of American golf.

For a while, another Texan, a tall, intense young man from Dallas, looked like he would pick up where Jones had left off. In tournaments in the early '30s, he appeared to be ahead of the other, eventually better-known pretenders. He was an unbeaten member of two Walker Cup teams, won a score of big amateur tournaments—then, like Jones, he disappeared from the golf scene. His name was Gus Turner Moreland.

Moreland had two nicknames. "Gus the Walker" referred to his habit of strolling along with the putt he had just hit, to facilitate the early removal of ball from hole. When Moreland walked after a putt, he knew he'd made it. It was a supremely confident gesture, infuriating to his opponents. "When Gus Moreland got that putter going, he was unstoppable," recalls LPGA Hall of Famer Betty Jameson. "He was the most remarkable putter I ever saw."

Moreland's other nickname was "Victrola." This moniker is still apt; he talks in a loud, clear voice despite his eighty-one years and requires no prompting to tell story after story, or describe round after round. Flick a switch, put the needle on the record, and the Victrola is on: "Okay, so I'm two down now and he says, 'Who's away?' and we're about even so I said, 'I'll go ahead if that's okay, so I hit it about six or seven feet and he hit it about twenty feet. Well, he missed and I made it so now I'm one down. On the next hole I'm under a tree . . ." The effect is numbing.

If you didn't know this competitive, garrulous man was a golfer, perhaps the best amateur in Texas history, you would guess that he was a salesman. He was. Moreland, in fact, gave up golf for a sales job in 1934. He was twenty-three and in his young career had beaten Byron Nelson, Ben Hogan, Ralph Guldahl, Lawson Little, Johnny Goodman, Francis Ouimet, and several other of the best players of the day. He then abruptly left the international golf scene to go to work for the Fleming-Potter Lithograph and Printing Company of Peoria, Illinois. Moreland explains:

"I was on my way back from the Walker Cup in England when I decided to play in the Western Amateur in Peoria even though I was a little tired and homesick. A fella invited me to dinner; he was going to start a lithograph-printing business—he wanted to print the Walker whiskey labels—and he wanted someone to play golf with important customers and be a salesman.

"Gosh, they only made one hundred or two hundred dollars when they won on the tour back then. I had to decide if I wanted a pro career or wanted to get married when I found the right girl and raise a family. I decided I wanted a wife and a family."

Moreland got the wife (Marion, from Peoria), family (five children), and career (twenty-eight years with Fleming-Potter) he wanted. No regrets: He tells stories of his successes as a salesman with the same relish with which he recounts his match-play wins over Nelson and Hogan. These tales have a recurring theme: Someone said Moreland couldn't do something, so he did it. Whether it was his success in a golf tournament, wooing and winning his spouse, or landing a big order for his employer, Moreland always saw himself as the underdog succeeding against long odds.

Moreland grew up around Stevens Park golf course in Oak Cliff, near Dallas. He caddied for his stepfather, who rebuffed little Gus when he asked if he might join the foursome as a player sometime. "No, we are too good for you. You'd better stick to carrying my bag," Moreland quotes his stepfather. The day came when Gus was allowed to play; he shot 43 and beat two of the foursome's regular players. "They never invited me to play again," Moreland says.

Before his match with Ralph Guldahl in the semifinals of his first big tournament, the 1929 Southwestern Amateur in Shreveport, Louisiana, Moreland recalls overhearing a man predict the tournament outcome. "Guldahl will be in the finals, as he's playing someone he's been beating," the man said. His companion replied, "Yes, you're right, but Hogan will get the silver tea set [first prize]." Moreland felt compelled at this juncture to introduce himself to the men. "I told them I would be the winner of the tourney and they could come to the dinner to see me get the silver tea set." Moreland got by Guldahl, who would be the 1937 and 1938 U.S. Open champion, in the semifinals. He faced "Benny" Hogan in the finals—and beat him. "Skill from the tee to the cup triumphed over the slugging type of golfer here today as Gus Moreland, nineteen-year-old of Dallas, defeated Ben Hogan, sixteen-year-old of Fort Worth, four up and three to play," said the story in the Shreveport paper the next day.

Upon his return to Dallas, Moreland was informed that Titanic Thompson, the legendary gambler/golf hustler, wanted to meet him and play a round of golf. "I told him I'd play with him but I didn't have money to cover any bets and that I'd prefer just a friendly game," says Moreland. Thompson agreed; Moreland shot 66.

"What say you hit the road with me, son," said the soft-spoken Thompson. "We'll both make lots of money and I'll take care of any bets we might lose." Moreland was skeptical; who would want to bet against the game's best-known gambler and the Southwestern Amateur champion? Thompson had it figured, of course: "He said that when we reached a golf course, I would go to the caddie yard with my old set of four irons, a wood, and a putter, and my small canvas bag," Moreland recalls. "Then Thompson said that when he couldn't get the right game, he would say, 'If you guys put up some bigger bets, I'll take a caddie from the caddie barn and play you.' Then he would call me, and the guys on the tee would not be able to get their bets made fast enough . . . I told him thanks, but I couldn't leave Dallas for this kind of match."

Moreland was happy to bet on a more straightforward competition, however. He and Guldahl were then living in Dallas; Hogan and Byron Nelson resided in Fort Worth. Soon after he won the Southwestern Amateur, a city-versus-city match was arranged, with big stakes. "We were supposed to play a home-and-home," he recalls. "Well, Guldahl got an ace and a couple of birdies on the front nine, and I got three more birds on the back nine, and we polished them off, twelve and eleven, if I remember correctly. They didn't even play us the second time."

In 1932, Moreland tied for second (with Gene Sarazen) in the Texas Open, then a tour event, and won the Western Amateur, the Houston Invitational (beating Johnny Goodman, who was to win the 1933 U.S. Open, in the finals), and the Texas State Championship. He also beat Byron Nelson on Nelson's home course in the finals of the Glen Garden Invitational; Moreland holed putts of twelve, twenty-eight, and thirty feet on the last five holes to win one up. He hoped that by winning the Trans-Miss, one of the last big amateur tournaments of the summer, he would be named to play in the Walker Cup, the biennial competition between the best U.S. and British amateur golfers. Things didn't work out that way, however.

Moreland won the tournament, held at Oklahoma City Country Club—he shot a course record 63 in the semifinals—and beat David "Spec" Goldman in the finals. HE WON'T WALK HOME, read one newspaper headline the next day, for the first prize in the tournament was not the usual trophy or plaque; it was a yellow, twelve-cylinder, $3,000 Cadillac roadster. Moreland proudly returned to Dallas with the top down on his new car "and a record that I felt would put me on the Walker Cup team," he says. "Then things got sticky. A week later I was told by a friend with contacts in the United States Golf Association that keeping the car would make me ineligible for the U.S. Amateur and the Walker Cup . . . 'Give the car back and you are on the team,' he said." Moreland returned the car. A week later, the Walker Cup team was announced. "But my name wasn't on the list," Moreland recalls. "I couldn't hold the tears back."

The resultant furor—over Moreland's nonselection to the Walker Cup team and the brouhaha over the Cadillac—was fodder for the sports pages and golf magazines in the weeks to come. *Golf Illustrated,* for example, applauded Moreland for returning the car and blasted those who gave away the "vulgar gift . . . Thus a mere boy . . . has by his honorable action been the one to put the finishing touch to a disgraceful situation . . . We trust Mr. Moreland's example will be mentioned honorably whenever any similar attempt is made to exploit amateur golf for the benefit of any advertising or commercial scheme." But the drama wasn't over.

The Western Amateur, held in Rockford, Illinois, in 1932, was the final big tournament before the Walker Cup. "I wanted to win and at least prove to the selection committee that they hadn't done a very good job," Moreland says. He got the chance to make his point in the semifinals, when he played Charles Seaver, who was picked No. 3 on the Walker Cup team (Seaver was a semifinalist in the U.S. Amateur in 1930, the year of the Jones Grand Slam, and would be the father of Tom Seaver, the baseball pitcher). Moreland was two down with five holes to play, but, as was typical of him, he made a series of unlikely putts to win the match. He defeated Ira Couch of Chicago in the finals, accepted the trophy, and was handed a telegram. It was from H. H. Ramsay, captain of the Walker Cup team. It read, in part: WOULD GREATLY APPRECIATE IT IF YOU COULD REPORT AT BOSTON IMMEDIATELY AS

MEMBER OF WALKER CUP SQUAD. Moreland won his singles match at Brookline and teamed with Seaver to beat the No. 1 British team nine and eight.

Moreland beat Lawson Little one up in successful defense of his Trans-Miss title in 1933, finishing with seven threes on the final ten holes. He also tied for seventh (with Walter Hagen) in the 1933 U.S. Open. And while there were more honors and tournament wins for Moreland in '33 and '34—he had another successful run in the Walker Cup and played in Bobby Jones's inaugural Masters tournament—his career on the national golf stage was almost over. Notwithstanding his considerable skills, Moreland's best finish in the U.S. Amateur was a fifth-round elimination in 1936, when he lost to eventual winner Johnny Fischer.

Moreland turned pro in 1963, at the age of fifty-three, saying: "Better late than never—I always wanted to be a golf professional."

The Hustler

Russ Pate

D magazine, March 1987

Start with Dick Martin's hands. In *Pigeons, Marks, Hustlers and Other Golf Bettors You Can Beat,* Sam Snead warns golfers to be wary of betting with anyone whose left hand has calluses at the base of the ring and little fingers. Martin's left hand is callused there. His hands are also incongruously large for a man no more than five-foot-five and 140 pounds, having been built up by gripping golf clubs each day for the past six decades.

Then there's Dick Martin's skin. Snead advises golfers to be wary of making bets with anyone who has a darker tan than theirs. And although Martin's complexion is too fair to tan deeply, his weathered skin testifies to the years he's spent in the unforgiving Texas sun and wind. The lines at the corners of his pale blue eyes suggest the hundreds of thousands of times he's squinted to see his golf ball arc against the horizon.

And don't forget Dick Martin's clubs. Martin carries a putter that can double as a driver and a rusty, lightweight nine-iron that has deep grooves in the club face and can make the golf ball hop, skip, and dance on its way to the hole. These are the tools of a real pro.

Unfortunately, many golfers are unaware of Snead's warning signs of a golf hustler. From the '40s well into the '70s, whenever golf hustlers arrived in Dallas they invariably asked two questions: How do I get to Tenison Park? And Where can I find Dick Martin?

The answer was simple. To find Tenison Park, a municipal course just off Grand Avenue in East Dallas, was to find Dick Martin. For decades he would arrive by midmorning each day, and when he wasn't out on the course looking for lost golf balls or empty Coke bottles—anything he could convert into cash—he held court in the grill.

Martin was without peer at poor-mouthing his own game while giving a pigeon false hope. "There's a sucker born every minute," he would say with conviction, if not originality, and then he'd proceed to demonstrate an uncanny sense of who they were. And how to pluck them.

When the propositions had been made and accepted, Martin would step up on the first tee and begin to operate on his opponents with the precision of a surgeon. "Dick Martin didn't ever try to drain a guy's blood," says his friend and frequent two-man partner Jerry Biesel. "But he'd take a drop or two—every day."

Martin generally played matches for $10 or $20 a side, with a few side bets. He'd take home maybe $200 a day, and with his frugal habits—perhaps the only thing Martin does better than play golf is live cheaply—he accumulated enough cash to begin investing in rental properties in far Northwest Dallas. It sure beat working nine to five.

Martin wasn't a long hitter, but he was straight off the tee. Accuracy was paramount at Tenison Park, a tight course with enough trees to give Smokey the Bear an anxiety attack. Once Martin was within 125 yards of the green, he picked up his trusty nine-iron, which he bought in the late '20s for fifty cents.

That four-bit club, which he paid out over five weeks at ten cents a week, has helped Martin win maybe a million dollars, cash, in golf bets. "Dick's nine-iron has crippled more guys than polio," says one Tenison Park veteran.

Martin, who turned seventy-three last December, now plays at Great Southwest Golf Club in Arlington, usually in a gangsome game with some of his old pals from Tenison. There's money riding every time a ball is in the air. Not big money, necessarily, but enough action to keep everyone interested—except Martin, who's prone to wander off looking for golf balls.

Gambling is a tradition in golf, a tradition-rich sport. Centuries ago the founding fathers in Scotland, the golfers at Muirfield and St. Andrews, kept a record of their golfing wagers on the town scroll. Today, whether the stakes are ten dollars a hole or ten cents, most golfers play the game for more than the exercise. Perhaps seventy-five percent of all golf games have something more riding on the outcome than a pat on the back. That estimate could be low.

Martin still takes an occasional trip to Las Vegas, which Dan Jenkins calls the most likely place to find a fourteen-handicapper who shoots 71. It was in Vegas, where Martin made a habit of winning tournaments for high rollers sponsored by casinos like the Sahara and Desert Inn, that a sportswriter dubbed him "Dandy Dick Martin, the scourge of the Texas amateur golf circuit."

It was also in Vegas that Martin once lost a $10,000 game in the biggest match he ever played. Martin was summoned to Vegas by Johnny Moss, a poker player nonpareil with Dallas connections, for whom Martin had caddied in high-stakes golf games in the late '40s and early '50s. Moss paid Martin caddie fees of $20 a day plus ten percent of his winnings, which were considerable at times, since Moss liked to play for $1,000 (and up) a hole.

Martin couldn't come through for Moss that day. Martin's misadventures in the greenside bunkers cost Moss the $10,000 (Martin says he won several hundred on his own money on the back nine) and convinced Dandy Dick to add a sand wedge to his bag.

At seventy-three and with a touch of arthritis in his back, Martin can't drive the ball as he once did. But put him within a hundred yards with his nine-iron in his hand and he remains Doctor Death. And he can still putt an opponent's lights out, as he did at the fund-raising tournament Lee Trevino sponsored last spring for Texas Wesleyan College in Fort Worth. Martin's team in the four-man scramble birdied sixteen consecutive holes, with Dandy Dick sinking "at least ten" birdie putts from fifteen to twenty feet.

Trevino, who got a putting tip from Martin ("stand more directly over the ball") on the eve of the 1971 U.S. Open and proceeded to beat Jack Nicklaus in a memorable playoff, praised Martin in his autobiography written with Sam Blair: "Dick Martin was probably the best player I ever saw until Jack Nicklaus."

Trevino and Martin saw each other mostly at Tenison Park, where the cast of hustlers and con artists came straight out of a Ring Lardner novel. It was at Tenison Park that Trevino fashioned his definition of pressure: having to make a five-dollar putt with only two dollars in your pocket.

And it was at Tenison Park that Dick Martin was king. He'd beat the low handicappers and scratch players, Lee Trevino included, straight up. And he'd "even things up" with high handicappers by inventing hustles like the game "Putting for Birdie." Under the rules, Martin had to play from the back tees, while his opponent was given a putt for birdie on each hole. The catch was that Martin was allowed to place his opponent's ball on the green. Martin knew the Tenison greens so well he could place the ball where his pigeon had no chance to make the birdie putt and a better-than-average chance of three-putting. The pigeon would shoot 76 or so, a score Martin had no trouble beating.

Playing Dick Martin at Tenison Park was like going one-on-one with

Larry Bird at Boston Garden. Any way you hooked or sliced it, you had virtually no chance to win.

Martin began playing golf full-time in the early '30s. He tried his hand at gainful employment on occasion—he worked for a laundry service and an auto-body shop, and during World War II he transported recruits arriving in Dallas over to Camp Wolters near Mineral Wells—but mostly he played golf. He caddied and hustled bets, and he began winning golf tournaments. The first was in 1931 at the old Parkdale course in East Dallas. Martin has won so many tournaments in the interim that he's lost count of the exact number, though he suspects two hundred might be close. He has a collection of golf trophies that cover nearly as much of Texas as AAA road maps.

In Odessa in 1949, Martin added to his reputation by making a hole in one on the final hole to win the tournament. Informed that his team needed a birdie two on the final hole to tie, Martin said, "Okay, boys, let's win this thing."

When the first member of the foursome hesitated in making his club selection, Martin kicked his ball off the tee and threw down one of his own. "What club do I hit?" mocked Martin. "Hell, just knock the goddamn ball into the goddamn hole." With that, he hit a four-iron that landed on the green 213 yards away, took one bounce, and disappeared into the cup.

On the days Martin doesn't play at Great Southwest, he piddles around The Golf Shop, which sits on his property on Southwell, near Walnut Hill and Harry Hines. In addition to several small rental houses, the property is cluttered with broken-down golf carts, rusted appliances, and scrap metal. Fred Sanford and son would love it.

The walls inside The Golf Shop are covered with photographs tracing Martin's career. There's a picture of him with Ben Hogan at the 1945 Victory Open at Dallas Country Club, and a publicity photo of Wahoo McDaniel, the football player/wrestler, a frequent Martin playing partner. It's said that McDaniel broke two or three clubs a round.

The main attraction at The Golf Shop, though, is golf balls. Martin finds them himself, wraps them in *Dallas Times Herald* rain protectors, and sells them below retail.

Martin attributes some of his success on the Texas tournament trail, the so-called "barbecue circuit," to clean living. He has never smoked, rarely drunk alcohol, and generally stayed away from the socializing that made Texas club tournaments notorious. "I've seen too many guys rum-dumb on the first tee the next morning," he explained. "Not me."

In addition to the first-place trophies Martin won, he often was given the choice between a new set of golf clubs or sterling silver. For Martin, who grew up poor, there was no choice involved. He would select the golf clubs, which he'd take back to Tenison Park and sell out of the trunk of his car, a movable pro shop of sorts.

Once, after winning a tournament in Corsicana, where he was born in 1913, Martin explained his rationale. "If I took the silver, Marguerite [his wife since 1947] would have to spend all her time polishing it. As it is, she's got to keep the grass cut while I'm out playing golf."

Don Cherry

Curt Sampson

Golf Journal, *April 1992*

Don Cherry was the amateur golfer and nightclub singer who almost won the U.S. Open. He was the prematurely bald man who married Miss America. His closest friends were hard-partying gentlemen from the worlds of sports (Jimmy Demaret, Mickey Mantle, Bobby Layne) and entertainment (Phil Harris, Dean Martin). But Cherry never smoked, never drank. He was an introvert who made his living on the stage, and a self-described family man who was married and divorced four times. He was drawn to golf, the ultimate game of self-control, but had only a loose grip on a temper that was frighteningly intense.

The unlikely life of Donald Ross Cherry began in 1924 in Wichita Falls, Texas, a medium-sized city one hundred miles northwest of Fort Worth. Fatherless since age two, he was raised by his doting but extremely strict mother, Ross Alma Cherry. "I could always sing," Cherry recalls. "Not that I wanted to. But my mother insisted that I sing for the ladies she did some sewing for. 'The Whiffenpoof Song' . . . 'Irish Lullaby.'" He was twenty-three when he accepted the invitation of a bandleader named Jan Garber to hit the road with his troupe. But Cherry was shy and somewhat stiff in front of an audience. Did he really want to be a singer? After a week, Garber gave Cherry $39 and a bus ticket back to Wichita Falls.

"He was backward," says entertainer Phil Harris. "Although, of course, he's one-hundred-percent better now. I'd tell him, 'When you're up there, you're a servant.' But I remember one Saturday night in Vancouver, this lady kept requesting 'Hello, Dolly,' and Don kept ignoring her. Finally he looks at her and says, 'I don't sing 'Hello, Dolly.' Not as long as I live. I hate that song.'"

Golf was a refuge, from singing and from his lonely home life. He won about eighty amateur tournaments, most of them on the Texas barbecue circuit, and some big ones, too, like the 1953 Canadian Amateur. Yet, as he was on the stage, Cherry was at war with himself on the golf course. Did he really want to be a golfer? "The worst temper the world has ever seen," Cherry says. "I made Tommy Bolt look like Little Red Riding Hood."

Byron Nelson confirms the diagnosis. "I always thought Don was an excellent striker of the ball, but he got too upset. Something would happen, and he'd just say, 'It's not my day.'" Cherry could hit the full shots when he was mad, but not the short ones. Many of his putters were broken asunder, or were launched with force at trees, tees, and ball washers.

He had a temper on the stage, too. He couldn't abide hecklers at all. Demaret, who was Cherry's mentor, father figure, and direct opposite in disposition, loved to take advantage of this. On one occasion, Jim and his party of giggling golf pros smuggled a ship's foghorn into the hotel nightclub in Houston where Cherry was the featured performer. Just as Cherry, in an unconvincing hairpiece, was midway through a song called "Ebb Tide," Demaret blasted the boat horn. Cherry stormed off the stage, the laughter of the merry pranksters ringing in his ears. A few minutes later, Demaret got his offended protégé on the phone—and gave him another burst from the foghorn.

From 1952 to 1962, Cherry played the PGA Tour as an amateur. This was the golden age of Don Cherry, when he enjoyed his greatest success as a singer and a golfer. Turn on the radio and there was Cherry singing "Band of Gold," or "Ghost Town," or "Wild Cherry," or "Namely You." He also performed his hits on the Arthur Godfrey and Ed Sullivan television shows. Meanwhile, he was an undefeated member of two Walker Cup teams, and almost won a tour event in Milwaukee. And in the 1960 U.S. Open at Cherry Hills, in Denver, Cherry found himself one stroke behind the leader, Arnold Palmer, with just two holes to play.

"I made a forty-footer for par on fourteen, and Sam [Snead] looked at me and said, 'You're gonna win the tournament,'" he remembers. "But I missed birdie putts from four feet on fifteen and eight feet on sixteen." Snead and Cherry were playing behind Nicklaus and Hogan; they stood by their drives on the par-five seventeenth hole and watched as Hogan, from about forty yards, pitched his third shot into the water hazard that surrounds the hard, tiny green. After Hogan and Nicklaus holed out, Cherry uncovered his three-wood, going for it. But he topped the shot into the water and made seven. He finished ninth, tied with Hogan.

Time resolved the major conflict of Cherry's life. His golf game deserted him years ago, but his voice, amazingly, improved with age. He is working six nights a week, Tuesdays off, at one of the better Las Vegas venues, the Desert Inn. The voice is smooth as silk, sort of a cross between Mel Tormé and Vic Damone, but more powerful than either. Phil Harris doesn't quite agree. "His style is all his own," he says. "Cherry is the last guy in the world who would copy anyone."

Part Seven

From Champions to Goat Hills

Hagen Defeats Turnesa, One Up

Milt Saul

Dallas Morning News, *November 6, 1927*

At Cedar Crest Saturday afternoon, the tumult and the shouting of a week of a PGA Championship tournament play ended, the captains and king of all golfers, Walter Hagen, departed.

Hagen bore off in triumph, as a result of his defeat of Joe Turnesa of Pittsford, New York, on the thirty-sixth green, the PGA title for the fifth in four times in succession: first prize of $1,000 in cash, four diamond studded gold medals emblematic of his PGA victories, and perspective exhibition engagements worth more than $100,000 for the entire year.

Hagen's victory Saturday was by another narrow squeak. He met his match in the final, one of the stoutest contenders he has ever played. Turnesa at one time had the champion apparently "in the sack" again but by a sensational rally in the morning round, Hagen scored three birdies in a row to come out of it and take the lead from his younger opponent.

This was the big break in an all-day seesaw combat. After it was over, Hagen modestly said he was lucky again to win over his skilled adversary. With Turnesa, however, a different view rested.

"He was just too good for me, that's all," said Turnesa. "I did my best, but it simply wasn't good enough to beat Walter Hagen."

Two moderate putts for birdie threes on the thirty-fifth and thirty-sixth greens were missed by Turnesa. Had either of these gone down it might have changed the complexion of the championship. The title literally hung in the balance on the two final carpets of green.

Hagen went one up at the thirteenth hole. They halved the remaining holes in par golf, with the exception of the thirty-third, where both missed one-foot putts, either of which might have changed the final result. Here they took fours on the par-three link.

With this crisis in the exciting combat driving a gallery of two thousand or more nearly frantic, they came to the thirty-fifth tee. Their drives were perfect and their pitch shots to the green were about on a level in regard to distance from the pin. Both tried for the birdie three but missed.

One hole remained. They drove perfectly and again each laid his ball within putting distance of the cup, and once more each missed the putt for the birdie. The game had ended, however, as no more holes remained and Hagen had won the match.

The final match developed many episodes that made the galleryites gasp. With its changing aspect, the combat was thrilling enough without frills, but these flashes nevertheless bobbed up to make it more so.

Hagen squared the match at the twenty-ninth hole when he made a typical Hagen shot across trees into the face of the par-four hole. Joe played safe, up the middle and around the dogleg. This left him a 120-yard pitch to the pin. Joe pitched ten feet above the hole and could not trickle the ball down the slight hill into the cup. Walter chipped dead and squared the match.

Turnesa threw away a grand opportunity at the thirtieth green by missing a three-foot putt and allowed Walter to halve the short hole in one above regulation figures.

At the thirty-first hole, a dogleg of 391 yards, Joe pulled his second slightly off the green, and it came to rest six inches from a tree. He had a difficult shot and could get only fifteen feet from the pin. Walter's second was thirty feet below the cup, and he putted dead for a four. Joe took three putts for a big six and went one down, a position from which he could not recover.

Joe had three opportunities on the last three holes to sink putts of four feet, eight feet, and three feet, respectively, to square the match. He was always inside on these holes and putted firmly, but the little pill would not drop.

Hagen, after the match, walked over near the clubhouse and as the sun was fading out behind a clear sky, allowed the photographers to snap him with his coal-black caddie boy—a real Texas Negro, who stuck to Hagen throughout the tournament. The boy got a $20 note for Sunday's work.

Hagen was the same stoic in Dallas Saturday afternoon at the thirty-sixth green that he was in England years ago, in the East this summer, and all over the universe. He was physically fit and his mental poise was always under control. At the thirty-fifth green when Joe started a four-foot putt uphill to the cup and it jumped over at the very last turn, Walter remarked, "Too bad Joe; you should have that one."

PGA officials and Dallas Chamber of Commerce officers gathered after the match and presented Hagen with all the trophies and prize money that goes with the championship.

Turnesa took his defeat graciously, wringing Hagen's hand over the thirty-sixth cup. The two then walked to the clubhouse shoulder to shoulder, where Hagen was handed a check for his prize of $1,000 and Turnesa a check for the runner-up position, which amounted to $600.

On the lawn, Alex Pride, president of the PGA, gave Hagen the loving cup, one of the many side prizes he will receive. Hagen, in thanking the president for the cup, made a little speech in which he complimented Turnesa highly, concluding:

"He showed that he is a player of rare mettle and I hope when I relinquish my title, Turnesa will be the man who receives my congratulations."

Among those banked around the last green on Saturday were Bobby Cruickshank, Tommy Armour, Gene Sarazen, and a host of others, some of them earlier victims of Hagen in this tournament.

Bobby Cruickshank Says Tough Grass Made Espinosa Lose

Bobby Cruickshank

United News, November 5, 1927

PRESS TENT, CEDAR CREST COUNTRY CLUB, DALLAS, November 4—This was a fine day for golf. A bright sun shone down over this wonderful course and reminded one of the winter games we have in Florida. There was a tremendous gallery out to see Hagen and Espinosa and Turnesa and Golden play their matches.

It was my good fortune (?) to join the galleries Friday and study the players from a distance. Looking around me at the many faces following the matches, I found that it is not all important to be beaten. I was just one of many golfers, some of them holding many titles, following the matches Friday. There was Tommy Armour, the National Open champion, and my partner on this winter's exhibition touring; Johnny Farrell, another sterling boy and player of equal ability; Gene Sarazen, Mortie Dutra, Francis Gallett, and a host of others.

In the Turnesa match, it seemed big John Golden could not control his putter. That 80 he shot in the morning is not Golden golf. I have met this man at all kinds of play and know he just had an off day. Joe was good. And when Joe is good, that means a lot.

The Espinosa-Hagen match was a "thriller" all day. Hagen usually maintained a slight lead, but never enough for him to feel safe. It is a fact—and golf record—that Espinosa really lost the match at the thirty-sixth hole when he was short on his putt. But it must be remembered that he was putting almost forty feet from the pin, uphill into the brustle of the Bermuda grass, which will completely baffle any golfer at times. I was close to Al when he tapped that putt, and the click of the blade seemed firm enough to send it hole high. Instead it stopped four feet short. Hagen won the hole, and Al's short putt at the first extra hole put him out.

The match Saturday between Turnesa and Hagen should be one worth anyone's attention. They are both of championship ability, Hagen has proven many times.

(Babe Ruth, Gene Tunney, Jack Dempsey, Lou Gehrig, please note: I, Bobby Cruickshank, wrote this story myself, in a press tent at Dallas. I did not get a thousand dollars for it. I did not get a hundred dollars. In fact, I'm afraid I won't get a cent.)

Forget the Alamo . . . Just Remember 1922!

Frances Trimble

Golfiana, *1992*

At the Texas Open players' dinner of 1922, young Gene Sarazen took the floor. "Instead of going to Florida next year to get in shape for the Texas Open, we are coming directly to San Antonio for a month at least," he suggested.

But a funny thing happened to Gene on his way to San Antonio that next year: He won the 1922 U.S. Open at Skokie and the PGA Championship at Oakmont. With his time more in demand in the winter of '23, Sarazen felt justified in wiring ex-cavalryman Jack O'Brien: WILL PLAY IN SAN ANTONIO IF YOU POSTPONE THE TOURNAMENT FOR ONE WEEK. SARAZEN.

O'Brien's terse reply was: WHO'S SARAZEN?

From 1923 through 1931, Sarazen bypassed Texas on his way from California to Florida. Whether it was O'Brien's reply or the lure of the Florida golf circuit which prompted Sarazen's actions is unclear.

In 1932, Sarazen mysteriously reappeared in the field. He finished second, tied with Texas amateur Gus Moreland at 288, one shot back of winner Clarence Clark.

In 1969, *San Antonio Light* sportswriter Harold Sherwitz (who worked for the paper during the period of Sarazen's absence) explained the apparition thusly: "Once, contacted by phone in Los Angeles, Gene Sarazen said he had made up his mind to pass up all tournaments between Los Angeles and Florida. The Texas Open people regarded this as a distinct challenge. A committee took the westbound Southern Pacific train to New Braunfels, thirty miles up the line, then boarded the eastbound on which Sarazen was a passenger. Exactly what happened between New Braunfels and San Antonio has never been explained, but Sarazen got off here and played in the Texas Open tournament."

The Texas Open once again brought Gene good luck, for he won his second U.S. Open title that summer at Fresh Meadow Country Club and the British Open at Sandwich.

Linksmanship

Turk Pipkin

Texas Monthly, *May 1993*

When I was a skinny kid growing up in San Angelo, there was still a raw spirit about the game of golf. I took my first lessons at age six, the exam being a tournament with kids twice my age. Not knowing the rules for an unplayable lie, I took sixteen strokes getting the ball out of a thick patch of Johnsongrass . . . and into a pond. I went on to shoot 127 and was awarded the last-place trophy, a statue of a boxer, for fighting the course. I threw the statue into the pond.

In the years to come I learned to love golf in West Texas. A number of courses still had greens made of sand, and, unlike today, you could clean a ball by licking it (without risking tongue rot). I caddied for hustlers—one now plays on the Senior Tour—and for ranchers who wore cowboy boots with spikes. Golf was a way of life: I would tote a heavy bag for thirty-six holes, then get out my own clubs and play until it was too dark to find the ball. I didn't know it then, but I was making a spiritual connection with the ancient traditions of the game that would stick with me for a long time.

In recent years, golf has changed into a business of manicured real estate, sporting motorized minibars, cellular phones, and greens fees reminiscent of the national debt. But in small towns across Texas, there is still a game that is more about character than coin. The locals call it pasture pool. They play on nine-hole courses, most of which offer golf in its basic form. When you're in the rough, you know you're in the rough. When you're in the hole, you're darn glad.

Lest you think nine holes is only half the game, keep in mind that golf was played in Scotland for nearly four hundred years before the standard number of holes became eighteen. Previously, courses varied from five to twenty-five holes. The famed Old Course at St. Andrews played for a century with twelve holes, was expanded to twenty-two, and was finally reduced to eighteen, which was then adopted as the norm. In America, even North Carolina's famed Pinehurst Country Club started with sand greens and nine holes.

One of the problems with eighteen-hole golf is finding the time to play. Hitting practice balls, playing rounds that get slower every year, and settling the bets over a cold one is practically a full-time job. But playing nine holes can be like swimming laps, especially if you play early or late, when birds and animals abound but other golfers are few and far between. Best of all, you don't have to take out a loan to hit the links. Average greens fees at Texas' some 250 nine-hole courses are about $10 (and some charge nothing at all).

Seven of my favorite courses are described below. Only one of them still has sand greens, but each is a step back into a primitive golden era of the game. Check them out before some fool adds a back nine.

McLean Lions Golf Association. Yes, you can get your kicks on Route 66, and your golf licks too, because America's most famous highway passes within shouting distance of the last sand greens in the state. Grass greens require an enormous amount of water and an expensive irrigation system; one alternative is to pack in greens of sand and spray them once a year with a light coat of oil to keep them from blowing away. Sand greens are rapidly disappearing nationwide, so you had better hurry if you want to play them at McLean.

Finding the course is no problem. Go to McLean ("Muh-clane"), eighty miles east of Amarillo on Interstate 40, drive north to the edge of town, and there it is in all its minor glories: no clubhouse, no greens fees, just a wide expanse of sloping farmland with fairways mowed fifty yards wide through a rolling wheat field.

There is also a good chance that you'll be the only golfer on the course. If you get the opportunity, I highly recommend that you play it alone or with one friend. Playing here is a reminder of the special pleasures to be had walking an empty course alone with your finest swing (or finest friend), serenaded all the while by the songs of unknown birds.

Fallen to the ground by the first tee is a hand-painted sign that says, #1, PAR 4, 320 YARDS. Hit a sweet shot, then pick up your bag and start down the rough-hewn fairway, and you'll feel as if you have gone back to the raw beginnings of something grand, as if you were the first golfer in Texas.

Putting on these sand greens is all in knowing the ropes—literally. The sand is uneven and foot-printed, with a single smooth track crossing the hole. Attached to the bottom of the pin is a long cord. Rather than drag your own track on every green with the heavy iron rake lying nearby, you use the cord to measure the distance from the hole to your ball, then place the ball at the same distance in the already smooth track. It is less work, and you can see the faint trails of others who have putted before you, giving you a distinct advantage in reading the break. Still, these are the most difficult putts you'll ever know. Even the holes are smaller than regulation, with homemade cups that look as if they were welded by an oil-field roughneck.

Take extra balls and don't forget to scout out the location of the par-three eighth green; there is a sucker's pile of sand about forty yards in front of the real putting surface, so hit plenty of club.

On my last visit, the sunset turned the clouds of an approaching cold front a blazing red as I pulled the pin on the ninth green. Just before putting, I glanced toward the hole and saw the full moon climbing huge and golden over the hills to the east. It took my breath away and covered me with goose bumps normally reserved for a hole in one. I knocked my putt dead in the cup for a three-over-par 39, and—thanks to a nine-hole course—shot my age.

The Lajitas Golf Course. A veritable oasis in the desert of Big Bend, Lajitas Golf Course is on the banks of the Rio Grande just below the Badlands Hotel and Restaurant, the RV park, and Laundromat. It may be a tourist trap, but it's a hell of a setting for one. Dry, barren mountains of rock rise on all quarters, and the entrance to the course is protected by a fence of ocotillo.

But the desert stops there, for lush cottonwoods, tall palm trees, and gnarled grapevines line the green fairways, and occasional grape-covered arbors provide shady relief from the sun. A couple of holes are so close to the Rio Grande that it seems as if a really bad shot might land in Mexico and a half-bad one might float all the way to the Gulf of Mexico.

As on many nine-hole layouts, two sets of tee markers make it possible to play two somewhat distinct nines, with longer tees on some holes changing par-fours into par-fives. If there is no one behind you, you can even play two balls a hole—one from each tee marker—carding an eighteen-hole score in just two hours.

When you are finished, you can wander over to the Lajitas Trading Post and share a longneck with Clay Henry Jr., the beer-drinking goat. The hotel has rooms overlooking the golf course, with the bar and restaurant only steps away. Life should always be this good.

The Alpine Country Club. The golf course is inside the city limits near a red-sandstone-and-glass-block architectural delight called Kokernut Field, which housed a semipro baseball team in the '40s. The country club is equally inviting. Its natural design dances in and around a wide golf ball–eating creek bed, while the fast and true greens resemble Indian burial mounds, somewhat flattened but sloping away on all sides. You have to rap the ball hard to get it to the hole, but not too hard or the ball accelerates down the opposite side. It's a little like putting on a bald guy's head.

On a recent visit, I played a few holes with the assistant greenskeeper. Bill Murray's *Caddyshack* character kept flashing through my mind, but I was disappointed when he failed to blow up even one of the pesky gophers tearing up the course. We did, however, enjoy watching the red-tailed hawks diving at the little rodents as they peeked from their burrows.

On the third hole, a *viejo,* searching the creek bed with a ball scoop made from a long cottonwood branch and a tin can, sold me four good balls for a dollar. "*Gracias*" and "*Buena suerte*" accompanied our brief variation on the free-trade agreement.

The generally excellent condition of the course just goes to show that natural maintenance does work, something the high-dollar, eighteen-hole courses are just rediscovering after a twenty-year love affair with the chemical industry.

Archer City Country Club. Archer City may have seen its last picture show, but golf plays on. In Scotland, the term "links" originally described the gorse-and-sand-covered land that links firmer ground to the seas. But the Archer City Country Club, like many nine-hole courses in Texas, was built on land that links the town to the country. The course defines the outskirts of town, with horses in the field beyond the mesquite-lined fairways. Rusted iron ladders are strategically placed on the barbed-wire fences that surround the course so that golfers can fetch their errant golf balls without tearing their Sansabelts or jeans. Tee boxes are baked so hard that the locals offer you not just a tee but a hammer as well. And the bare ground on the parched Bermuda fairways is sun-dried and windblown to a hardwood sheen.

If you join in a friendly neighborhood game, remember that a little local knowledge is as good as gold: On the seventh hole a red metal disk that looked for all the world like a hundred-yard marker was only thirty yards from the green. Sprinkler guards masquerading as yardage markers do not bode well for out-of-towners. On the other hand, win or lose, all things tend to balance out in the new clubhouse, where a cold beer goes for a buck and a quarter.

Pedernales Country Club. Willie Nelson's golf course is one of Texas' best nine-hole courses, if for no other reason than its friendly clientele and central location, thirty-five miles northwest of Austin off Texas Highway 71. Willie (once again the owner, with all that IRS nastiness over back taxes behind him) has shaped this course philosophically. The rules state: "No more than twelve in your foursome." Such large groups are called a gangsome. Beer drinkers are referred to as float-sam. Maybe that's why the scorecard admonishes you to "please leave the course in the condition you'd like to be found."

There are other variations on the standard game. The unofficial rule from the first tee is, Hit till you're happy. The course is always open to the public ("Come on out!" says resident pro Larry Trader), and newcomers are often shown the Pedernales Stroll. Facing an unplayable lie, you just pick up the ball and stroll to a spot you like better. It may be against United States Golf Association rules, but it beats ruining a club on the rocks.

And the company is tops. I've played more than a few rounds with Willie (who putts one-handed and sometimes sings as he jags from shot to shot), and I have taken chipping lessons from Lee Trevino, driving lessons from Darrell Royal, and gambling lessons from Trader (the lesson on gambling with Trader is "Don't!"). Willie even let me in on what he calls the true secret of golf. "Swing hard," he said with a sly smile. "You might hit it."

Nongolfers frequently ask what the big deal is about golf. I've given up trying to explain the haunting feel of a perfect shot: the magical flight of the ball as it defies gravity, wind, and all things physical in search of the tiniest of goals. Instead, I tell them that golf is a great excuse to get outdoors. And while most of man's athletic competitions imitate war, golf imitates life, each player pitting his own skills against the hazards of the way. On the basic nine-holer, as in days of old, it is you against the lay of the land; and if bad breaks conspire against the player, they also show whether you have what it takes to overcome them. Golfers wouldn't have it any other way.

I just wish I had kept that childhood trophy of the boxer, because after all these years, I'm still fighting the course.

Houston's Odd Couple

Nick Seitz

Golf Digest, *June 1969*

The photographer is set up to take the picture of Jimmy Demaret and Jack Burke Jr., who conceived and developed the Champions Golf Club in Houston, site of the United States Open Championship, June

12–15. Demaret is late. He is almost always late, usually because he is cheerfully permitting himself to be delayed by some guy in magenta pants who has had four drinks and who saw him win the Masters in 1947. "Jimmy makes you feel that he has all the time in the world to talk to you, and that there is nothing he would rather do," says a friend of Demaret.

Burke, a more impatient type, is restively wearing out shoe leather near the putting clock, on which one nouveau riche oil man, his two jumbo-size diamond rings glinting in the sunlight, is matter-of-factly saying to another as he pushes a twelve-footer past the cup: "This new deal will make me twenty-five thousand dollars a month for life." The mention of money does not ease Burke's roily mood. One of Houston's best-known bankers has complained of slow play at Champions and sworn to quit the club and take all of his influential friends with him, or something, and Burke is furious.

Now Demaret, dressed in assorted shades of green (he was dressing this way before Doug Sanders saw his first rainbow), ambles out of the clubhouse. He smiles and waves, and greets the group with an amiable "Whaddayuh say, ole buddies?" Eventually the photographer poses the two, bidding them just to relax. In Demaret's case, the suggestion is ridiculous; telling Demaret to relax is like telling Wilt Chamberlain to be tall, or Raquel Welch to be sexy. Burke is another matter. A scowl clouding his handsome face, he is railing at Demaret about the banker.

"Beats any damn thing I ever saw," Burke snaps. "Who does he think he is, threatening me?"

"I can't figure him," says Demaret, agreeing but not angry.

"I was playing right in front of him yesterday, and nobody kept me waiting," Burke goes on.

"He's comin' on stronger'n train smoke," says Demaret, shaking his head in exaggerated concurrence.

"Smile, Jackie," implores the photographer, who by now has already shot a roll of film to no avail.

"I'm going down to that bank when we finish this and take out a hundred and seventy thousand," Burke growls.

"What's all this I stuff?" Demaret kids Burke with a wink at the photographer. "I thought we were partners."

"You come with me. We're not doing any more business with this guy."

"Okay, but let's wait till tomorrow. I've got a game in twenty minutes, and I need to win a little walkin'-around money. We'll get together with him tomorrow and see what he has to say." Demaret's tone is pacifying.

Burke, partially mollifed, grunts agreement, and in response to another plea from the photographer, manages a half-sardonic smile. The session over, Demaret, who has been beaming throughout, goes off to join the three Champions members with whom he will play a round. Burke, still shaking his head in mock disbelief, stalks back to his office in the clubhouse to return a list of phone calls.

It would be difficult to find in the business world an odder couple than Jack Burke and Jimmy Demaret. As unlike as a campus radical and the cop on the beat, they have worked closely for a dozen years, building one of the finest, most prestigious young golf clubs in the country, and—through foresighted investments in neighboring real estate—becoming exceptionally wealthy. Burke, wavy-haired and looking thirty-six instead of the forty-eight he is, is an intense, opinionated, sometimes impetuous driver of a man, who slams through a working day and then, dutiful father of four, goes home at exactly five o'clock and usually stays there through the evening.

The silver-haired Demaret, by contrast, is older by thirteen years, had to struggle as a youngster where Burke did not, is avuncular and easygoing and an enthusiastic after-hours socializer (his daughter is grown). It has been said, with considerable justification, that he has more friends than anyone else in the game. He is probably the funniest man in golf with his drawling, extemporaneous one-liners that land on every available target. "I'm overgolfed," Demaret once said. "I just had lunch with Claude Harmon." (Harmon, being a ranking teacher of the game, will debate theory for hours.) At the Masters one year Demaret smiled and waved at the jovial Roberto De Vicenzo of Argentina, then said, solemnly: "Play good. I got a bet on you for low Mexican." Not even Ben Hogan is spared Demaret's long needle (Demaret is one of a handful of men close to Hogan). Hogan, so the story goes, built a marvelous $200,000 home in Fort Worth, and included only one bedroom. "Hell, Ben," Demaret laconically said to Hogan the next time he saw him, "you could have put another bedroom in that place. I wasn't goin' to come and visit you, anyway." His nimble wit has made Demaret a popular and highly paid ($100,000 a year reportedly) television commentator on the *Shell's Wonderful World of Golf* series.

Telling Demaret stories is the second-most popular indoor sport in Houston, behind only talking about money. There was the time Demaret was on the Johnny Carson show, and Carson asked him to analyze his swing. Demaret said fine. Carson swished a club through the air and looked at him expectantly. Demaret thoughtfully stroked his chin and moved around on Carson's other side.

"Swing again," said Demaret.

Carson did. Demaret moved to still another angle of observation.

"Swing one more time, John," said Demaret, arching his eyebrows.

Carson did.

"What do you think?" he asked Demaret.

"Tell you what, John," Demaret drawled, sucking on his teeth. "If I were you I'd lay off for a couple weeks." He paused. Then he added: "And then I'd quit." The audience fell all over itself.

Playing in an early Texas Open in San Antonio, Demaret was beset by stomach difficulties, and was briefly confined in the hospital. Released, he was not sure he would make it through his practice round the following day. He did, but leaving the eighteenth green his stride had none of its familiar zest, and his normally florid complexion was pale. A rookie photographer from the local newspaper, unaware of Demaret's condition, rushed over and informed him that his editors needed a good action picture for the next edition, and would Demaret please comply. Demaret blanched, insofar as that was possible. "Son," he moaned, "whaddayuh want me to do? Throw up?"

The funny Demaret, the fiery Burke. Wherefore this unlikely consortium? Its roots are planted in the mid-1920s in Houston, where both were born. Burke's father, Jack Burke Sr., runner-up in the 1920 U.S. Open, but better known as a crack instructor, was head professional at the exclusive River Oaks Country Club, and was sort of a combination teacher, hero, and father-confessor to the young pros in Texas. Demaret caddied at River Oaks as a youngster, and at eighteen became an assistant to the elder Burke.

Jack Burke Sr. refined Demaret's game (and his social graces) in long sessions on the practice tee and in the Burke living room. Demaret passed many evenings with the Burke family, talking golf and bouncing around with Burke's young son, Jackie, who affectionately called him "Uncle Jim." Demaret and Jack Jr. did not see so much of one another when Demaret later went to work in the East and joined the PGA Tour, but Jimmy would not return to Houston without visiting the Burke home.

In 1943, Jack Sr. and Demaret were to play an exhibition match against Byron Nelson and Harold (Jug) McSpaden, the famous Gold Dust Twins. But Jack Sr. died shortly before the match, and Jack Jr., at the time a judo instructor in the Marines, filled in as Demaret's partner. The two were more or less a team from then on.

Upon his discharge from the service, Burke went on the tour. Demaret guided him, repaying the favor Burke's father did him. The two traveled together and, driving along, would discuss the other players, various competitive situations, and the different courses they played. Especially they were intrigued by the courses.

"The touring pros today fly everywhere and don't realize what it was like to drive hundreds of miles between tournaments," Burke says. "It could get pretty tedious. We would play this game with the countryside speculating on what kind of golf hole a stretch of land would make—whether we could cut a green into the side of a certain hill, or a fairway through a certain wooded area. That's where we got the idea to build our own course, drawing on our knowledge of the good and bad features of courses we had seen."

Meanwhile, Demaret and Burke established themselves as top players, winning, between them, forty-three titles. Demaret comes very, very close to being one of the few genuine greats of golf, having won three Masters Championships and twenty-eight other events, including a Vardon Trophy. Additionally, he was the most colorful performer the game has seen, with the possible exception of Walter Hagen. (Demaret once was turned out in two-tone shoes of deep purple and rose pink, pink slacks, and a sea-green shirt with white trim. For a long time the regular writers on pro golf lived off Demaret copy.)

Burke, seemingly doomed to be known as the perennial rookie of the year, blossomed in 1950 and '51 into, if not a Demaret, a fine player, winning four tournaments in succession. His big year was 1956, when he won the Masters and the PGA Championship.

That very same year, Demaret and Burke announced their virtual retirement from the tour, a surprising move by Burke, then in the prime of his career. But he wanted to be with his family, and felt that the time was opportune for a new golf club in Houston, where both he and Demaret had won tour events and were widely liked.

Nevertheless, their decision several months later to build a course in northwest Harris County was generally regarded as ill-considered. "They'll lose their butts," one Houston tycoon pronounced, and he had a point. The locale they had chosen was a remote, undeveloped sector twenty-five miles from downtown Houston and farther than that from the south part of town, where live the people with the money to support a first-class golf club. And this before a modern freeway network linked the loosely connected environs of the sprawling, 440-square-mile city.

Houston is a place that admires the big thinker and the big spender (see Judge Hofheinz and his Astrodome), and is a city in a hurry, seeking to out-culture New York overnight (there is an apocryphal story about the leading socialite in Houston who only five years ago was a madame in a house of ill repute). But it also is a city with deeply ingrained views about which are the "right" parts of town. Demaret and Burke were, it was agreed, making a disastrous mistake.

But they had carefully studied the situation for nearly a year, and had sufficient reasons for their choice. "It was the so-called wrong side of the tracks," says Demaret, "but it was also the only pretty section, the only place with woods and rolling ground. It was higher than the rest of town, and drier; there was less fog and smog. The land was cheap. There was no doubt in our minds that the freeways would come, and that if we gave people the greatest golf club in the world, we'd do all right."

For financing, Demaret and Burke and a half-dozen partners, who included Jack Valenti, turned to the memberships of the elite Houston Club and Petroleum Club, among others, and sold their idea to 500 golf-minded, well-to-do businessmen who, for a $500 initiation fee, became charter members of . . . well, a patch of wilderness.

"We raised a quarter of a million dollars in initiation fees, and hadn't knocked down a tree," Demaret says. "This club was built on trust and friendship."

The original eighteen holes? The Cypress Creek Course, where the Open will be played, opened in 1967. To hasten the development of the surrounding area, Demaret and Burke launched high-priced housing projects related to the golf club—Champions West, Champions South, et cetera. To protect themselves against a nearby incursion of cheap housing, they took options on more land.

Today, the few lots that remain in the vicinity of the club are valued at as much as $15,000 an acre. Demaret and Burke originally bought at $500 an acre. They have expanded their original holding from 529 to 1,400 acres, have sold 400 expensive homes, and have planned an additional 1,400, some on a new twelve-acre artificial lake. Another developer is building 1,800 homes that will start at $35,000 and scale upward to $200,000. Too, there are cottage complexes, apartments and townhouses, and planned is a racquet club with townhouses and twenty tennis courts, two indoors. Freeways run almost to the door of the clubhouse, and by the time of the Open this month, the vast new Houston Intercontinental Airport should be in business just up the road, which could well make the previous boom sound like a cap pistol. "It has been pretty much a development for people with no children," says a chamber-of-commerce official. "Now you see schools, shopping centers—the works. It's the fastest-growing part of Houston."

And in large part because Demaret and Burke had a dream to build a championship golf course. "The club is all we ever really wanted," Burke says. "The housing made us some money and helped the club, but we're selling our real estate interests to Pat Morgan, who used to be an executive with the First Flight Company, and our main involvement will be with the club. We had to cut a lot of corners at first, to spend our money on the golf course. Now we're spending two hundred fifty thousand dollars to expand the clubhouse. It will be finished for the Open." . . .

. . . If everything is prosperity and light today for Demaret and Burke at Champions, the early years were a constant struggle, and no one begrudges them their success. The turning point came in 1964, when the second eighteen, the Jackrabbit Course, opened, giving Champions perhaps the finest thirty-six holes in the Southwest—if not the country. "We can give our members a choice between two distinctly different courses," Demaret says. "Cypress was designed by Jack and I and Ralph Plummer. George Fazio did the Jackrabbit Course with us. Cypress is more modern, with wide, tree-lined fairways, large, subtle greens, not many bunkers, and five lakes. Cypress puts a premium on the well-played second shot. The Jackrabbit, which we believe will be just as good a tournament course when it matures, is more of an Eastern course, with elevated tees and greens, tighter fairways, smaller greens, and more bunkering. It is as different from Cypress as we could make it."

With the opening of the second eighteen, the membership soared, and has since been cut off at nine hundred. The initiation fee is now $3,000 plus dues of $48 a month. For their money, members get what Ben Hogan has privately called the finest golfing atmosphere he has experienced. The L-shaped locker room is comfortably immense, with a large horseshoe bar, color television sets, a lot of wood paneling and lush carpeting and leather furniture, and card tables that encourage pre-

and post-round relaxation (one unfortunate fellow is said to have lost his $90,000 home one night in a particularly wild card game).

The glass-walled pro shop looks into the lodge area—containing the unpretentious dining room and main bar—and shop assistants are instructed by innovative head professional Jimmy Burke, Jack's brother, to keep an eye out for a member in the locker room who acts as though he would like a game but does not have one. They are to politely take him in hand, and arrange him a game. Immediately, if not sooner.

Outside, the fine touch of Demaret and Burke is everywhere apparent. As you move around the perimeter from the locker room, you come, consecutively, to the caddie and golf-cart area, the practice tee, the putting clock, a snack shop complete with rest rooms, and the first tee of the Cypress Course, so that you are eased smoothly into your round with scarcely a wasted step.

One course always is stag. One week, the men play Cypress and the women and mixed groups Jackrabbit; the following week the roles are reversed, and so on. There is a handsome swimming pool on the far side of the clubhouse, but Champions is essentially a golf club (no dance floor and no social activities not directly tied to golf events). All nine hundred members play, and their average score is claimed to be 78. Demaret doubts that any other similar-size membership can match this scoring. Says Burke, "Our members are serious players. They're not out there to sell some poor slob an insurance policy." Demaret and Burke do not give formal lessons, but one or the other is almost always at the course and available to members who want to introduce them proudly to friends, relatives, and business associates.

Burke is the business arm of the operation. Possessed of terrific energy and imagination, he is president of the club and cochairman this year of the Open with Earl Elliott of the Houston Golf Association. He personally oversees the club books, and is the man the community turns to when money is involved. He is always outspoken, but Houstonians have come to know and appreciate his good qualities, which are many. "Jack has always been one to say what's on his mind without a second thought," says a charter member of the club, "and he offends some people who don't know him well. He'll get a hundred ideas a day, and ninety-nine of them will stink, but you'd better listen to that other one, because it's liable to be a bomb. Jimmy knows how to listen to Jack and sort out the good ideas from the bad, all the while kidding and pretending not to take his partner seriously. That's one reason they make a great team."

Demaret, on the other hand, is officially in charge of the course and unofficially in charge of management-member and management-public relations. Not infrequently he finds it his lot to brush down feathers that Burke, in his straightforward, sometimes blustery manner, has ruffled. No one could be better at getting along with all kinds of people. At the Ryder Cup banquet in Houston two years ago, Burke, unimpressed with the work of a high PGA official, was going to "forget" to introduce him on the dais, until dissuaded by Demaret and others. "We disagree like any other business partners," says Burke, "but it's impossible to get mad at Jimmy. He'll have you laughing first."

The members have nothing to say about the conduct of their club. There are no committees. Burke and Demaret make all the major decisions, insuring a continuity of policy and management that other clubs are hard-pressed to equal with temporary, amateur committees. The twosome receives few complaints; the only one I heard was that some members would just as soon the Open be played on an oil tanker off the coast of Galveston, so they wouldn't have to give up their course that week. This equable atmosphere is largely due to Demaret's good-natured camaraderie. He often plays golf with the members, and will swap stories with them at the bar until closing time. (Not at all sympathetic with the anti-liquor movement that keeps Houston's liquor laws anything but liberal, he has four bars in his own home.) At a slight provocation, he will break into a nicely rendered song—he turned down offers to sing with the big bands of Jimmy Dorsey and Lawrence Welk. If Burke and Demaret have thought of everything for their members, they cater to visiting tournament players just as attentively, as contestants in the Open will quickly discover. Jack Tuthill of the PGA field staff, in his weekly memorandum to PGA headquarters, has referred to the Champions International, a regular tour event that will be dispensed with this year in deference to the Open, as the finest tournament in the world for the players.

A wing of the locker room is closed off, and a table of food and drink set out for the players, guaranteeing them the privacy they seldom can find at tour stops. A training room is staffed by the head trainers of the Houston Astros and Houston Oilers. Many tour regulars complain about pro-ams, and so there are no pro-ams. Instead, there are photo days for the fans, followed by clinics featuring Burke and Demaret, at which Demaret is liable to wear almost anything. One year he showed up in a shirt, tie, sport coat, and a pair of psychedelic walking shorts that would glow in the dark, and the conservatively dressed Burke, at the microphone, shrieked, "Jimmy . . . you forgot your pants!"

This improbable pair, Burke and Demaret, their improbable golf club and related investments making them wealthy, Texas wealthy, are motivated by a common goal, and it is this that has welded them into the enduring team they are. "We both want Champions to be the finest club there is," Demaret says. "We both have rich tastes, as different as we are in most ways, and we like the best in everything. In that respect, we are a lot alike."

If there was any doubt about Champions's credentials, they were obliterated with its selection for the Open. While this is not your usual Open course, steeped in tradition and staid as a twenty-year-old pipe, Champions has a great deal going for it. Come the week of the Open, and Jimmy Demaret, resplendently attired, will be on the front lawn by the clubhouse as players, officials, and fans begin to arrive, and he will be smiling and waving and warmly exclaiming, "Whaddayuh say, ole buddies?" And all will be right in one small corner of the world anyway.

(Editor's note: When Steve Elkington won the 1995 PGA, he became the fourth member at Champions to win that tournament, the others being Burke, Marr, and Jay Hebert. "Isn't that kind of unusual, having four members who won the PGA?" observed Tim Melton, a Houston sportscaster.

"That's not so unusual here," Burke quipped. "We've got three members who walked on the moon."

In case you're wondering? The three astronauts are Alan Shepard, who hit a golf ball up there with a six-iron, Charles Duke, and Gene Cernan.)

Preston Trail: Last Bastion of Male Chauvinism

Blackie Sherrod

Golf Digest, *May 1973*

The elegantly gowned dowager stalked across the stone entranceway, pulled open the ornate door, waltzed inside, and braked to a stop in horror. Sprawled in a leather chair, jaybird-naked save for a towel, was a man calmly talking on the telephone. His eyebrows shot up in shock and he clutched the towel as if Hannibal's elephants were dragging it from him. Then both, stifling genteel little screams, fled in opposite directions.

The lady was a lost guest who had mistaken Preston Trail Golf Club for the neighboring Prestonwood Country Club, where she had a luncheon date.

The unsuspecting nudist was a Dallas oil millionaire making a business call, and if he wished to talk buff bare, then by damn that was his right. He paid dearly for the Preston Trail privileges, one of which is a strict ban on women visitors.

This was one of few occasions when a woman has seen the inside of Preston Trail Golf Club, one of the richest and most exclusive in the nation, and site of the upcoming Byron Nelson Golf Classic.

Preston Trail is not just for men only; it dang near is for millionaires only. Of the limited two hundred fifty memberships, one-fifth can be safely classified as millionaires and another one hundred are flirting comfortably with that neighborhood. The Preston Trail parking lot looks like a Cadillac dealership. All us rich Texans drive nothing but Cadillacs, baby. You know that.

First rich Texan: "I bought a new car today."

Second rich Texan: "Sure 'nuff? What kind?"

First rich Texan: "Blue."

Memberships in Preston Trail, now traded on a bid basis whenever one surfaces, have gone as high as $22,000. And even then you must pass a screening committee that could give lessons to the CIA.

An ordinary day might find Lamar Hunt, the international oilman/sportsman, lining up a putt on one green, while Mickey Mantle whacks one of his prodigious drives off the next tee. And conglomerate master Jim Ling is eating a $2.50 bowl of chili in the grill, waiting for Herman Lay, the potato chip king, to arrive. On the practice green is former pro football star Buddy Dial, now on his way to high brackets as a clothing manufacturer. (Dial's membership cost him $20,026, the odd $26 being a sentimental addition in memory of his old football-jersey number.)

Clint Murchison, owner of the Dallas Cowboys, is changing shoes in the locker room, and so is John Niland, his all-pro offensive guard. Both are Preston Trail members, albeit with a slight difference in bank statements. Bob Strauss, the Democratic Party national chairman, is soaping up, and Jack Stroube, the resident needle, is barking to a fellow member, "Don't get smart with me! My daddy has more money than your daddy!"

Downstairs in the pro shop someone admires the garments of Ed Haggar, of the menswear family.

"I've been trying to find a pair of Haggar slacks exactly like that," says the guy. Whereupon Ed unzips, steps out of his pants, hands them to his friend, and stands there in his jockey shorts, never pausing in conversation.

The unique Preston Trail operation is patterned partly after Burning Tree in Washington and Bob O'Link in Chicago, but it has become nationally established in its own right. The eight-year-old course, located some twenty miles north of Dallas, exists for golf only. No swimming pool. No tennis courts. Oh, you might get a gin game around the heavy wooden locker-room tables, if you don't mind going up to seventy cents a point.

But the $500,000 clubhouse is plushly business. A pro shop, bag and cart storage downstairs; locker room, bar and grill, sauna, and offices upstairs. Gene Shields, a husky, affable politician, presides over the pro shop. Royce Chaney runs the clubhouse. Twenty-seven employees are on the payroll.

Plush as it is, Preston Trail runs a tight ship. No dinner parties, buddy. No night meals. You can have brunch or lunch. A cheeseburger, $1.50, and a bottle of beer, sixty cents. Not too bad when you've just finished putting together a multimillion-dollar merger. Or brought in a new oil field, like maybe Jake Hamon or Al Meadows are wont to do. Or won another big-stakes race as happens frequently to Buddy Fogelson and his missus, Greer Garson.

Preston Trail is the product of four Dallas golf enthusiasts, all of whom are reasonably well aware of where their next sirloin or yacht is coming from. John Murchison, of the legendary Murchison fortunes, is one. Oilman Stuart Hunt, newspaper publisher Jim Chambers, and oilman and developer Pollard Simons are the other three founders.

The story goes that these guys became weary of waiting for tee times at busy Dallas Country Club and Brookhollow, two other hoity-toity clubs in Dallas. So they decided to build their very own little playground, where never is heard a hurrying word and the fairways are not crowded all day.

Murchison and Simons owned a couple of farms some discreet distance from crowded Dallas real estate. They whacked 161 acres out of the middle, threaded by temperamental White Rock Creek, and sold it to the project at cost, around $2,000 an acre. The gently rolling, wooded slopes have a history dating back to 1840, when a military supply road, linking Texas forts on the Brazos and Red Rivers, ran through this property. It was named Preston Road because of its destination: Fort Preston on the Red River.

Byron Nelson, the immensely popular Mr. Golf around Dallas, was engaged as consultant and Ralph Plummer as architect. Construction started in 1962 at a course cost of $1.5 million.

Preston Trail supposedly is a collection of Nelson's favorite holes around the world; a number of the greens are similar in design to those at Augusta National. From the member tees, the par-71 layout plays at 6,636 yards. For the professionals in the $150,000 Byron Nelson Classic, the test is a par 70 over 7,076 yards.

Forty-eight charter members put up $4,000 each to start the project. Membership limit was established at two hundred fifty. Members own their own stock, and in the event of death or withdrawal, the stock may sell to the highest bidder approved by the membership committee. The last membership-winning bid (one comes up about every six months) was $10,000. The club retains twenty percent of the stock-transfer price, but still Preston Trail remains one of the few golf organizations wherein a member may realize a handsome profit on his investment. Monthly dues are $100.

A special arrangement was made for the cluster of tour golfers who headquarter in Dallas. They paid $1,000 initiation and their monthly dues are $25; because of their travels they are classified as nonresident members.

The late Champagne Tony Lema, a Dallas resident, was a Preston Trail member, and his locker has been kept intact; his clothes and golf shoes are still there. Nelson, whose plaques and trophies line the entrance corridor, is the only honorary member.

When the club began operation in 1965, wives were invited to a gala opening night and then officially banned forever. Not even during the Byron Nelson Classic are women allowed inside the clubhouse. Hundreds of pretty miniskirted "Nelsonettes" serve as scorekeepers, guides, and hostesses during the event, but they are relegated to tents and trailers and porta-cans. Of course, these are no ordinary porta-cans, my dear. Each has a sedate little pot of ivy bolted to an inside wall.

There have been two official exceptions to the ban against women. Rev. Billy Graham, a Nelson pro-am participant, brought his wife inside to show her the Nelson trophies, not realizing it was a men-only operation. Tony Lema's mother, who presented the club an oil painting of her famous son, was given a tour of the premises on a Monday, when the course is closed.

Oh yes, one other female made a semiofficial visit. She parked her car outside, dashed to the door, and was informed of the club embargo on women. Whereupon she announced loudly that she didn't give a damn, that she had to go wee-wee and this was the only cover for miles around. An amused member cleared out the locker room and escorted her to the john. He forgot one member who was inside a stall and who almost set a club record for cardiac arrest when he heard high heels on the tile floor.

Preston Trail members got their wish for privacy and uncrowded conditions. During the spring and summer months, Preston Trail will host only fifty golfers on an average weekday, maybe 125 on weekend days. In 1972, for example, the pro shop counted only 13,500 total rounds for the twelve months. Another rather exclusive place, Shady Oaks in Fort Worth, Ben Hogan's hangout, had 22,000 rounds during the same period. In further contrast, a Dallas municipal course named Elm Fork recorded 76,000 rounds in 1972.

Greens fees for guests are $10 during the week, $15 on weekends, and, of course, each guest must play with his member host. The guest list is autograph territory. Bob Hope often plays there on his visits to Dallas, and he's been a frequent participant in the Nelson Pro-Am. A couple of years ago, Hope was paired with Rev. Graham.

The minister hooked a high tee shot that had the gallery moaning as it disappeared into a tree bordering the rough. Suddenly there was a loud crack as the ball struck a limb and reappeared, bouncing out on the fairway. Hope clapped palm to forehead, wheeled, and shook hands with the preacher.

"Tell me," Hope asked the gallery, "did he slip to one knee?"

"This guy is always pulling miracles," Hope continued. "He can find a four-leaf clover in a sand trap."

There is a constant air of looseness, born of greenback pollution. When Notre Dame coach Ara Parseghian guested there after his Irish lost a Cotton Bowl game to Texas, club jester Stroube greeted him with, "Congratulations on going for a loss instead of a tie."

Of course, with men of independent wealth, there also are independent ideas on how a club should be run and maintained. Shields, now in his sixth year, is only the club's second pro, but the grounds-and-greens committee has run through five greenskeepers.

"It's not the biggest job financially," said the pro, "but there's a lot of freedom. I get to play a lot of golf, the members all support the pro shop, and I get to meet everybody who comes to town." . . .

. . . Preston Trail may have lifted certain ideas from Burning Tree and Bob O'Link, but now it serves as an all-male model in its own right. A Kansas City group made six trips to the Dallas club to study its operation, resulting in construction of the Wolf Creek Golf Club, south of Kansas City. Interested parties in Oklahoma City and Columbia, Missouri, also have researched the Preston Trail format.

As for the course itself, it is becoming as plush as the facilities. It is long and spacious, a special favorite of Jack Nicklaus, who won back-to-back victories here in 1970–71. Jack's first triumph came in a dramatic playoff with old rival Arnold Palmer, won with a birdie on the first extra hole.

The tremendous, sometimes errant drives of Mickey Mantle are a constant locker room topic. Mantle once played in a Nelson Pro-Am with long-hitting Martin Roesink of Holland, supposedly the distance king of all. Mantle held his own with Roesink and outdrove him on several holes. On the fourteenth tee, facing a 430-yard challenge, Mantle was afraid to use his straying driver because of the spectators lining the fairways. So he took a three-wood and smote a shot, by actual measurement, 398 yards. . . .

. . . As for the Byron Nelson Classic itself, the tournament is an offshoot of the old Dallas Open, started in 1956 by wealthy industrialist Jim Ling. A decade later, the event was adopted by the affluent Salesmanship Club of Dallas and moved to Preston Trail in 1968. Newspaper editor Felix McKnight, a Preston Trail member, suggested the name change to honor Byron Nelson. That alteration, plus considerable muscle from heavy names in the Salesmanship Club, resulted in better spring dates for the tournament and a springboard to national prestige.

That first event, won by Miller Barber, is remembered not for the golf shots themselves, but for the pretournament testimonial banquet honoring Nelson. It probably drew the biggest collection of famous golf names ever gathered under one roof. Jimmy Demaret sang. Ben Hogan spoke. Palmer, Nicklaus, Player, Casper, and Trevino were merely members of the audience. . . .

. . . The Salesmanship Club itself is unique. The organization is misnamed; it is a collection of the most influential, commanding names in the city, all dedicated to a single project, rehabilitation of boys with problems. The $400,000 yearly budget includes a beautiful camp in East Texas woodlands and a rehabilitation house in Dallas.

All Salesmanship Club members are assigned posts during the Nelson Classic. It is nothing to see Paul Thayer, board chairman of LTV, raking a sand trap, or Toddie Lee Wynne Jr., heir to an oil throne, serving as a marshal.

In 1968 there was such a huge gallery following Arnold Palmer that Preston Trail member David Thornton foresaw a spectating problem. He approached the caddie who was carrying the score placard, offered him $20 for his job, and enjoyed a tiring but unobstructed view of the round.

Several years ago, Jack Tuthill the foremost fussbudget of tour officials, was fretting over the trailer designated as his PGA headquarters. He nervously informed W. L. Todd, the tournament chairman, of his need for another desk.

"Just a minute, Jack," oilman Todd said pleasantly. "I'll see if I can get a couple of bank presidents to move one in for you." And he did.

If You Don't Like What You See, You're Too Old to Be Looking

Gary Cartwright

Texas Monthly, *May 1978*

I don't know what was going through John Schroeder's mind as 20,000 spectators watched him line up a putt worth $18,000 on the final hole of the final day of Colonial Country Club's 1977 golf tournament, but I was thinking about my old Granny. The twenty-five-foot putt would enable Schroeder to tie for first place and force a sudden-death playoff with Ben Crenshaw. It was easily the most important putt in Schroeder's eight years on the professional tour: Although Schroeder's yearly earnings have climbed as high as $67,000, he is considered an unknown.

In contrast, Crenshaw, the young Austin High and University of Texas graduate, has won more than $500,000 since turning pro in 1973 and is considered the Jack Nicklaus of his generation. I knew what my old Granny would be thinking as Schroeder drew back his putter. She would be thinking: Miss it, turkey. And so he did, by a fraction of an inch.

Granny used to think that golf was a cream-puff game redeemed only by the fact that it occupied the weekends of men who would otherwise be foreclosing on small farms and roping widows and orphans (Granny was both) to railroad trestles. Then about 1960, television introduced her to Arnold Palmer. Palmer reminded sportswriters, and by extension my granny, of a blacksmith hammering out his trade on an anvil, and on that image the masses rose up and swallowed the game as mindlessly as they would have swallowed a new brand of shrimp-flavored almonds.

Golf had its good guys and its bad guys—Granny never cared much for Gary Player because he dressed in black and was a foreigner (from South Africa), and it took her a spell to adjust to the news that Jack

Nicklaus had once been a fraternity boy at Ohio State. Golf was both childishly simple and vicariously egalitarian, so long as it was exercised, as Granny exercised it, in front of a seventeen-inch TV screen. It was a remarkable sight to walk into Granny's tiny living room, cluttered with yellowing photographs of catfish she had caught and relics preserved from the 1936 Texas Centennial, there to find the old lady playing out her remaining weekends perched in front of her Montgomery Ward ("Monkey Ward" she called it) black-and-white set, dipping Garrett snuff, and pontificating such wisdom as, "Arnie was making a run on the field till he chili-dipped that wedge on fourteen."

Granny lived all of her life in or around Fort Worth but never saw a Colonial, except on TV. When I was a sportswriter, I offered to take her, but I might as well have asked her to put on her best housedress and come meet the queen of England. "What would I do out there with all them high-muckety-mucks?" she wanted to know. Granny wasn't a social climber: Her idea of high rolling was taking a city bus to Leonard's Department Store's free parking lot, catching the subway that connected to the store's huge basement, purchasing a spool of No. 1 thread, dining on fried perch and peach cobbler at the Leonard's cafeteria, and returning home in time to watch *Arnold Palmer's Tips on Golf,* which preceded the tournament of the week.

Once, when we were driving through Forest Park, I turned off impulsively on Colonial Parkway, which skirts the rosebush-laced fences of the golf course and circles in front of the country club's faintly antebellum red-brick clubhouse. "You're fixin' to get us arrested," Granny warned. I told her that Colonial Parkway was a public thoroughfare, the same as her own modest street. If that was so, she asked, then why did a high muckety-muck like Marvin Leonard, the department-store mogul and founder of Colonial, live there? I said that Marvin didn't actually *live* at Colonial. It was true that he built Colonial and supervised its rebuilding after a series of fires and floods, but now he had built a second country club, Shady Oaks, and it was my understanding that he made his home somewhere in that neighborhood. Shady Oaks was now *the* club in Fort Worth. I asked if she was interested in seeing Shady

Oaks, but Granny's old eyes had wandered through the stately oaks and elms and out to the perfectly manicured seventeenth fairway, where a group of men in Ban-Lon shirts and straw hats were preparing to hit their drives. "It's the most beautiful thing I ever saw," she said.

As I watched John Schroeder miss the most important putt of his life, my heart sank in a small, permanent way. Granny had hexed him from the grave. Arnie and Jack weren't even in the field, but I knew Granny would already have taken Ben Crenshaw to heart with the same unwavering zeal that she felt back in the '20s the first time she watched the Fighting Texas Aggie Band parade through Fort Worth. Crenshaw had that special zing. If Palmer was a blacksmith, Crenshaw was a sculptor. Twenty thousand groaned as Schroeder missed his big putt, but later, when everyone was drunk and mellowed out on a hard week of socializing and name playing, all you heard was, What a great finish for a great tournament.

Poor Schroeder. I guess second place wasn't so bad, seeing as how he won $22,800 and got to appear on national TV in the shadow of Ben Crenshaw.

Inching along with the tournament traffic on Colonial Parkway early in May, I observed residents hawking parking spaces on their front lawns for five dollars. A few hundred yards from the clubhouse was a barricade guarded by a policeman who rerouted all motorists not possessing Super Saints badges. All other categories—the ordinary Angels, Patrons, club members, and plain folks with fifteen-dollar tickets—were directed to the TCU Stadium parking lot where buses waited to ferry them to the golf course. There are 1,600 members of Colonial, and a waiting list of six months, but only a few hundred wear the gold badges of Super Saints. Aside from the color of their badges, there is one other way to recognize Super Saints. They don't sweat. It is an acquired art. For the privilege of playing in the pro-am, enjoying valet parking, and gaining entrance to the exclusive Terrace Room overlooking the seventeenth tee and eighteenth green, Super Saints purchased $1,500 worth of tickets. Mere Angels absorbed only $750 in tickets, and so on down the pecking order. In a way, the police barricade near the clubhouse represented a final bastion separating the plutocrats from the plebeians. It was somehow sad to watch an exquisitely proportioned young woman with the word SPOILED printed on her T-shirt being turned away.

The Terrace Room is not a good place to watch a golf tournament, but it has been my observation that Super Saints do not come to watch, but to be watched. From the ground you can look up and see them cool as cloisonné behind tinted glass. In case anyone has a passing interest in the tournament, there are TV sets strategically situated in every room of the clubhouse: the Chalet Room, the Mirador Room, the Gold Room, the Cork Room, the 19th Hole, and the Men's Card Room—these being the hangouts of Angels and mortals—all of them packed with revelers, make-out artists, and wool inspectors. Wool is a sporting-world euphemism for . . . well, for good-looking women. One former tournament chairman is known affectionately to the press as Old Wool. A Fort Worth doctor caught in the act of leering at a nifty in a thin halter told me: "It's okay. I have a clearance from my wife to leer at anything above a 36-B cup." There was an oilman who used to position himself in the 19th Hole with a prepared sign that said: TELL THE ONE IN BLUE TO TURN AROUND. Probably the most memorable scene in Colonial archives was an act of flagrante delicto near the fifteenth fairway, captured, quite by luck, by an ABC cameraman testing his equipment: This classic piece of photojournalism has since been shown—privately—worldwide, and the performers, who were not married to each other, are no longer married to anyone. And Cullen Davis, the multimillionaire charged with murdering his stepdaughter and his wife's lover, used to park his trailer near the clubhouse and treat his guests to private screenings of *Deep Throat.*

Cullen was in the jailhouse and not available for this year's tournament, but his estranged wife, Priscilla, star witness in the murder case, was highly visible in tight white pants and a blouse that covered the scar on her stomach and very little else. Priscilla was accompanied by her bodyguard, an off-duty homicide detective, and her presence in the Terrace Room less than a year after the murders created the kind of stir you would expect on finding Truman Capote in Gloria Vanderbilt's shower. A few Super Saints openly greeted her; the rest openly snubbed her: There wasn't a trace of indifference. Tom McCann, former mayor of Fort Worth and a man who himself has known adversity, sat holding Priscilla's hand and telling her how the tournament just wasn't the same without Cullen; though of course he was delighted to see her alive and maybe when this thing was all over everyone could get together like in the good old days.

In a sense Priscilla Davis epitomized the style and spirit of Colonial. If it was true that the real pooh-bahs of Fort Worth now formed their alliances in the sedentary lounges of Shady Oaks, Colonial was still where things happened. CBS sports commentator Tom Brookshier, who has been around, observed that Colonial was "the halter-top capital of the world," and Norm Alden, a former Fort Worth disk jockey who went on to become a minor actor best known for his Aamco commercials, noted, "If you don't like what you see at Colonial, you're too old to be looking." I don't have the figures to prove it, but I'd wager that a majority of the members at Shady Oaks hold dual memberships at Colonial, if for no other reason than to be a part of the yearly rites. One of the city's better-known gamblers was doing a few card tricks for the oilmen in the Men's Card Room, and Hayden Fry, athletic director at North Texas State, lobbied appropriate powers on behalf of his school's campaign to join the Southwest Conference. Willie Nelson was supposed to be at Colonial, but he overslept.

Back in the days of Ben Hogan the biggest celebrities you were likely to encounter inside the clubhouse were golfers, but that practice seems to have gone the way of all things. I didn't spot a single golfer in any of the hangouts, not that I would necessarily recognize one. Golfers used to have names like Hogan, Snead, Nelson, Palmer, and Nicklaus—these days they are called Tewell, Cerrudo, Kratzert, Zoeller, and Curl, and if that sounds like a seat on the New York Stock Exchange my point is made. Golf is the only sport I can think of where success is measured almost entirely by how many trips you make to the bank. Where once a man had to be rich to play golf, now the reverse seems true. No less than a dozen golfers currently on the tour have pocketed more than a million dollars. (There now are fifteen over the million mark.) When you're playing for those kinds of stakes, who has time to sit around jabbering with local Super Saints?

Though he lives in Fort Worth, Ben Hogan no longer plays or even attends Colonial. He can't stand the crowds. During the tournament I asked a friend of Hogan's what the great man was doing with himself these days. "Practicing," the friend said. "Sometimes he'll play a few holes, alone with his caddie, but his legs won't make it through eighteen. But there's not a day goes by you won't find him on the practice tee. If he hits twenty balls on the green, you can cover them with your coat."

In recognition of the fact that he has won the National Invitation Tournament, as Colonial is officially known, a record five times, and also because he redesigned several of the holes—supervising the removal of a number of trees including the big oak on No. 1 fairway that he used to hit regularly—Colonial is known as "Hogan's Alley." Almost all of Hogan's trophies are on permanent display in a room adjacent to Colonial's main lobby, but hardly anyone stops to look. Breaking one of my two cardinal rules for watching Colonial, I decided to visit the Hogan Trophy Room. As I stood there admiring a phonograph record with a sterling-silver label identifying it as "an address by Dr. Granville Walker [Ben's pastor] in commemoration of Ben Hogan's British Open victory, July 27, 1953," I was suddenly aware of two young girls in shorts. They were breathing on the display glass and drawing hearts in their own fog. They asked me to get them a couple of beers.

"You can sign my daddy's name," one of them told me. I asked if either of them had ever seen Ben Hogan, and after some reflection one answered: "I think I used to watch it on TV." Poor Hogan.

In the final day of the tournament I violated my second cardinal rule—I stepped outside where it's hot and where the plebeians with $15 tickets get so caught up in looking at each other's backs they are liable to trample you. Earlier, from the third-floor balcony, I had observed this seemingly endless stream of humanity that poured over the horizon like the Great Wall of China and had reflected on their motives: Perhaps they came on the off chance that they might see someone hit a golf ball. Standing now in the crush, I realized the folly of this reasoning. Nobody who is not being paid guild wages (a sportswriter, for example) should ever take it on himself to walk on a golf course. I remembered how I hated Colonial when I worked for the old *Fort Worth Press,* how my main job was to roam the fairways and jot down notes that would appear at the tail of someone else's story. I remembered how easy it was to hang close to the pressroom bar and let them come to me.

The best place to watch Colonial was, and still is, the pressroom, located directly above the eighteenth green. If you stand at the window long enough, you'll see everyone worth seeing. There is a bar, a buffet, a roving waitress to take drink orders, a color TV, a giant leader board, a communications officer who knows instantly every bogey and birdie going down, and enough mimeographed material to fill a garbage truck. In the old days, if you wanted to talk to a certain golfer, you had to find him yourself. Now they deliver him to the pressroom like room service. Years ago a kid named Lehmmerman drove a cab and moonlighted as a sportswriter for the *Press,* but someone caught him talking to Hogan and they had to let him go. Trouble was, he was talking as he marched stride for stride with Hogan down the eighteenth fairway in the final crucial minutes of a tournament. He was saying, "C'mon, Ben, open up. What are you really feeling inside?"

Poor Lehmmerman.

Colonial members pay the lowest dues in town, one member told me. This is consolation for the fact that it is nearly impossible to use their magnificent golf course—in order to play golf on Saturday it is mandatory that club members queue up every Wednesday at five P.M. and draw for starting times. I don't know if this was as Marvin Leonard intended when he opened Colonial in 1936, but given his rag-merchant proclivities, I expect it was.

Anyway, you can see why Mr. Marvin had to build himself a second country club.

Marvin Leonard is dead now, and the once-great department store that he and his brother founded sits on the north edge of downtown Fort Worth boarded and abandoned like an old amusement park. During its heyday twenty or thirty years ago "Leonard Brothers'" (as Granny called it until the day she died) was the prototype of the modern shopping mall, with everything from gourmet food to overalls available under one roof. Leonard's had the first escalator I ever saw, and the first subway. Mr. Marvin made his mark among retailers by purchasing enormous quantities of a single item (he once bought fifty carloads of lard from a bankrupt San Antonio grocery chain and sold it thirty-three cents a gallon below wholesale), using these as leads to bring people like Granny to town. Those who knew Marvin Leonard well called him the Kingfish.

"There was something magic about the Kingfish, something that inspired everyone around him," says Berl Godfrey, Colonial's first president. Berl recalled the Saturday during World War II when he and Marvin sat up all night watching the clubhouse burn down. Because of the war all building materials were restricted. While everybody else was throwing up their hands and bemoaning a duration without cocktails and grilled sirloin, the Kingfish slipped over to Stamford and purchased a condemned schoolhouse. He tore it down, shipped the best heavy timber to Colonial, and sold the salvage to cover construction costs.

Berl remembered why the Kingfish built Colonial in the first place. Aside from the fact that the old dairy where it is now located and the adjacent farmland that is now Tanglewood were dirt cheap and the nearest thing to a sure bet any businessman could pray for, a country club, even if it was nonprofit, could generate truckloads of profits for the man who developed the land around it. But money was only one of the Kingfish's motives. Bent-grass greens. That was his real reason. Bent grass, if you can figure out how to keep it watered and drained, stays green all year. Unable to convince the board members at River Crest Country Club to install bent grass, the Kingfish bought the land along the Trinity River and built his own golf club. With revenue from the slot machines that once lined its lobby, Colonial paid for itself in three years.

In 1941, five years after the club opened, the Kingfish lured the U.S. Open to Fort Worth, the first time golf's most prestigious tournament was ever played south of the Mason-Dixon line. By 1946 Colonial was a regular event on the pro golf tour, years before Houston and Dallas became tour stops. Having Ben Hogan around didn't hurt Colonial's image. Nobody said no to Hogan, except the Kingfish. When Leonard decided to build Shady Oaks as a lead item for a housing project on 1,400 acres of land he owned in Westover Hills, Hogan helped design the course; but it was the Kingfish who personally supervised the bent-grass greens.

Colonial lost something when the Kingfish died. Cecil Morgan Jr., a University of Texas basketball player from the early '50s, son of one of Colonial's charter members and himself a current member of the club's board of governors, recalled, "My dad wouldn't let me play until I had first walked the course with Mr. Marvin and learned the ethics of the game. Don't stand behind a player who is hitting . . . don't stand on the opposite side of the cup when a player is putting . . . things people don't always teach anymore. Even after I mastered ethics, I still had to take ten lessons from the club pro before my dad ever let me strike a ball on the course."

By Saturday afternoon John Schroeder was making a shambles of the competition and the party in the Terrace Room was beginning to look like Red Square on Lenin's birthday. Jaded and bored by what was (or was not) taking place on their golf course, Super Saints jostled for a place at the bar and waved fistfuls of dollars at immobilized waitresses. What they needed was a miracle. The miracle's name was Ben Crenshaw. There is some dispute whether Crenshaw won the tournament or Schroeder lost it, but it amounts to the same thing. Even when Schroeder was leading by five strokes and threatening the course record, Crenshaw was hovering over Colonial like a monster hawk. Schroeder started the day with a one-shot advantage, but when he faced that final putt on eighteen, Crenshaw had a one-shot advantage and was already in the locker room watching it on TV. If he had hit the ball a fraction of an inch to the left, Schroeder would have forced Crenshaw into a sudden-death playoff. I'm not sure Schroeder wanted that. I know the mob in the Terrace Room didn't. . . .

Hustle Park: Where They Ship the Pros Home C.O.D.

Gary Cartwright

Golf Digest, *June 1969*

There is a large pecan tree on the crest of a hill beside Tenison Park's No. 12 fairway. That is where they first saw him that Sunday afternoon eleven years ago.

This foursome, consisting of ex–big league baseball player Davey Williams and three other action lovers, were about to play their second shots on 12 when The Redeemer (as some would call him later) appeared from behind the pecan tree. He must have been a fearsome and sobering sight: dressed all in black, they say, and holding a Bible in one hand, his arms raised so high that his bushy black beard seemed to grow from the neck of his frock coat, eyes burning like the windows of hell.

"Repent!" he shouted. "Lay aside the sticks of the devil!"

Well, they should have known better. After all, this was Tenison Park, the garden spot of East Dallas, the flower of fortune and fate, a sort of municipal casino-on-the-green where, if a man sticks around long enough, someone is sure to make it even money that the sun will set in the south. Tenison Park, "where they go home C.O.D." Tenison Park, where the resident Robin Hoods have names like Fatman and Dogman and The Fly, where the legendary gambler Titanic Thompson keeps hours as solicitous and regular as your downtown bank president, where in days past a Mexican urchin named Lee Trevino would offer to beat your best ball using a Dr. Pepper bottle off the tee.

Tenison Park; they should have known better. And they did. "They say you can't hustle an old hustler," observes a hanger-on in Tenison's flagstone clubhouse with the Virginia steeple. "Hell! That's exactly who you can hustle." So it was that Sunday afternoon eleven years ago.

After about two minutes of ideology mixed with some praying and cussing under the pecan tree, they got it on. The Redeemer, who swore then and there he had never taken grip on a "devil's stick" (in that case, a three-wood) in his life, made an exception right then.

"He played just good enough," Davey Williams recalled later. "There was a lot of hallelujahing and 'Lord, put the right club in your servant's hand,' but if we hit a fat one he hit one a little fatter, just to build up the money."

When it was over, the original foursome was several hundred dollars poorer but wiser. Nobody ever saw The Redeemer again, or if they did they didn't recognize him.

There is not a golf course in the civilized or savage world which has failed to attract its share of sports, but since the late 1920s Tenison has been known in select circles as a free port of open action. Such famous names as Jack Carson, Audie Murphy, Ted Lewis, Kyle Rote, Mickey Mantle, and Dizzy and Paul Dean have tested their various skills at Tenison. Two U.S. Open champions, Trevino and Ralph Guldahl, played here in their formative years.

Just after World War I a Dallas banker named E. O. Tenison purchased 128 acres of wooded, rolling land a few miles east of downtown Dallas. What old man Tenison had in mind was a memorial to his son who had died in the war. He donated the land to the city with the understanding that it would be perpetuated as a municipal recreation area for men of all persuasions, and that is an accurate description of what

Tenison Park has become. (Later, the city purchased an additional 180 acres and commissioned Ralph Plummer to design a second eighteen-hole course.)

Years ago this was a wealthy section of Dallas. Stately old mansions and high ivy-walled estates still grace the Lakewood area just north of Tenison, but the backside of the park is pocked by slum neighborhoods and tough bars that seem forever situated next to railroad tracks. Richard Speck, convicted killer of five nurses in Chicago a few years ago, grew up around here. Clyde Barrow sometimes hung around the joints on East Grand. In this climate, where the have-nots were constantly mingling with the haves, the almighty dollar had the capricious allure of frost on a windowpane.

"I guess a lot of us were pretty hot-blooded way back there, back in the late 1920s, through the Depression years," says Erwin Hardwick, who has worked at Tenison forty-one years, the last twenty-five as head professional.

"But that's water under the bridge. They used to play for a hundred dollars a nine, ten dollars a hole with presses. That was when a man was working his tail off for thirty-five dollars a week, too. But now I'd say there is less betting at Tenison than at any country club in town."

Hardwick says that he put a stop to the heavy gambling in 1953, about the same time two FBI agents came around asking after a certain fellow. The agents first flashed this picture of a bald-headed man—nobody recognized him. Later they produced a picture of the same guy wearing a wig. "Why, that's old Nassau Nick!" Hardwick gasped. "He ought to be on about seventeen right now." The last time anyone saw Nassau Nick they were leading him off in handcuffs. It turned out he was an ex-FBI man using his old identification card to cash checks to finance his growing golf-hustling empire.

"It was hard to tell how much big money changed hands," says Hardwick. "There was a lot of big talk, you know, and there was plenty of side action. It got so bad that they were using cars to follow the players around the course. I put a stop to that, and I started charging green fees for anyone who wanted to watch. What really made it bad, the kids from Woodrow Wilson [a nearby high school] took to coming over and following the action. They'd hear all that big talk, and they'd think: Why go to school if money is that easy? It was bad for golf."

Trevino recalls: "I didn't really play Tenison much until after I came out of the service. There wasn't a lot of hustling going on that I could see, just the hustlers hustling the hustlers. Shoot, I didn't have no money to hustle. We'd play a dollar medal and quarter skins. I'll say this—there were a lot of good players around Tenison. They're still there, too."

The best of them is Dick Martin, a frail, skittish little man in his mid-fifties. Far as anyone knows Martin has never worked a day in his life, unless you call golf work. "Somebody asked me one time why I didn't turn pro," says Martin. "Man, I can't afford it." Trevino prudently avoided matches with Martin for years; now Martin avoids Trevino. . . .

. . . Probably the most distinctive thing about Dick Martin is the fact that he sometimes fleeces the Hustler of Hustlers, Titanic Thompson. That is to say he has been known to get away with it. This is because Martin makes it his policy to never bet on anything but golf, Titanic's one weakness.

Now in his late seventies, Titanic has gambled on everything from his skill as a pistol shot to his ability to estimate the number of white horses between Dallas and Fort Worth. When he first "opened store" at Tenison about 1947, Ti's favorite tactic was to lose a bundle the first day to a local duffer, then challenge him to a second match . . . left-handed, all bets doubled. They soon learned that he was a natural left-hander. When this no longer worked, Ti would bet he could sink a twenty-five-foot putt using his instep as a putter, a feat he could perform almost every time. He could also throw a playing card over the clubhouse, or hit a snuff can with a quarter from thirty feet.

"Ti hasn't been around in a while," assistant pro Dutch Boyd was saying a few months ago, "but they still wait for him out under that big oak tree. He used to sleep till noon, then at twelve-forty-five on the button he'd fall out of his Cadillac and have a hundred bets before he hit the ground. On the course he was always overmatching himself, but he'd get it back, and more, some other way."

One way was to bet a fellow sportsman that two of the first thirty persons they met and spoke to would have the same birthday. Fired on the notion that he had 365 days running for him, the second hustler was pleased to accept. For the price of the bet, Titanic threw in a free lesson in math: The chance against him at first was 364/365, which, when multiplied by succeeding chances (364/365 x 363/365 x 362/365 x . . . etc.) squirreled down to better than even money after twenty encounters.

Not that he was above subterfuge. Titanic once bet Nutts Nitti, a New York dice player, that he could find a hairpin in each block on a twenty-block stretch of Manhattan. Having planted the hairpins himself, Titanic was not surprised to win. On another occasion he wagered some high rollers that he could find a dead rat in the basement of the plush club where they happened to be at the time. Sure enough the rat was there, under a barrel in the basement. Exactly where Titanic placed it.

There is skill and there is skill. Ti once bet a group of Dallas real-estate brokers that he could throw a quarter from fifteen feet and stick it in a potato at least once in seven attempts. He scored on his fourth throw.

Ti was on the putting green one day practicing with a long-handle shovel when a wealthy Dallas car dealer approached him with a sizable proposition. See that kid over there putting with a sand wedge and picking the balls out of the hole with the toes of his barefeet? How would Ti like a piece of him?

"In a New York minute," Titanic replied. "I'll play anybody that can't afford shoes."

Unfortunately for Titanic the young man turned out to be Dickie Crabtree, one of the best junior golfers in the state. He was too strong and Ti lost. For a couple of hours Ti moped around the clubhouse, pitching coins at a crack in the floor, while the powerful junior golfer played another round. Suddenly, Ti got an idea. Pulling the wealthy car dealer to one side, he offered to challenge the young tiger a second time.

"And this time," Ti said, letting his wounded pride show, "I'm gonna let him take three drives on every hole and play his best."

Though the kid piled up a good lead on the first nine holes of the rematch, the day took its toll. By the tenth or eleventh hole his arms were so tired from three full swings, plus a day of golf, he could hardly draw back his club. Titanic skinned him on the back nine, more than saving the day.

Tenison's reputation for being "where it's at" permeates golfdom's more adventurous souls like the song of the sirens. Frequently, though not invariably, the music is sweeter than the reward.

Cynical as pawnbrokers, Tenison regulars maintain a state of readiness. Your standard gypsy hustler in the Texaco uniform with Billy Frank stitched over one pocket will stick out like a gold tooth, yet this fails to explain what happened not long ago when a stranger from Mississippi put the touch on them for several bills.

"He was a real charmer," says Dutch Boyd. "He claimed to be an ex–all-American football player from Ole Miss who was on his way to Hollywood to be a movie star or something. In one afternoon he made a half-dozen guys for a hundred bucks each. The boys are still waiting to see him in the movies."

More in character is the case of the well-known pro who took a leave of absence from the tour four years ago and headed for Tenison, where he understood the quick money was laying around like pecans. Call him Roy. He hit town, according to Dutch Boyd, with "thousand-dollar bills stuffed in his watch pocket." And he went back as they say, C.O.D. . . .

. . . Dizzy Dean and some of his high-rent pals from nearby Lakewood played Tenison until two monumental examples of bad luck convinced them to look elsewhere. The former baseball star always requested a special caddie, a veteran named Bud. It was a well-known fact that Bud bet against Dean, but this failed to shake the famous Dean confidence until one day in a tight situation Bud handed Dean a four-wood where a five-iron would have been more than enough. On another afternoon and in another financial crisis, Ol' Diz came to the eighteenth tee dead even with his opponent, home pro Erwin Hardwick. Eighteen is a short par-three, blind and tricky. Both men hit good tee shots, but as they approached the green only one ball was in sight. It rested less than six feet from the hole.

"Man alive!" Dean chirped, "I believe that's my ball!"

"I hope so," cracked Hardwick, "'cause if it is, mine's in the hole." And it was indeed.

The games people play at Tenison depend as much on imagination as skill. They tell of the day that Fatman was $600 down to The Fly when a hijacker stepped out of the woods near No. 3. (This is not as uncommon as you might suppose. Where there are high rollers there are likely to be hijackers. Titanic Thompson once shot and killed a robber on a course in Tyler, Texas.)

"Your money or your life!" the robber is supposed to have said to Fatman and The Fly, at which time Fatman took out his roll, peeled off six bills, and handed them to The Fly, thus settling up before subsequent transactions commenced. . . .

The Glory Game at Goat Hills

Dan Jenkins

Fairways and Greens, *1994*

Goat Hills is gone now. It was swallowed up almost four years ago by the bulldozers of progress, and in the end it was nice to learn that something could take a divot out of those fairways. But all of the regulars had left long before. I suppose it will be all right to talk about it now, about the place, the people and the times we had. It could even be therapeutic.

Maybe it will explain why I don't play golf so much anymore. It's swell to get invited to Winged Dip and Burning Foot and all those fancy clubs where they have real flagsticks instead of broom handles, but I usually beg off. I'm still overgolfed from all those years at Goat Hills in Texas. You would be too if . . . well, let me tell you some of it. I'll try to be truthful and not too sentimental, but where shall I begin? With Cecil? Why not? He was sort of a symbol in those days, and . . .

We called him Cecil the Parachute because he fell down a lot. He would attack the golf ball with a whining, leaping move—more of a calisthenic than a swing—and occasionally, in his spectacular struggles for extra distance, he would soar right off the end of elevated tees.

He was a slim, bony, red-faced little man who wore crepe-soled shoes and heavily starched shirts that crackled when he marked his ball, always inching it forward as much as possible. When he was earthbound, Cecil drove a delivery truck for Grandma's Cookies, and he always parked it behind a tall hedge near the clubhouse, out of sight of passing cars, one of which might have Grandma in it.

Anyhow, when the truck was there, you could be pretty sure that not only was Cecil out on the course but so were Tiny, Easy, Magoo, Foot the Free, Ernie, Matty, Rush and Grease Repellent, Little Joe, Weldon the Oath, Jerry, John the Band-Aid, and Moron Tom—and me. I was known as Dump, basically because of what so many partners thought I did to them for money.

There would be an excellent chance that all of us would be in one hollering, protesting, club-slinging gangsome, betting huge sums of money we didn't have. In other words, when Cecil's truck was hidden behind the hedge, you knew the game was on.

The game was not the kind the United States Golf Association would have approved of, but it was the kind we played for about fifteen years at the windy, dusty, seldom-mowed, stone-hard, practically treeless, residentially surrounded public course named Worth Hills in Fort Worth.

Goat Hills, we called it, not too originally.

It was a gambling game that went on in some form or another, involving anywhere from three to twenty-two players, almost every day of every year when a lot of us were younger and bored silly. The game not only survived my own shaft-breaking, divot-stomping, club-slinging presence, it outlasted rain, snow, heat, wars, tornadoes, jobs, studies, illnesses, divorces, births, deaths, romances, and pinball machines.

Nearly all the days at the Hills began the same way. Some of us would be slouched in wicker chairs on the small front porch of the wooden clubhouse, smoking, drinking coffee or Cokes, complaining about worldly things, such as why none of the movie houses in town had changed features in five or six weeks, and why most of the girls we knew only wanted to hump rich guys—they didn't care anything about debonair?

Say it was August. We would be looking across the putting green and into the heat. In Texas in the summer, you can see the heat. It looks like germs. In fact, say it was the day of the Great Cart Wreck.

There on the porch, Matty, who had a crew cut and wore glasses, was playing tunes on his upper front teeth with his fingernails. He had learned how to do this in study hall in high school, and for money he could play almost any tune, including "Sixty Minute Man," and "Sabre Dance," and you could actually recognize it.

I was reading a book of some kind as usual. Something light by a Russian or a German.

Tiny, a heavyset railroad conductor, came out of the clubhouse in his flaming red shirt and red slacks, and said, "Dump, what you gonna do with all that book crap in your head?"

"None of it stays there," I said.

Foot the Free, which was short for Big Foot the Freeloader, was there, practice-putting at a small, chipped-out crevice in the concrete, a spot that marked the finish of the greatest single hole I've seen played—but more about that later.

Little Joe was on the putting green, trying to perfect a stroke behind his back, a trick shot, in the hope that somebody would one day suggest a behind-the-back putting contest.

Magoo was sitting next to me on the porch.

"Anything about God in that book?" he asked.

"Some."

"Anything in there about what God did to me on the back nine yesterday?"

Around the corner came John the Band-Aid, cleats on, clubs over his shoulder, handkerchief around his neck, impatient as always.

"You, you, you, and you and you, too," said John. "All of you two, two, two automatic one-down presses, getting evens on nine and eighteen. Whipsaw everybody seventy or better for five."

We began tying our shoes.

John the Band-Aid removed three clubs from his bag, dropped the bag on the gravel, and started swinging the clubs in a violent limbering-up exercise.

"Me and Little Joe got all teams for five match and five medal—dollar cats and double on birdies," he said.

Little Joe, who played without a shirt and had a blond ducktail, said, "Damn, John, I'd sure like to pick my own partner someday." Then he said, "You gonna play good, or scrape it around like yesterday?"

John the Band-Aid said, "Well, you can have some of me, if it'll keep your interest up."

"I'll try five," said Little Joe in his high-pitched voice. "Five and a R-ra C."

Little Joe and I took a cart. So did John and Magoo. We had won money the day before, so we could afford to ride. The others walked, carrying their own clubs. We were an eightsome, but others would no doubt join us along the way. It wasn't unusual for other players to drive their cars around the course, find the game, hop on, and get it on.

It was Matty one afternoon who drove his red Olds right up to the edge of the third green, jumped out with his golf shoes and glove already on, and said, "Do I have a duck in the car?" He had driven straight to the game from the University of Oklahoma, a distance of some two hundred miles, and he had the duck in the car in case someone wanted to bet him he didn't have a live duck in the car.

We played the first eight holes, then came the long interlude of bookkeeping on the ninth tee.

John the Band-Aid had earned his nickname by bleeding a lot, such as he did this day because he had shot even par, but was losing to everybody. Which was why he had teed up his ball first—the game worked in reverse etiquette.

"All right, Magoo," he said, "you got me out, out, even, even, one down, and one down. I press your young ass for ten. Foot, you got me out, out, out, and one down. You're pushed for eight. Window closed?"

And so it went.

The ninth tee at Goat Hills was on a bluff, above a steep drop-off into a cluster of hackberry trees, a creek, rocks, and weeds. It was a par-four. The drive had to carry the ravine, and if you could hit it far enough, you had about a seven-iron to the green, going back toward the clubhouse.

John the Band-Aid tightened his straw hat and dug in for his tee shot.

"I'm gonna hit this summitch to Dallas," he said.

"Outhit you for five," Magoo said.

"You're on. Anybody else?"

"I try five," Little Joe said.

"You're on."

He curved a wondrous slice into the right rough, and coming off of his follow-through slung his driver in the general direction of Eagle Mountain Lake, which is thirty miles behind us.

He just missed hitting Little Joe, who was nimble enough to dance out of the way.

Little Joe said, "Man, they ought to put you in a box and take you to the World's Fair."

John's arms were folded and he was staring off in an aimless direction, burning inside. Suddenly, he dashed over to his bag, jerked out his two-iron and slung it against the water fountain, snapping the shaft in half.

"That club cost me a shot on the fourth," he explained.

I wasn't all that happy myself. One under and no money ahead. Maybe that's why I pointed the three-wheel electric cart straight down the hill, full speed ahead, a getaway cart.

Over the rocks and ditches we went darting, and that's when the front wheel struck a large stone in the creek bed. All I recall hearing was Little Joe's voice.

"Son of a young . . . !"

We both went over the front end, headfirst, the bags and clubs flying out over and behind us.

I guess I was knocked out for ten seconds. When I came to, the cart was pinning down my left leg, battery acid was eating away at my shirt, and broken clubs were everywhere.

Little Joe was sitting down in the rocks, examining his skinned elbows and giggling.

The others were standing around, looking down at us, considering whether to lift the cart off my leg, or leave me there to lose all bets.

Magoo glanced at Little Joe's white canvas bag, which was already being eaten by battery acid.

"Two dollars says Joe don't have a bag by the fourteenth," Magoo said.

My ankle was swollen. I had to take off my shoe and play the rest of the round in one shoe.

It is a remarkable footnote in golfing history that I birdied the ninth hole, to which Matty said, "I done been beat by everything now. Dead man comes out of the creek and makes a birdie."

Little Joe's bag lasted exactly until the fourteenth hole. After holing out a putt, he went to pick it up but there was nothing left but the two metal rings and a shoulder strap.

"Two says Joe is stark naked by the seventeenth," Magoo said.

That day, Little Joe and I both managed birdies on the eighteenth, winning all presses and get-evens, and Magoo and John the Band-Aid talked for weeks about the time they got beat by a cripple and a guy who was on fire.

On other days at Goat Hills, purely out of boredom, we played the course backward, or to every other hole, or every third hole, or entirely out-of-bounds except for the greens, which meant you had to stay in the roads and lawns. We also played the course with only one club, or just two clubs, or sometimes at night.

One game we invented was the Thousand-Yard Dash.

This was a one-hole marathon that started on the farthest point on the course from the clubhouse—beside the twelfth green—and ended at the chipped-out crevice in the concrete on the clubhouse porch.

I'm not quite sure, but I think this game was the brainchild of either Foot the Free, Matty, or me. We had once played through six blocks of downtown Fort Worth, from Seventh Street to the courthouse, mostly on Commerce Street, without getting arrested.

On the day of the first Thousand-Yard Dash, some of us went to the left of the rock outhouse perched atop the highest point on the course, and some played to the right of it. I followed Foot the Free because he could never afford to lose—he carried the same five-dollar bill in his pocket for about eight years.

We hooked a driver, hooked another driver, hooked a third driver, then hooked a spoon—you had to hook the ball to get distance at Goat Hills—and this got us within a pitching wedge of the front porch.

Most of the other twelve were out of it by now, lost in the creeks or flower beds of apartment houses bordering the first fairway.

My approach shot carried the porch, slammed against a wall of the clapboard clubhouse, chased Wells Howard, the pro, inside the front door, and brought a scream from Lola, his wife and bookkeeper. The ball came to rest about twenty feet from the crevice and was puttable if I moved a chair.

Foot played a bounce shot at the porch. He lofted a high wedge, let it bounce off the gravel. It hopped up over the curb, skidded against the wall, and stopped about ten feet from the crevice.

We borrowed a broom from Lola and swept the dirt particles out of our putting lines.

The other players gathered around to make side bets. Two rent-club players came out of the clubhouse and stepped in our lines.

"Hey," I said to them. "This is business!"

"Smart-ass punks," one of them mumbled.

I gave my putt too good a rap. It went past the crevice and wound up in a row of pull carts at the end of the porch.

"Unnatural hazard," I said. "Free drop."

An instantly formed rules committee consisting of Magoo, Matty, and Grease Repellent, who worked at a Texaco station, basically decided that my request was bullshit.

I had to play it out of the pull carts, which was why I eighteen-putted for a twenty-three.

Against anyone else I might still have had a chance, but Foot was one of the great putters in history, on any kind of surface. If anything, the concrete looked like bent to Foot, compared to the texture of the gnarled Bermuda greens out on the course.

He calmly tapped his ten-footer and it wobbled slowly, slowly, slowly over the concrete, wavered, and went in!

That was one of the two greatest holes I ever saw played. The other was when my friend Bud Shrake made a 517 on a five-block hole that stretched from Goat Hills's first tee to a brown leather loafer in another friend's apartment.

The longest hole we ever played was from the first tee at Goat Hills to the third green at Colonial Country Club, roughly sixteen blocks away.

The first time we played it, Rush's dad, a retired oilman, caddied for him in a black Lincoln, and Cecil got bit by a cocker spaniel.

Playing through neighborhoods required a unique shot, we discovered. A blade putter was an ideal club to keep the ball low so it would get extra roll on the pavement.

Some of us went down Stadium Drive, past the TCU football stadium, then left on Park Hill and over the houses. Others went the back way, down Alton Road.

I happened to have sliced a blade putter into a bed of irises on Alton Road and was looking for it when I saw Cecil down the driveway.

He was contemplating a shot that would have to rise quickly to clear a Cyclone fence, then duck sharply under an oak, then hook severely to get around a tile roof, then slice to land in the street.

As Cecil studied the shot, a dog was barking at his ankles.

Cecil leaped at the ball in his customary manner and drove the ball straight into the fence, about eight feet in front of him, and his follow-through carried him forward and onto the ground on his elbows and stomach. He slid into the fence, and the spaniel chased after him as if it were retrieving a sock.

Cecil scrambled to his feet and tiptoed back down the driveway, and withdrew from the competition.

"Hurried the shot," he said. "That sucker was a-growlin' at me, and just when I started to swing, I seen a lady cussin' me through the kitchen window."

Tiny quit at a fishpond. Grease Repellent lost his ball when he struck a sundial. Easy Reid met a fellow and stopped to sell him some insurance. John the Band-Aid broke his blade putter when he sailed it at a chimney. Foot and Magoo were the only two who finished, and they had to play out after they climbed over the Colonial fence because some members sent a caddie back to the clubhouse to get the club manager, who would, in turn, call the police.

There was an argument about who won, and a playoff was decided upon. Magoo wanted to play back to Goat Hills, to the cold-drink box in the lunchroom. Foot wanted to play to Herb Massey's Café, about three miles away, to the third leg of the Shufflebowl machine. Herb's was where Matty showed up one day with his shirt and pants on backward and his glasses on the back of his head, and posted a score of 280 on the Shufflebowl, sliding the puck backward.

Foot and Magoo wound up splitting the money, and we all went back to Goat Hills and got in a putting game that lasted until midnight.

Why we did such things was because we lived in Fort Worth, the town that gave you Ben Hogan and Byron Nelson, and offered little else to do.

Besides, it was Texas.

Golf had always received lavish attention in the newspapers, and it was at a very early age that you knew about Hogan and Nelson and others: Jimmy Demaret, Lloyd Mangrum, Ralph Guldahl, Jackie Burke, Gus Moreland, Harry Todd, all Texans.

There was also a vast amateur circuit you could travel, if you wanted to take your game out of town. All summer long, you could go play in invitation tournaments in towns like Ranger, Midland, Abilene, Wichita Falls, Waxahachie, Longview, Corpus Christi, everywhere.

In these tournaments, you would win shotguns, radios, silverware, lawn tools, and quite a bit of money in calcutta pools.

It was this amateur circuit that gave you Hogan, Nelson and Demaret from the good old days, and then Jackie Burke Jr., Tommy Bolt, Billy Maxwell, Don Cherry, Don January, Earl Stewart, Dave Marr, Bill Rogers, Charlie Coody, Bobby Nichols, Miller Barber, Howie Johnson, Ernie Vossler, Homero Blancas, Fred Marti, Jacky Cupit, and then in later years your Ben Crenshaws, Tom Kites, and John Mahaffeys.

Ernie Vossler, who got richer than A-rabs in Palm Springs, came right out of our game at the Hills.

Even then, he was a relentless competitor who never understood why anyone but him ever made a putt.

Sometimes, when Weldon the Oath, a postman, made a putt, Ernie would walk off the course fuming.

Ernie was never as proficient as myself or John the Band-Aid at breaking clubs. I once broke the shaft on my eight-iron nine days in a row at the seventeenth because I couldn't make the ball hold that green, a par-three. But Ernie had his moments. He bladed a six-iron one day in the sixth fairway and almost killed everybody. He hurled the club into the brick fairway, and the shaft snapped, and both parts of the club went into the air, and one jagged end sprang back and hit Ernie in the palm, causing five stitches, and another jagged end caught me in the leg. As the shafts sparkled in the sun, it was as if we were being attacked by lightning bolts.

And this was one man who knew nothing of golf before I recruited him for the golf team at Paschal High. He went on to win the Fort

Worth city championship, which was something that Hogan, Nelson, and I could never do—we all finished second in our best effort—and Ernie won the State Amateur, and then some tournaments on the PGA Tour, and then he got into real estate and bought Oklahoma City and Palm Springs. Ernie Vossler became our honor graduate.

But our most intriguing graduate was Weldon the Oath.

Weldon had talking fits—talking to the ball.

He would take oaths. He would rush out to the game so quickly, he would play golf in his postman's cap and without golf shoes, which could have had something to do with his chronic slice.

"All right, this is your last chance," Weldon would say to the ball as he waggled his driver. "You lousy little crud, if you slice on me just one more time I'm gonna bite you right in half and chew your rubber guts up. You're going straight this time, you hear me? You hear me tellin' you this? All right, then. Geeeeooood, daaaammmmmm, aaaaiii, ga!"

And Weldon would hit another slice. It would cross two fairways to his right, a marvelous half-moon of a shot.

The ball would scarcely leave the club face before Weldon would start to spin around in circles, pawing at the air, slugging at imaginary evils. Frequently, he would dash over to the tee marker and start beating the driver on it. He would stomp on the club.

Then just as quickly, he would calm down and say, "Let me hit one more. I got to figure out what I'm doin' wrong."

And he would slice again.

That's when he would break the shaft over his knee. "Geeeeaaa, rrreeeeaaa, aaaddd," he would snarl. "This is my last time on a golf course, you can book it! Gaaddd raaaap son of a baddered bat rop ditch bastard." When Weldon was hot, the words didn't come out right. "You picks have guyd me damn stick—this rotten, stinking, miserable, low-life spicky dop whore bubbin' game—feck it, babber sam."

Weldon would hike to the clubhouse, but of course he would be back the next day.

It was in the last couple of years at Goat Hills, shortly before the city sold those 106 acres to TCU so the school could build more cream-brick buildings, that the games grew too big, too expensive, for working men and college students.

Some of the guys got to where they couldn't pay when they lost, and others didn't want to collect it, and some of us were developing other interests—snooker, eight-ball, newspapers, divorces.

Moron Tom had something to do with the games disappearing, going the way of other endangered species.

He was a muscular, likable West Texan who had come to Fort Worth on a football scholarship at TCU, but had quit football when he found out you had to work out every day in the fall. He hit a long ball and he loved to bet, on anything. He could hold his breath longer than anybody, for money, or inhale a can of beer in four seconds, for money, and he rarely spoke English.

Everything was quadruple unreal to Moron Tom, or "Hit it fine, pork-e-pine," and many of the words he uttered were something else spelled backward.

"Cod Ee-rack Fockle-dim," for instance, was Dr. Cary Middlecoff spelled backward.

The day of one of the last big games, Moron Tom walked onto the porch and said, "I'll take toops and threeps from Youngfut, Youngjun, and Youngdump."

This meant Moron Tom wanted two up and three up from young Foot, young John, and young me.

"Ten and ten with Grease's men," he added, "and two and two with Joe-Magoo."

Everyone drifted out to the first tee.

Wagers were made, partners chosen, practice swings taken.

Moron Tom brought a big hook in from over the apartment houses and found the fairway.

"Think I can't, Cary Grant?" he said.

Magoo and I wound up as partners against all other combinations, and this was not altogether good—neither of us knew how to play safe, and Magoo was also unlucky. Once in the Glen Garden Invitation in

Fort Worth—that's the course where Hogan and Nelson caddied as kids—Magoo hit a 285-yard tee shot but found his ball in a man's mouth, being cleaned.

We were in good form today, however. Teamed well for a blaze of birdies and had everybody bleeding to death by the time we got to the eighteenth.

I would hit a good drive and Moron Tom would say, "Cod Ee-rack Fockle-dim," and Magoo would hit a good drive, and Moron Tom would say, "Wod Daw-ret-sniff," meaning Dow Finsterwald spelled backward.

When either of us holed a putt, Moron Tom would say, "Take a nap, Einra Remlap," which was Arnie Palmer spelled backward.

By the time we came off the seventeenth green, Magoo and I had somehow birdied six holes in a row, and we calculated that if we only parred the eighteenth, we would win so much money we wouldn't be able to haul it home in Cecil's cookie truck.

Everybody pressed to get even, of course, on the eighteenth tee.

John the Band-Aid summed it up for most of the players, who must have numbered twelve in all, when he said, "I'm out, out, out, out, out, and out, and one down, one down, one down, one down, one down, and even. Want me to bend over?"

The eighteenth at Goat Hills was slightly uphill. You drove from a windy knoll with the south wind usually helping and aimed across a tiny creek and a couple of sycamore trees. A big drive would leave you only thirty or forty yards short of the green, a flip and a putt from a birdie or a slip and two putts for an easy par.

Not to birdie the eighteenth often resulted in a wedge being broken, and not to par the eighteenth was unthinkable.

The only conceivable trouble was far, far to the right, across the tenth fairway, where Stadium Drive was out of bounds. But nobody had ever sliced that badly, not even Weldon the Oath, until Magoo did.

At the height of his backswing, when he was coming out of his shoes to try to drive the green and make us richer, Moron Tom quietly said, "Tissim, Oogam." Which was Miss it, Magoo, backward.

Needles were commonplace in the game. Coughing, sneezing, dropping a full bag of clubs, yelling, burping, all such things could be heard on backswings at times—you took it for granted and dealt with it.

But Magoo came apart with laughter at Moron Tom's remark and almost fell down like Cecil when he swung at the ball.

Even Magoo had to laugh again when Moron Tom said, "Oogam dewolb the Nepo," which translated into "Magoo blew the Open."

To say this put extra pressure on me, with Magoo out of the hole, would be to say that the meat loaf in the lunchroom at Goat Hills contained grease.

Right here, I should explain that on the other side of the creek at the eighteenth, set upright into an embankment, was a storm drain about three feet in circumference. We often pitched at it with old balls from the ladies' tee, but it was a remarkable thing if anybody ever got one in there.

And from up on the men's tee a hundred yards or so back, it was an incredibly small target. In fact, I didn't even think about it as I got set to drive the green and make another birdie, or know the reason why. All I wanted to know was what everybody wanted engraved on their tombstones.

But at the top of my swing, Moron Tom whispered something else.

"Clutch, Mother Zilch," he said.

The club head hit about two inches behind the ball, and the drive snap-hooked into the ground just in front of the ladies' tee, took a big hop to the right off of some rocks, and—I swear to you—went straight into the storm drain.

It remains the only hole in one I ever made, and it was, you might say, the shot which semiretired me from golf forever.

About the Authors

Skip Bayless is fearless. He tackles every column at warp-speed and aims for the gut. A Dallas fixture, he lets you see another side of Lee Trevino—one that's not so merry. The author of three books on the Cowboys, including the recent *Hell Bent,* Bayless is also on ESPN.

Tom Callahan and Dave Kindred. Pardon me, but I think of them as a pair. They rode elephants together, waited for a shrouded corpse to pass before they could tee off in Kathmandu, got a bit tongue-tied when they met Hogan, and managed to play all around the world and get paid for it when they wrote *Around the World in 18 Holes.* Thus, they became golf pressroom heroes. Together or apart, they're two great writers—Kindred currently (actually again) for the *Atlanta Journal Constitution;* Callahan for *Golf Digest* and *U.S. News & World Report.* They team for a piece on Shady Oaks and Hogan (which includes Kindred's memories of Hogan in '67) and Callahan explains why Tom Kite is "The Rarest Kind of Genius."

Now a senior editor at *Texas Monthly,* **Gary Cartwright** got his start as part of that infamous *Fort Worth Press* staff of the 1950s. He takes you inside the Colonial National Invitation, circa Priscilla Davis, and looks at Tenison Park, which, along with Houston's Memorial Park, were two of the best places for pros to lose to amateurs. Cartwright is working on a book about his own heart bypass surgery, titled *Better Than Ever.*

Just think of **David Casstevens** as a mad scientist/professor. That's what he looks like when he's writing. His eyes are wild. His hand shoots through his hair. He says he's struggling. You know it's great. David has a wonderful touch with words—and people—and draws you into the scene with keen observations. Here, he captures then-aging Legend Bolt at the Legends of Golf and looked at what was—and could have been—for Orville Moody. Casstevens worked in Houston and Dallas and is now with the *Phoenix Gazette.*

Myron Cope was the most popular man—and his story on Lee Trevino the best read—during U.S. Open week at Oakmont in 1968. Cope's profile on the soon-to-be-Merry Mex came out the week of the U.S. Open and darned if Trevino didn't go out and win it. Cope dabbled in writing, but his true love was broadcast. Now in his twenty-eighth season as color analyst for the Pittsburgh Steelers, Cope has given up those days when he was also a talk-show host and did radio and television commentaries. He calls himself semiretired. We know he's not.

Peter Dobreiner had more than just a way with words. He was funny. He was a bit whimsical. And he was darned good. His tribute to Jimmy Demaret makes you realize there was much more to him than his Technicolor wardrobe and songs.

The *Dallas Morning News*'s coverage of Texas's first major championship—the 1927 PGA—included the work of **Bobby Cruickshank** and **Milt Saul.** Saul was a staff writer for the *News,* while Cruickshank, a player and the professional at Progress Club in Purchase, New York, provided a little expert commentary. Their stories reflect the style of writing in the 1920s.

Larry Dorman loves the game and loves writing about it. Is there a better combination? After doing time in Miami, Fort Lauderdale, *The National,* and the *New York Times,* Dorman is vice president of advertising, press, and public relations at Callaway Golf Company. He visited Byron Nelson during the fiftieth anniversary of his streak and gives you a feel for the man and that never-to-be-broken record of eleven straight. His biography of Ely Callaway is scheduled for release in 1998.

Gene Gregston may have known Hogan better than anyone, even better than Jenkins. The late *Fort Worth Star-Telegram* reporter even wrote a biography of the Hawk, but after that they didn't speak. He looks at the way New York embraced Hogan after he won the only British Open he played in (1953) and completed the Grand Slam.

Editor **Melanie Hauser** was born in Pennsylvania, but that was simply an accident, since she moved to Texas at age five and hasn't left. She spent a combined twenty years at the *Austin American Statesman* and the *Houston Post,* and while her job took her from swimming pools to Super Bowls and NBA Finals, she always spent her springs and summers on the nation's golf courses. Now a Houston-based freelance writer and contributor to *Golf World, Golf Digest, Sports Illustrated,* and *CBS Sportsline,* she profiles fellow University of Texas alum Ben Crenshaw, former University of Houston players Fred Couples and Steve Elkington, and takes you inside Crenshaw's magical week at the 1995 Masters. This is her first book.

Mickey Herskowitz, one of the country's most prolific authors, has written more than thirty books under his own name and one as Michael Herskowitz. Why? Well, Bette Davis made him change his name because she just didn't think a collaborator named Mickey was quite appropriate. Herskowitz, who started at the *Houston Post*—unpaid—at fourteen, profiles legendary teacher Harvey Penick and the father of college golf, Dave Williams.

Ed Hinton and **Mark Stewart** of *Sports Illustrated* turned out one of the best—and most heart-wrenching—stories of 1996 when they told the sad story of LPGA Hall of Famer Betty Jameson.

It would be easy to fill an anthology like this with pieces by **Dan Jenkins.** And he's done it several times. He made sportswriting—and particularly golf writing—what it is today, and whether we owe it to those long afternoons at Goat Hills, Morris Williams erasing the best shot of Jenkins's career with a better one, or just plain talent, he took us—ever so irreverently—inside those drives and wedges to two feet and most of all the people. From his look back at his first Colonial to one more trip around Goat Hills, Jenkins captures Texas golf like no one else—who grew up in Fort Worth and turned into a novelist, anyway. That's why there are so many delightful pieces by him in the book. You've read most of them before, but they're all worth another curtain call.

Sports Illustrated's **Franz Lidz** may do quirky better than anyone. And it doesn't come much quirkier than "Holy Cow," the story of Azle farmer Robert Landers. He didn't have a full set of clubs and he practiced around cowpatties and cows at his ranch, but he made it to the Senior Tour with wife Freddie in tow.

Nothing takes you inside Hogan's accident better than the excerpt from

Bo Links's novel *Follow the Wind.* A California attorney, Links is an avid golfer and photographer and is a photo contributor to *Golf Journal* and *GolfWeek.*

Barry McDermott takes a look at LPGA legend Kathy Whitworth, the all-time winningest golfer in history. She was born just the other side of the Texas border, but spent most of her time across the state line.

Jack Murphy may be the only sportswriter to have a stadium named after him. Well, now it's just the field, but, yes, the man who wrote about Hogan is that Jack Murphy. He started his career as a reporter at the *Fort Worth Star-Telegram,* then went to San Diego where he became sports editor of the *San Diego Union* and was a key figure in bringing the Chargers and the Padres to Southern California. Here, he puts you beside Hogan as the Hawk, still battered and broken from his car accident fifty-nine days earlier, returns to Fort Worth by train and heads to a makeshift hospital in his house.

He's been everywhere and done it all. Like Jenkins and Sherrod, you could fill books with great **Jim Murray** columns. He covered Hogan like a blanket, but here, he takes you inside the world—circa 1963 and segregation—of Charlie Sifford, the first black player on the PGA Tour.

Russ Pate is quiet, soft-spoken, and talented. A frequent contributor to *D Magazine,* Pate has written four golf books including *Greener Pastures* with Robert Landers, and *The Mental Game Pocket Companion for Golf* with Dr. Fran Pirozzolo. Here, Pate, who lives in Dallas with his wife Becky, takes a look at the Lone Star State's best-known hustler, Dick Martin.

Dick Peebles started his career in San Antonio and finished it as the executive sports editor of the *Houston Chronicle.* Peebles was at Champions the day Hogan walked off the course for the final time in competition, and he visits with the Legend in the locker room.

Harvey Penick used to be the best-kept secret in Texas. Now his books are national golf treasures. Just about every great golfer in Texas knew or was a student of the legendary University of Texas golf coach and instructor—his most famous students being Tom Kite, Ben Crenshaw, and Betsy Rawls. But it wasn't until he collaborated with **Bud Shrake** on his Little Red Book that Penick drew national attention. He died in 1995, but his lessons on golf and life live on in his books.

Turk Pipkin stands out in this crowd—for many reasons. One thing, he's basketball-tall and has a long gray ponytail. For another, he didn't spend his young days writing, but rather juggling and working as a mime in Austin. And that was after a tour of service. How does that diverse background fit with writing about golf? Pretty well. The author of *Fast Greens* looks at his younger days as a caddie, then takes you to some of Texas's treasures—nine-hole courses where there's a *Tin Cup* everywhere you look.

Grantland Rice. They called him Granny and he was just about the most famous sportswriter of his time—and the man that Dan Jenkins, Blackie Sherrod, and that gang grew up reading. Here he looks at Jimmy Demaret.

Charles Price was one of the most respected writers in the game. In an excerpt from one of his "At Large" columns, he looks at Lloyd Mangrum, a great player who was lost in the Byron Nelson–Ben Hogan–Jimmy Demaret era.

Tim Rosaforte once spent the night trying to escape from the L.A. Coliseum—and some nearby gangs—after covering a Fort Lauderdale Strikers soccer game. Not long after that, he wisely turned his full attention to golf. Formerly with *Sports Illustrated* and now a senior writer at *Golf World,* Rosaforte profiles Lanny Wadkins. He is the author of *Heartbreak Hill* and *Tiger Woods: The Makings of a Champion.*

Curt Sampson. He may be best known as the author of *Hogan* but here he gives you a peek at such diverse characters as Lefty Stackhouse, Gus Moreland, and Babe Didrikson Zaharias. He is currently working on a book on Augusta National and the Masters.

One of the oddest couples in the game? Jackie Burke and Jimmy Demaret, who wound up building a heck of a golf-only country club in Houston. *Golf Digest* editor **Nick Seitz** explains the unique relationship between the pair.

Blame Dan Jenkins on **Blackie Sherrod.** He's the guy who plucked Jenkins off the TCU campus and gave him a job at the old *Fort Worth Press.* Thought the kid could write. Sherrod's eye for talent—he hired Jenkins, Gary Cartwright, Bud Shrake, and all-star PR man Jerre Todd on his Murderers' Row staff in the 1950s—should tell you all you need to know. There will never be a single staff that talented ever again. The dean of Texas sportswriters, Sherrod has survived the death of two newspapers, a zillion Super Bowls, countless Dallas

Cowboys scandals, and more than his share of Odessa Pro-Ams, Colonials, and Byron Nelsons. When I got my hands on "Blackie's Texas" there was never any question that it should open this book.

No one knows more about the history of golf in Texas than **Frances Trimble.** The director of the Texas Golf Hall of Fame since 1992, Trimble has written for *Golf Journal* and *Golf Digest.* Her contribution to *Under the Lone Star Flagstick* is a short story on the day Gene Sarazen was hijacked to play in the Texas Open.

He went by Van, but his real name was **Sid Van Ulm**. Van was both a cartoonist and a writer, and was a Houston legend during his long stint at the *Houston Press*. Here, he tests the first sand wedge, which just happened to be invented in Houston.

As for so many other writers on this list, covering golf is only a part of what the *Chicago Tribune* asks **Bob Verdi** to do each year. Yet it's the one sport nearest to his heart. His column on Kite finally winning the Open says what everyone thought for a long time and we all tried to write. We just didn't do it half as well.

Permissions *(continued from page 4)*

"Hagen Defeats Turnesa, One-Up" by Milt Saul. Copyright © *Dallas Morning News,* 1927. Reprinted with permission. All rights reserved.

"For Merry Mex, the Laughter Only Hides the Tears" by Skip Bayless. Copyright © *Dallas Morning News,* 1980. Reprinted with permission. All rights reserved.

"Bolt's Life Is His Curse" by David Casstevens. Copyright © *Dallas Morning News*, 1982. Reprinted with permission. All rights reserved.

"Moody's March to the Top Was Brief" by David Casstevens. Copyright © *Dallas Morning News,* 1984. Reprinted with permission. All rights reserved.

"Well-Wishers Greet Hogan at End of Fifty-Nine-Day Journey" by Jack Murphy, *Fort Worth Star-Telegram.* Copyright © *Fort Worth Star-Telegram,* 1949. All rights reserved.

"Flattery" by Gene Gregston, *Fort Worth Star-Telegram.* Copyright © *Fort Worth Star-Telegram,* 1953. All rights reserved.

"Golf's Teacher of the Century" by Mickey Herskowitz. Permission *Golf Digest.* Copyright © 1977 The New York Times Company Magazine Group, Inc. All rights reserved.

"Houston's Dynamic Duo" by Nick Seitz. Permission *Golf Digest.* Copyright © 1969 The New York Times Company Magazine Group, Inc. All rights reserved.

"Preston Trail: Last Bastion of Male Chauvinism" by Blackie Sherrod. Permission *Golf Digest.* Copyright © 1973 The New York Times Company Magazine Group, Inc. All rights reserved.

"Hustle Park" by Gary Cartwright. Permission *Golf Digest.* Copyright © 1969 The New York Times Company Magazine Group, Inc. All rights reserved.

"Blackie's Texas" by Blackie Sherrod. Permission *Golf Digest.* Copyright © 1985 The New York Times Company Magazine Group, Inc. All rights reserved.

"The Rarest Kind of Genius" by Tom Callahan. Permission *Golf Digest.* Copyright © 1997 The New York Times Company Magazine Group, Inc. All rights reserved.

"Dave Williams's Houston Dynasty" by Mickey Herskowitz. Permission *Golf Digest.* Copyright © 1987 The New York Times Company Magazine Group, Inc. All rights reserved.

"America's Most Wanted Match Player: Lanny" by Tim Rosaforte. Copyright © *Golf Illustrated.* Reprinted with permission from *Golf Illustrated.*

"Babe Could Play" and "The Trials of Lefty Stackhouse" by Curt Sampson, 1991. Copyright © *Golf Journal.* Reprinted with permission of *Golf Journal,* the official magazine of the USGA.

Excerpt from "Lord How That Man Could Play" by Charles Price. Copyright © 1973 *Golf Magazine.*

"One from the Heart" by Melanie Hauser. Copyright © *Golf World* 1996. Reprinted with permission.

"A Tribute to Demaret's Greatness" by Peter Dobereiner. Copyright © *Golf World* 1983. Reprinted with permission.

"Hogan Even Took an Eleven on One Hole" by Dick Peebles. Copyright © 1971, *Houston Chronicle.* Reprinted with permission. All rights reserved.

"A Golfer Second to None" by Melanie Hauser. Copyright © 1989 *Houston Post*. Reprinted with permission. All rights reserved.

"Newest Contribution to Golfdom Invented by Houston Golfer" by Van. Copyright © 1930 *Houston Press*. Reprinted with permission. All rights reserved.

Excerpt from "Hogan," "Old Tom," excerpt from "A Semi-Tough Return to Golf," and "The Glory Game at Goat Hills" by Dan Jenkins, *Fairways and Greens,* Doubleday, 1994. Copyright © Dan Jenkins. Reprinted with permission of Dan Jenkins.

"Another Day, Another Man" by Dan Jenkins, *Fort Worth Press,* 1959; "Magic Deal" copyright © Dan Jenkins, 1991. Reprinted with permission of Dan Jenkins.

"Call Him 'Lucky'" by Jim Murray. Copyright © 1963 *Los Angeles Times.*

"Gentle Ben" by Melanie Hauser, 1992; "What You See Is What You Get" by Melanie Hauser, 1994; and excerpt from "Paying Attention to Details" by Melanie Hauser, 1996. Reprinted with permission of the PGA Tour from *On Tour,* the official publication of the PGA Tour.

"The Hustler" by Russ Pate, *D Magazine,* March 1987. Copyright © Russ Pate. Courtesy of Russ Pate.

"Linksmanship" and "Once Upon a Green" by Turk Pipkin, *Texas Monthly,* 1993, 1994. Copyright © Turk Pipkin. Courtesy of Turk Pipkin.

"Gus Moreland" by Curt Sampson, *Golfiana,* 1994. Courtesy of Curt Sampson.

"On Awe: The Babe and Making Money Playing Golf" by Blackie Sherrod. Copyright © Blackie Sherrod, 1991. Courtesy of Blackie Sherrod.

"The Accident" excerpt, *Follow the Wind.* Reprinted with permission of Simon & Schuster from *Follow the Wind* by Bo Links. Copyright © 1995 by Bo Links.

"Betsy Rawls." Reprinted with the permission of Simon & Schuster from *Harvey Penick's Little Red Book* by Harvey Penick with Bud Shrake. Copyright © 1992 by Harvey Penick and Bud Shrake.

"John Bredemus." Reprinted with the permission of Simon & Schuster from *Harvey Penick's Little Red Book* by Harvey Penick with Bud Shrake. Copyright © 1992 by Harvey Penick and Bud Shrake.

Excerpt from "Our Daughter Sandra." Reprinted with the permission of Simon & Schuster from *For All Who Love the Game* by Harvey Penick with Bud Shrake. Copyright © 1995 by Harvey Penick, Bud Shrake, and Helen Penick.

"Holy Cow, Robert!" by Franz Lidz. Reprinted courtesy of *Sports Illustrated,* December 4, 1994. Copyright © 1994, Time, Inc.

"Fading Fame" by Ed Hinton and Mark Stewart. Reprinted courtesy of *Sports Illustrated,* May 6, 1996. Copyright © 1996, Time, Inc.

"Wrong Image but the Right Touch" by Barry McDermott. Reprinted courtesy of Sports Illustrated, December 4, 1983. Copyright © 1983, Time, Inc.

"Forget the Alamo . . . Just Remember 1922!" by Frances Trimble, *Golfiana,* 1994. Courtesy of Frances Trimble.

"Bobby Cruickshank Says Tough Grass Made Espinosa Lose" by Bobby Cruickshank. United News, 1927. Copyright © United Press International.